The Bell Helicopter Textron Story

Changing the Way the World Flies

David A. Brown

Book Design and Typesetting: Jerry Moore
Text Editors: Harry "Ned" Gilliand, Carl Harris, Jay Miller, John Williams
Photo Support: Ted Hayes, Jay Miller

Library of Congress Cataloging in Publication Data
    David A. Brown, 1934
        The Bell Helicopter Textron Story
        Changing the Way the World Flies
        Includes index.
        1. *Bell Helicopter Textron*–History. I. Brown, David A. II. Title
        Library of Congress Catalog Card Number: 95-075395
        ISBN 0-942548-61-2 hard
        ISBN 0-942548-60-4 soft
U.S. Trade Distribution: Specialty Press Publishers & Wholesalers,
North Branch, MN 55056; Tel.: 612 583-3239
European Trade Distribution: *Midland Publishing Ltd.*, Earl Shilton,
Leicester LE9   7NA England; Tel.: 01455 233747
Printed in Hong Kong
First edition

CONTENTS

Foreword

I believe that no one could have possibly imagined how much positive impact Bell products, and the people who make, sell and support them, would have on the world. In March 1946, the first helicopter – an odd looking contraption with a bubble nose and a tail boom resembling an oil derrick – became the first vertical flight machine to be certified for use in civil aviation. It was, of course, the venerable Bell 47 helicopter.

Our company's history has been filled with achievements and accomplishments that have not only advanced vertical flight technology, but enriched the very way we live our lives. Our journey has not been easy. Successes have been tempered by tragedy, our humor diminished by seriousness, and even our doing things "the Bell way" uprooted to ensure survival in an ever-changing world marketplace. But, over time, Bell products and people have changed the way the world flies.

Born in wartime, reared over the battlefields of Korea and Vietnam, and nurtured in civilian life, this technology is now used hundreds of ways with little thought given to its miracle. What made the helicopter truly unique was its use in moving wounded soldiers from Korean battlefields to frontline tent hospitals. Now helicopters move the critically injured to fully equipped hospitals. Tactics and techniques honed in battlefield surveillance are now used daily by airborn police officers as they patrol our cities, helping to keep our families safe. Heavy duty lifters of soldiers, cannons and rocket launchers now move crews to off-shore oil rigs and lift giant logs from primeval forests. Our helicopters have come a long way in relatively short period of time. We can take pride in these noble accomplishments.

But, I believe we have only begun. The next 50 years holds even more promise for an ever-expanding use of the technology, in ways not yet even imagined. The helicopters and tiltrotors of the future will have even greater impact on our lives.

What better way is there to celebrate 50 years of progress than to reflect on Bell's glorious heritage by reading a book filled with reflections and reminiscences by Bell's own storytellers. After reading it, you'll discover that the best parts of the Bell story are not in the descriptions of the many Bell products developed and built over the years, but the words of the people who are , were and will always be the heart and soul of Bell Helicopter. From its humble beginnings in an abandoned car dealership outside of Buffalo, New York, in the early 1940s to its move to Fort Worth, Texas, in 1951, to establish a vertical flight dynasty, many events and superhuman efforts have led to Bell taking its place as a leader in the world helicopter community. This book is dedicated to all those who take pride in themselves as a member of the Bell Helicopter Textron family. Please read this book to help you not only understand our company's past, but to encourage you to build on this solid foundation. Read to reflect on the glories and the agonies, the sweet victories and defeats. Take enthusiastic pride in Bell's past and complete faith in its future.

Webb F. Joiner
President
Bell Helicopter Textron Inc.

December 1991 reunion...Bart Kelley and Arthur Young at Bell Helicopter Textron.

Preface

One word kept turning up as I researched this book. The first time or two I heard it, I dismissed it as an aberration or thought that the person who said it had used it inadvertently. But it kept being repeated and finally I realized that the people speaking it were not using it lightly or incorrectly. They came from every level within Bell Helicopter Textron and they meant it.

The word is Love.

"I love this company. I love what I am doing. I love the people I work with. I love Bell." If you hear phrases like these often enough, you begin to get the message. Most of the people at Bell consider it not only an organization, but also an extended family.

Every organization has its own personality, whether it be a company, a choir, a sports team or a family. Bell Helicopter's familial aspect may not be unique among employers, but it is certainly the strongest and most deeply felt that I have encountered in more than 35 years of association with the aerospace industry. Bell Helicopter's personality comes through as one which embodies both respect for and concern about its people, its performance and its reputation in the world.

My major regret is that I could not work into this history anywhere near all the recollections, stories, details and facts that were provided to me by the Bell employees and retirees with whom I spoke. The space simply wasn't available. To those who sat with me for many hours recounting their memories and now cannot find any mention in this volume of what they told me, I can only apologize. Also, to those who served with the company for many years and did not have a chance to express their recollections, I again can only offer my regrets.

To those who endured the hours of discussion and many questions, some of them repetitive, I give my sincere and heartfelt thanks. There are those who will disagree with some of the things expressed in this history of Bell Helicopter and to them I can only say that nothing incorrect was intentionally written. However, memories fade with time and on a number of occasions, I was forced to choose between two or more differing recollections of the same event. If I chose wrongly, please forgive it as an honest error.

Finally, my sincere thanks to Carl Harris, Bell's director of public affairs and a friend of many years standing; to Bartram Kelley, Bell's first employee, whose wealth of knowledge about the company's early days led me down many paths of enquiry; and to Jim Atkins, Jack Horner and Webb Joiner, the presidents of Bell, past and present, for their assistance and support and never failing courtesy, even when they were concerned about the future of this project. Others who contributed significantly to this effort include Harry (Ned) Gilliand, Joyce Lyksett, Bob Leder, Terry Arnold, Dwayne Williams, John Williams, Betty Sanderson and Ted Hayes. My thanks to them and to all of the men and women of Bell Helicopter.

Love is the only word that describes it all.

David A. Brown
Roanoke, Texas
January, 1995

CHAPTER ONE

What is a Helicopter?

Larry Bell as a youth in a Curtiss B biplane of pre-World War 1 design (center). Clockwise from upper right: Bell Model 30, Ship 1, the first Bell helicopter; Ship 1 under construction; An assistant to Arthur Young and a helicopter research model; Larry Bell and the Collier Trophy.

Those who knew him well say they had seldom seen Larry Bell so mad.

It was not because of anything anyone had done. Rather, it was what they wouldn't do.

"I used to know everyone in the whole damn Army Air Corps by their first name," Bell fumed, "and now they won't even talk to me!" Bell's exasperation was understandable, but times and people had changed and so had the products Larry Bell was selling.

It was in August, 1950, just after the outbreak of the Korean War. And Larry Bell was working hard to keep his new helicopter manufacturing operation going. What was needed were military orders to bolster the flagging civil sales of Bell Aircraft Corporation's tiny helicopter program.

Larry Bell and two members of his

Arthur Young flying an early research model helicopter by remote control at his Paoli, Penna., farm.

team, pilot Joe Mashman and sales engineer Hans Weichsel, had flown to the U.S. Army's Continental Army Command headquarters at Ft. Monroe, Va., in a Bell Model 47, in hopes of convincing the brass there that a helicopter would be of immense value in a combat situation. Reconnaissance, utility work, rapid movement of commanders, medical evacuation, and other potential uses were on the list to present and demonstrate to the officers in charge of selecting new equipment for development and integration into the nation's post-World War 2 army.

The Army had been largely stripped of its aviation capability when the U.S. Air Force became a separate service in 1947. What was left consisted mainly of pilots who had flown light, single-engine fixed-wing aircraft during the war. These had been used for artillery spotting and medical evacuation and liaison and had proven very useful. Since the war, however, development of Army Aviation had lagged. The Army had only 99 Bell helicopters in its inventory when the Korean war broke out, and 16 of these were developmental models of types that never went into production. Of the remaining 83, 18 were development versions of the Model 47/H-13.

"There were a few Army aviators left over from World War 2, and they wanted to develop Army Aviation and equip it with helicopters," Weichsel recalled. None of them were of high rank and none of them had much clout in the Army's decision-making process.

"Bell tried to help by giving access to helicopters to the top brass, and that's what we were doing at Ft. Monroe," he said.

The problem was, the Army top brass was too busy with other things right then to take what they saw as a joy ride in a helicopter. The outbreak of the Korean War had taken just about everyone by surprise, and most attention was directed to the fierce combat then raging on the Asian peninsula.

After the trio landed the helicopter on the lawn outside the headquarters building, Larry Bell and Joe Mashman went inside to knock on doors. Hans Weichsel stayed with the helicopter and spent his time polishing the aircraft with a cleaning rag.

Inside, Larry Bell and Mashman found all doors firmly closed. Larry Bell

One of Arthur Young's research models being photographed during flight test at Gardenville.

called on old friendships, recalled past successes, and described glowing promises for the future. Nothing worked.

Outside, Weichsel was approached by a young girl of seven or eight years of age, duly equipped with a lollypop. Like all children of that age with a lollypop, she was a sticky mess. And like all children that age, she was curious about this strange machine parked on the grass in her neighborhood. She asked Weichsel what it did and how it did it and what was this for and what did that do. And she touched everything. Weichsel followed along behind her, wiping sticky fingerprints off the bubble, the skids and any other part of the helicopter the girl touched, all the while answering her questions.

"Finally, she laid her lollypop down on the passenger's seat — the one we were hoping to get a general to sit in — and asked if she could have a ride," Weichsel said. "I told her that if she could get her daddy to come ride in it, she could go along".

In truth, Weichsel was more interested in getting the child to leave than in giving her father a ride, especially since he didn't know who her father was. His ploy was successful. The girl left and shortly thereafter, an irate Larry Bell, with Joe Mashman in tow, came out of the headquarters building and said, "Let's get out of here."

"Larry wanted to leave right away, but I asked him to wait by the helicopter for just a minute," Weichsel said. Sure enough, the young lollypop girl soon returned, tugging at her daddy's hand. And Daddy had stars on his shoulders. "We gave the girl the ride we had promised," Weichsel recalled, "and Daddy went with her."

The general was duly impressed with what he saw. "He recognized what a helicopter could do," Weichsel said, "and that opened up the access to the top brass that we needed." Eventually, after some bargaining back and forth, the Army ordered some 85 of the Model 47s, with the understanding that Bell's advertising would stress that Army Aviation was pushing ahead technologically."

Arthur Young demonstrating his model's capabilities to Larry Bell (kneeling, left) and a group at the Gardenville development center.

Helicopter model designed by Arthur Young which later served as the basis for the first full-scale Bell helicopter.

Floyd Carlson hovers Ship 1A equipped with "spider leg" landing gear about 1944.

The Army had some valid concerns. Although helicopters had been flying for a decade in 1950, few people knew what this strange machine was and what it could do. Most people had never seen one and of those who had, most considered the helicopter a gimmick–interesting to watch but not really very useful.

But Lawrence J. (Larry) Bell was different. With the visionary's eye, he saw his first helicopter and was impressed. When he saw his second, he understood that here was an industry waiting to be born.

Larry Bell had the ability to look into the future in a way that few others could. He could see how things would be, or could be, or should be and then act to make his vision come true. In fact, Bell Helicopter Textron exists today because Larry Bell looked at a small, remotely-controlled model helicopter and saw an industry.

"He could look into the future, literally," James Atkins, who rose from cost accountant at Bell Aircraft to become president of Bell Helicopter, recalled. "Larry Bell's foresight never stopped. He had the greatest foresight ability in any man I have ever seen."

Larry Bell was one of the true pioneers of aviation in America. He saw his first airplane — they called them flying machines back then — in 1910. Not many people saw a future for the flimsy wood and fabric contraptions that could, if everything was just right, barely lift themselves off the ground. Larry and his older brother, Grover, attended the first major aviation exhibition in the U.S. It was held in Long Beach, California, and the Bell family drove down from Santa Monica to watch the airplanes and balloons that braved the sky that day.

The Long Beach exhibition set in motion a train of events that would direct the destinies of both Larry and Grover Bell. Grover, who had already finished high school, telephoned the Glenn L. Martin Company — it was listed under "Amusements" in the Los Angeles telephone directory — and enrolled as a student aviator. Glenn L. Martin himself taught Grover to fly for a fee of $500 and then, impressed by Grover's ability, hired him as an exhibition flyer and part-time instructor.

For two years, Grover Bell toured the western United States, giving exhibitions with such great pilots as Glenn Curtiss and Lincoln Beachy. At first he flew one of Martin's aircraft and later, he bought his own airplane from Martin. In 1912, Larry Bell graduated from high school and promptly joined his brother on the aeronautical tour circuit, acting as mechanic for Grover. In their spare time, they talked about forming their own company and building aircraft of their own design. But that was not to be.

In 1913, Grover was fatally injured in a crash at Petaluma, California. He dug in a wingtip while trying to avoid horses which had run out onto the field where he was landing. Larry Bell was devastated and vowed never to go near an airplane again.

But Larry Bell's interest in aviation proved too strong. He went back to Glenn Martin and asked for a job. Martin hired him as a stockroom clerk. Within

months he had been advanced to shop foreman, where he helped produce the first bomber to be designed and built as such in the U.S. It was built to the order of Mexican revolutionary Francisco (Pancho) Villa and delivered to his agents in Tucson, Arizona. They later smuggled the aircraft into Mexico, where it was used in Villa's fight against the Mexican government.

Larry Bell stayed with Glenn Martin until early 1925. During his tenure, in which he rose to be vice president and

general manager of the Glenn L. Martin Company, he had a hand in a number of significant events. It was Larry Bell who selected a young graduate of the Massachusetts Institute of Technology to be chief engineer of Martin's company. The young man was the first college-educated aeronautical engineer to be hired in the U.S. His name was Donald Douglas. It was Larry Bell who was instrumental in moving the Glenn L. Martin Company to Cleveland. And it was Larry Bell who helped sell a new bomber, the Martin MB-2, designed by Douglas, to the Army Air Service.

Finally, it was Larry Bell who made friends with a prominent Army officer and convinced him to use the MB-2 in some forthcoming tests. The officer was Col. William (Billy) Mitchell and the

tests involved seeing if an airplane could sink a battleship. The MB-2 could and did sink several battleships, starting inter- and intra-service rows over the value of airplanes that continued for years. It was during this period that Larry Bell met and came to know the officers and men of the Army Air Service, later the Army Air Corps.

In 1925, Larry Bell asked Martin to let him purchase stock in the Glenn L. Martin Company, and when Martin refused, Larry Bell quit. He was out of aviation for a few years, but was hired in 1928 by Maj. Reuben Fleet, president of Consolidated Aircraft. He came aboard as sales manager for the company, which was based in Buffalo, N.Y. Fleet agreed to sell Larry Bell stock in the company, allowing him to realize his long-held dream of being an owner of an aircraft company.

In 1929, Larry Bell became general manager of Consolidated and remained so until 1935, when Fleet decided to move the company to California in order to take advantage of better flying weather. Larry Bell resigned and decided to form his own company. Although it was not easy during the Depression, Larry Bell found financial backers organized the Bell Aircraft Company in July, 1935 and took over the old Consolidated factory.

The company specialized in the design and production of fighter aircraft, first the XFM-1 Airacuda, a twin-engine fighter to oppose attacking bombers, and then the famous P-39 Airacobra. Thousands of P-39s were built during World War 2, with many of them being sent to help Russia fight against the Germans. The company also designed and built the P-59 Airacomet, the first American jet fighter, and the P-63 Kingcobra, the successor to the P-39.

In 1938, Larry Bell was asked by President Franklin Roosevelt to join a group of American industrialists who had been invited to tour Nazi Germany. Larry

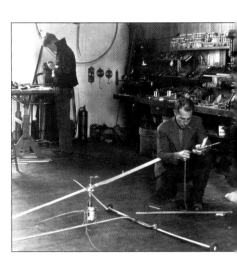

Research model helicopter being modified. Arthur Young used models extensively in solving the problems of vertical flight.

Transmission of the first Bell helicopter installed in the fuselage. The original transmission was copied directly from a model transmission.

Ship 1 is readied for a flight from Gardenville Airport probably in September 1943, Floyd Carlson is in the cockpit.

Arthur Young's patent covering the rotor and stabilizing bar system he developed to control a helicopter in flight. The application was filed on Nov. 10, 1941 and the patent issued Sept. 11, 1945.

Bell was asked to go along to help determine just what aviation capabilities Hitler's Third Reich really had. Bell later said that the most impressive thing he saw during this trip was the German Focke 61 helicopter. This twin-rotor machine could hover and had a top forward speed of 70 mph.

In 1941, just before the U.S. entered World War 2, Larry Bell saw another helicopter. This one was a small model, but it could fly forward, backward, sideways and hover under complete control and with complete stability. Its inventor, a young fellow from Pennsylvania, was looking for financial backing to build a full-sized man-carrying version and Larry Bell provided it.

The inventor was Arthur Middleton Young, who came from a financially independent family in Radnor, Pennsylvania, a suburb of Philadelphia and who preferred philosophy to aviation. While a student at Princeton University, he tried to formulate an original philosophic line of thought, but eventually decided he needed more experience in the real world. After he graduated from Princeton with a mathematics degree in 1927, he looked around for "some practical problem" to which he could devote 10 or 15 years in order to get a "better grasp on how things work." Then he planned to return to his first love, philosophy.

After a fruitless search lasting almost a year, Young happened to read a book by a German inventor, Anton Flettner, who had come up with an idea for improving the efficiency of windmills. His concept called for putting a small propeller at the tip of each windmill blade to provide a boost to the windmill's rotation. Young immediately saw this as a means of powering the rotor on a flying helicopter.

Young decided that the best way to develop a successful helicopter was by means of remotely controlled models. He built a number with rotors measuring some six feet in diameter and powered with electric motors. For the next nine years, Arthur Young worked unsuccessfully to get a fully-controllable and stable model to fly using the Flettner concept.

But the failure had a silver lining. By building models Young taught himself to calculate stresses and to build the metal components of such a craft with simplicity and precision. In designing and redesigning them, he developed many of the tools and concepts used to measure rotor lift, propeller efficiency and other phenomena, as well as the formulas needed to predict the lift capabilities and power requirements of full-scale helicopters. Without fully realizing it, Arthur Young had laid the theoretical and engineering groundwork for the development of a successful helicopter.

In the late 1930s, Young decided that the Flettner concept could never be developed into a successful helicopter and began to look at other concepts. He bought a small farm near Paoli, Pennsylvania, and turned the old barn into a workshop/ laboratory.

In 1938, he attended a meeting of would-be rotary wing designers and learned

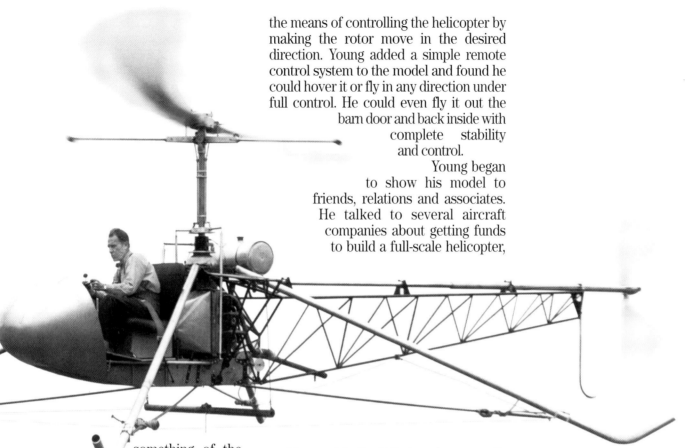

the means of controlling the helicopter by making the rotor move in the desired direction. Young added a simple remote control system to the model and found he could hover it or fly in any direction under full control. He could even fly it out the barn door and back inside with complete stability and control.

Young began to show his model to friends, relations and associates. He talked to several aircraft companies about getting funds to build a full-scale helicopter,

something of the work of others. At the meeting, he heard a talk by Igor Sikorsky on the possibility of using a tail rotor to control the torque generated by the main rotor. He also heard a paper read by Havilland H. Platt, another American helicopter pioneer, in which he commented on the concept of a hinged rotor, as distinguished from one fixed rigidly to the drive mast.

Intrigued by both concepts, Young built a small electrically powered model with a hinged rotor. It failed to fly because the hinged rotor was inherently unstable. But he recognized the need for a means to easily stabilize the rotor as the key to success. Young tried a half dozen ways of doing this before hitting on the idea of a stabilizer bar with weighted tips to act as a gyroscope and hold the rotor in the desired plane.

This device effectively overcame the rotor's tendency to follow the mast when the mast moved. It also gave the operator

and he went to the U.S. Army's aeronautical development center at Wright Field, Ohio, but he could find no one who would support him financially.

One of those who had seen the model helicopter fly was a physician, Dr. John Sharp, who knew Young and admired his work. Dr. Sharp had an unusual hobby. In his spare time, he devised gears and gearing systems. He had developed a new concept for a variable pitch propeller mechanism and was trying to sell it to Bell Aircraft. One day in 1941, Dr. Sharp told a Bell engineer with whom he was working, Jack Strickler, about Young and his invention, which he apparently described in glowing terms. Strickler mentioned Dr. Sharp's report to Larry Bell, who recalled being impressed by the Focke helicopter in Germany. He invited Young to come to Buffalo and demonstrate his invention.

Arthur Young arrived at the Bell Aircraft factory in Buffalo on September 3, 1941, and was ushered into a hangar

Arthur Young flying Model 30, Ship 1, at Gardenville. The absence of a Swedish Yoke on the rotor indicates this is an early, tethered flight.

Floyd Carlson hovers Model 30, Ship 1, with Swedish Yoke on rotor and wheeled landing gear. Straight tail rotor shaft shows this flight was made before the accident of September, 1943.

crowded with airplanes to demonstrate his helicopter model.

"They told us to quit whatever we were doing and help push P-39s out of the way in the hangar, so they'd have room for some sort of demonstration," Frank "Chick" LaJudice, recalled. LaJudice was then working as a crew chief on the Bell flight line, helping to ready P-39 fighters for delivery.

The Bell Aircraft employees cleared a space in the hangar and Young unpacked his model from the suitcase in which he carried it. Although Young later recalled that the space allotted for him to

demonstrate his helicopter model was "rather confined," the demonstration itself was a resounding success. Young showed that he could maneuver the helicopter model around the hangar r under complete control and that it would hover with total stability. After the flight demonstration, he showed a film he had made concerning the principles of stability and depicted his research work with a variety of models.

Larry Bell and Arthur Young met that day and discussed what it would take to develop the model helicopter into a full-sized, man-carrying machine. Larry Bell was impressed with the work Art Young had done, and Young liked Larry Bell from the start. Over the next few weeks, they worked out an agreement under which Arthur Young would move to Buffalo and head the Bell helicopter development effort.

Young assigned the patents he had already taken out on his work to Bell Aircraft. Larry Bell, in turn, agreed to fund the design, development and manufacture of two full-sized, man-carrying

Model 30, Ship 2, was, as required by Larry Bell, a two-seat helicopter. He wanted it that way so he could ride along. The pilot has not been positively identified, but may be Arthur Young.

helicopters. Young insisted on two helicopters in the contract "in case one should be wrecked." Larry Bell, for his part, insisted that the second helicopter be a two-seat machine so that he could go for a ride in it.

Young also talked Larry Bell into hiring his assistant, Bartram (Bart) Kelley, who had been working with him on helicopter models at the Paoli farm for several months. Kelley, who rose to be engineering vice president of Bell Helicopter, was hired at a salary of 90 cents per hour. "I was signed on as a draftsman, although I didn't know a thing about drawing," Kelley recalled. "And I was paid next to nothing."

The agreement was signed in November, 1941, and on Nov. 24, only two weeks before the United States entered World War 2, Young and Kelley arrived in Buffalo to begin work on a full-scale helicopter.

As it turned out, very little happened for the first few months. Both Larry Bell and Arthur Young had different understandings of the agreement they had signed.

Young thought that Bell would provide a team of engineers, technicians, pilots and mechanics to develop and then build the prototype helicopters he envisioned, with Young acting as technical director and overall supervisor. He realized that he and Kelley had no experience in fabricating parts for a man-carrying helicopter or in assembling and building such a machine. What they did have was technical data calculated from the performance of a small model and the proven ability to solve problems with a combination of mathematical calculations and experimental testing.

Larry Bell, on the other hand, expected Young to use the office space, drafting tables and other facilities provided to make drawings from which the factory could fabricate full-scale components which would then be assembled into a flyable helicopter. This helicopter would be based on the knowledge that Young had gained in his decade of theoretical work and model testing.

What neither man fully realized was that neither of these approaches was the correct one. Larry Bell failed to realize that techniques that work with a fixed-wing aircraft, which benefited from 40 years of practical experience, could not work with

a rotary-wing helicopter because there was no such experience. That body of knowledge would have to be attained through a development program that eventually took longer than either had anticipated.

A budget of $250,000 was established for the project, but little money actually was made available for helicopter development. The Bell Aircraft factory already was working on a three-shift basis for the growing war production effort and was expanding as rapidly as new workers could be hired and trained. Every supervisor and worker was already stretched to the limit, and nobody knew, or wanted to know, about a helicopter project, whatever that was.

After a couple of months, Art Young went to Russ Creighton, who was head of production at the Bell Aircraft factory, and pointed out that his agreement called for

Model 30, Ship 1, being readied for a flight in the backyard of the Gardenville development facility. Wheels replaced the spider landing gear after free-flights were well along.

building two helicopters, not just drawing plans for them. No such plans could be drawn, he pointed out, until it was known just what was needed. And that knowledge could come only when the problems and unknowns inherent in a new type of aircraft could be solved by experimentation and test flying. Creighton agreed to change the budget to provide money for the construction of two helicopters, but added that this would be acceptable only if it did not add to the existing burden of work assigned to the company's engineering staff.

Another roadblock which cropped up was Larry Bell's concern over the safety of a full-scale helicopter. He had asked himself what would happen if the engine quit in flight. He didn't know and asked Young if he could prove that the helicopter would be safe under such conditions.

Young promised a demonstration that would relieve Larry Bell's fears. He attached a spoon to one of his models and placed a raw egg in it. He earlier had added a slightly larger rotor to the model. Larry Bell watched as Young flew the helicopter model, carrying the egg, up top the roof of the hangar and switched off the electric motor. The helicopter autorotated down a guide wire to the floor until it landed so gently that the egg was not cracked.

With Larry Bell's fears allayed, work proceeded on the full-scale helicopter, but much more slowly than Arthur Young desired. All of the factory workers and officials were involved in urgent war work and seemed irritated if they were asked to help with some part of the helicopter. Little progress was being made and Young decided that the only way to get development of a real helicopter moving at a reasonable speed was to get the project completely out of the factory. After some searching, he found a vacant building which fit his needs in the suburban town of Gardenville, N.Y. The build-

Rebuilt after it crashed in September, 1943, the first Bell helicopter was redesignated Ship 1A. Modified landing gear had tail wheel moved closer to the rotor hub.

ing had been used as a Chrysler automobile dealership, but with automobile manufacturing shut down for the duration of the war, it was empty.

On June 23, 1942, almost exactly six months after Young and Kelley arrived in Buffalo, the helicopter project was moved to the Gardenville facility and work commenced in earnest. Since no one knew any other way, they took Young's latest and most successful model and copied it to a scale six times larger.

Young began by assembling a team of craftsmen skilled in making things quickly, by hand, sometimes with nothing more to base a design on than a verbal description or a rough sketch. A machine shop, office space, a wood shop for making rotor blades, a small drafting office and a model shop were all crowded into the old auto showroom and garage.

Mechanics, sheet metal workers, a welder, wood pattern makers, three tool makers and some designers were sent down to Gardenville from the main Bell factory in Buffalo or were hired on the spot. Five draftsmen were added to the team to make working drawings of the needed parts as the program progressed. A young man named Tom Darner, who had aided Young during his model-making days at Paoli, came to work in the wood shop.

In all, there were fewer than two dozen workers on the project in the first few months at Gardenville. During the entire three-year operation at Gardenville, there were never more than 32 workers on site at any one time, "and that included the security guard," Bart Kelley recalled. When needed for some special work, a limited number of workers would be brought down from Buffalo for a few days.

The development team was a very informal organization, and management was kept to a minimum. "There were no department heads or managers," Bart Kelley recalled. "Everything was directed by Art Young, and everyone reported

to him."

It was a team built on the idea that everyone did what had to be done, without regard to position or status.

"I remember one time a group of distinguished visitors came down to see Art Young, and his secretary took them out to the shop floor, where he was working at the time," Dick Ledwin, who was working as a mechanic on the team, recalled. "She pointed to a pair of legs sticking out from under the fuselage of a helicopter, and said 'There he is.' The visitors looked at each other and one of them said, 'No, you don't understand, we want to see Mr. Young who invented the helicopter.' And the secretary looked right back at them and said 'I understand perfectly. That's him.'"

"Arthur Young was a fun-loving person," Ledwin added. "He liked to party and he loved to Indian wrestle. He and Floyd Carlson used to really go at it arm wrestling."

Larry Bell sent one of his aides, David Foreman, down to "keep an eye on things" and Foreman eventually became director of the Bell helicopter division. However, Foreman was concerned primarily with fostering sales after a viable machine was developed and certificated and did not, apparently, try to exercise any direct control over the development team's efforts.

In just six months, the team designed and constructed the first Bell helicopter, designing and fabricating parts as they went and solving problems with the use of mathematics, model experiments, intuition and trial-and-error. The first helicopter was officially designated the Model 30 by the company and was christened *Genevieve* by the team that built it and would later fly it. The name never caught on, however, and the first Bell helicopter has been referred to consistently over the years by the highly appropriate name of Ship 1.

The fuselage was made partly of plywood beams. The original tail cone, which was made at the Buffalo factory, was of riveted magnesium. The rotor blades were a

Pump-handle control design in Ship 1/1A required all control functions to be done with the hands; there were no rudder pedals. This was the only Bell helicopter to have such a control design.

composite of fir and balsa wood, with a steel reinforcement bar down the leading edge. Ship 1 was powered by a 165-hp. Franklin engine mounted vertically. It drove both the 32-ft. main rotor and the anti-torque rotor at the end of the tail boom through a geared transmission sys-

The assembly shop at the Gardenville development facility was the place where the first three Bell helicopters were built.

tem. This had been copied directly from the transmission on Arthur Young's model, because no one at Bell knew how to design a transmission from scratch.

"What we had at Gardenville was a group of artisans," Joe Mashman recalled. "They were more than just engineers. But the engineers at the main Bell plant were disdainful of them and the Board of Directors had grave doubts they could produce. However, Larry Bell gave the program strong support. He would come down to Gardenville once or twice a week to encourage us. After we had the helicopter pretty well tamed, he would often come fly with us."

The landing gear initially consisted of four long, dural "spider legs," designed to prevent the helicopter from being inadvertently tipped over during early hover tests. They had to be removed and then replaced each time Ship 1 was taken out of or went back into the shop, because they were too long to fit through the door when attached to the fuselage of the craft.

Ship 1 was rolled out of the garage on December 18, 1942, but it was so cold in

Gardenville that day that the engine would not start. Use of a more powerful starter battery allowed the engine to be started and the first flight made on December 29, 1942. Since at that time there was no project test pilot assigned to the program, Arthur Young claimed the honor of making the first tethered hovering flight on that day. At the time, Young had never flown anything except the models.

Ship 1 was badly damaged in an unnecessary accident in late January. Robert Stanley, Bell Aircraft's chief pilot (and later chief engineer), came to Gardenville one day and said he wanted to fly the helicopter. As he was chief pilot, no one felt empowered to say no, so he climbed into the pilot's seat — without a seat restraint — and lifted Ship 1 off the ground.

In his attempts to hold Ship 1 in a steady hover, Stanley worked the collective control too violently and was tossed up out of the seat and into the whirling rotor. Fortunately, he missed the stabilizer bar and hit only the wooden blades. As it was, he was tossed several feet and suffered a broken arm. Both the rotor blades and the tail boom of Ship 1 were so badly damaged that they had to be replaced, and the test program was delayed for several weeks.

Stanley called Larry Bell from the helicopter development site before being taken to the hospital. "Larry," he said, "I'm sorry, but I think I've delayed your helicopter program a little."

The accident had a beneficial side, in that it brought two new members to the development team. Ed Unwin, who was a safety inspector at the Bell plant in Niagara Falls, was sent down to see what caused the accident and help prevent future mishaps. Floyd Carlson, a member of the Bell Aircraft test pilot group, was assigned as project pilot for the Model 30. Carlson, who earlier had been a test pilot at another Buffalo company, knew Dick Ledwin and urged that he be hired.

Slowly, the Bell Helicopter development team began to grow. Arthur Young and Bart Kelley were joined by Charles Seibel, recently graduated from the California

Institute of Technology, and Tom Harriman, a recent Massachusetts Institute of Technology graduate.

The five of them —Young, Kelley, Seibel, Harriman and Carlson — formed the nucleus of the development team which saw the Model 30 project through to a successful conclusion. The team operated on the principle that the quickest route to a successful helicopter lay in having complete flexibility. There were few rules and regulations. When the development team decided that something needed to be devised or changed, it was done quickly, with a minimum of paperwork.

Rough drawings were translated into hardware which was tested, revised and revised again, if need be. Only when the component was working satisfactorily were final precision drawings made. The small size of the team and the close relationships that developed between all the team members allowed the first Bell helicopter to be completed in an extraordinarily short time.

Repaired after Bob Stanley's accident, the Model 30 began a series of flights in which the development team first learned to fly the machine and then determined what needed to be done to perfect it. Early flights were tethered by a rope and pulley arrangement in the small back yard behind the car dealership building. Later, as confidence grew in the ability of the pilots to control the helicopter, it was decided to attempt a free flight.

"The little yard behind the building was too small but there was a larger field behind it and a fairly wide gate in the fence between the two," Bart Kelley recalled. Floyd Carlson, the project test pilot, lifted the helicopter off with a man holding each of the four spider legs. This was considered a tethered flight. With the "tethered" helicopter hovering high enough for the

Larry Bell sits in the cockpit of Model 30, Ship 2, possibly before his first flight in late 1943 or early 1944.

Floyd Carlson hovers Ship 1A, while Arthur Young looks on. The helicopter was rebuilt from the original Ship 1, with a redesigned landing gear and modified tail rotor shaft.

rotor to clear the fence, the four men walked it through the gate and set it down in the field, which was about eight or ten acres in size. There Carlson, on June 26, 1943, made the first untethered flight in Ship 1.

Five others on the developmental team, including both Young and Kelley, taught themselves to fly in Ship 1 while it was tethered.

Before long, confidence in the helicopter had risen to the point where it was routinely flown over the fence enclosing the small yard behind the development facility to the field. There, much of the earliest developmental flying was done and a number of unforeseen problems were discovered and solved. Chief among these was a high vibration level encountered when the forward speed approached 30 mph.

"Floyd Carlson came in one day with this surprised look on his face and said, 'I hit vibration that was out of this world,'" Ed Unwin, the safety inspector, recalled. The vibrations were so heavy that Carlson refused to try to go faster until the cause

could be determined and some sort of fix developed.

Using existing research data and advanced mathematical calculations, the team determined that the vibration was caused by an insufficiently stiff rotor. Carlson devised a brace to increase the stiffness, which was termed "the Swedish Yoke", because of his Swedish ancestry.

After this, flight at higher forward speeds was possible, but the field behind the development center was too small, so the helicopter was tied to a trailer and towed to Military Road Airport — a civil field despite its name — where it achieved speeds in excess of 70 mph. in forward flight. Later, flight test work was moved to the Gardenville airport, which was much nearer the development center.

At both airports, the curious gathered to see the strange machine fly.

"We started out very easy at Gardenville Airport," Unwin recalled. "There was very little air traffic and only a few spectators at first. But Ship 1 made a lot of racket when it flew, and that drew the curious the longer we flew there. We began to

Model 30, Ship 2, was the helicopter used for many of the early demonstration flights to potential customers.

encounter new problems with the helicopter, too. The one I recall most was excessive gear wear in the transmission. No one had ever experienced it before because no one had ever flown a helicopter this much."

Joe Mashman recalled the delays this entailed. "We had to stop flying every hour or hour and a half and tear down the rotor and transmission to see what wear had occurred," he said. "And there was no instrumentation in the ship. All the data came from the pilot's qualititative analysis."

While flight test work was underway on Ship 1, work on the second helicopter was progressing. Although they were both labeled Model 30, there were considerable differences between Ship 1 and Ship 2.

Ship 1 had a single seat in an open cockpit. There was no clutch in the rotor drive system, which forced someone to spin the rotor by hand when the engine was started. Also, it had a control system completely unlike any now flown. The system combined a cyclic control and throttle operated by the pilot's right hand and a collective control and anti-torque control operated by the left hand. It was called a pump-handle control system because it resembled an old-fashioned pump handle. There were no controls operated by the pilot's feet.

In line with Larry Bell's wishes, Ship 2 had two side-by-side seats in an enclosed cockpit. Ship 2 had a clutch in the power transmission system to facilitate starting the engine. The control system was similar to modern designs, largely because Floyd Carlson insisted on pedals for foot-control of the anti-torque rotor.

It proved to be fortunate that Ship 2 came along so quickly, because Ship 1 was wrecked in a flying accident in September, 1943. Carlson was attempting the first autorotational landings at the Gardenville Airport. He made the first two successfully, although at a fairly high forward speed. On the third attempt he flared the helicopter to kill off forward speed, bringing the nose up sharply just before reaching the ground. The helicopter's tail wheel, which was mounted fairly far back on the tail boom, touched the

ground before the main wheels and forced the tail boom up, where it collided with the rotor. The helicopter then rolled over on its side, where it was fairly well smashed up. Carlson was not injured and after sifting through the wreckage, the team members present decided that Ship 1 could be rebuilt. But for a time, all test work would have to be done on Ship 2.

By the time the Gardenville team was ready to try autorotational landings again, much later, using Ship 3, Joe Mashman was flying, and he and Floyd Carlson both flew that day. Carlson made the first autorotational landing, with Mashman sitting beside him calling out airspeed and altitude. Then they changed places and Mashman made the second autorotation.

Ship 2 was quickly finished and the test program restarted in the fall of 1943. In September, Larry Bell officially notified the Bell Aircraft board of directors that the company had a prototype helicopter successfully flying and that the company planned to enter the postwar helicopter market. A number of senior military and government officials were brought in to view the helicopter, including top researchers of the National Advisory Committee for Aeronautics (NACA), forerunner of the present NASA.

Late in 1943 or early in 1944, Larry Bell received his first helicopter ride, when Floyd Carlson took him on a short flight at Gardenville in Ship 2.

With all the public flying both at the Gardenville center and at local airports, keeping the helicopter under wraps became virtually impossible. People would drive out and park near the Gardenville site in hopes of seeing a flight. Finally, it was decided to publicly announce the helicopter program ,and the local newspapers were invited out to witness a demonstration flight and receive briefings on the project in May, 1944.

The company newspaper, The Bell Ringer, gave the helicopter project a two-page spread in its May, 1944, issue, with photos of Ship 2 in flight and a group photo of the Gardenville team. The team photo was printed so small, however, that only one person, Joyce Dennison, can be positively identified. She was Arthur Young's secretary and the only woman assigned to the team.

Also in May, the Model 30 made its first public demonstration when Ship 2 flew indoors at Buffalo's 65th Regiment Armory during a meeting of the Civil Air Patrol. This was first indoor flight in the U.S. by any type of aircraft. Several thousand CAP members and cadets were present. Floyd Carlson was the pilot for the demonstration, and although hampered by spotlights shining in his face and dust kicked up from the floor by the rotor downwash, he successfully completed several flights. The highlight of the demonstration came when Carlson hovered the helicopter with one wheel resting on Arthur Young's outstretched hand.

A few months later, on July 4, 1944, the original Model 30, modified and rebuilt after its accident and redesignated Ship 1A, performed before more than 4,000 spectators at a defense workers' rally at the Buffalo Civic Stadium.

As soon as the existence of the Bell helicopter program became public, the craft was called on to perform rescue and mercy missions. The first of these occurred on Jan. 5, 1945, when Bell Aircraft test pilot Jack Woolams was injured after bailing out of an early model of the Bell P-59, the first American jet fighter. He reached a farmhouse near Lockport, N.Y. after walking more than a mile through snowdrifts, but the heavy snow blocked all the roads into the area. Floyd Carlson picked up Dr. Thomas C. Marriott in Ship 2 and flew him directly to the isolated farm in about five minutes. There, he was able to treat Woolams hours sooner than if he had come in by road. The prompt treatment was credited with making unnecessary the amputation of Woolams frost-bitten feet.

The most famous of these early rescues occurred on the night of March 14, 1945, when Carlson in Ship 2 saved two fishermen who were stranded on an ice floe in the middle of Lake Erie for 21 hours. The request for assistance came from the U.S. Coast Guard, and Carlson later was awarded the Treasury Dept. Silver Medal for his efforts.

Before making the rescue attempt, Carlson had to do some impromptu test flying to see if someone could safely climb onboard a helicopter while it was hovering. This had never been done before. With his crew chief, Harry Finagan, posing as the prospective passenger, Carlson developed a flight technique which proved to his satisfaction that he could control the hovering helicopter while someone climbed on board.

"I recall the fisherman being mad as all get out," Ed Unwin recalled. "Floyd had to fly four or five miles out into the lake to get one and then repeat it to get the other. They had a pretty large string of fish they had caught and they wanted to bring them back, but Floyd refused to let them."

Early in 1945, the Gardenville team made a decision that eventually had a far greater impact than they anticipated. They decided to build a third Model 30, even though the agreement between Larry Bell and Arthur Young had provided that Bell Aircraft would pay for only two helicopters.

"We found out so much from the two helicopters already flying that it seemed a shame not to build one that incorporated all the lessons we had learned," Bart Kelley noted. "We got some great performance data by mounting two motion picture cameras on the helicopter to record instrument readings. It was surprisingly accurate. Some of the data would stand up in a development program today." So, in January, 1945, work quietly began on Model 30, Ship 3, which was as different from Ship 2 as Ship 2 had been from Ship 1. Like Ship 2, it was a two-place helicopter, but initially had an open cockpit. Ship 3 embodied all the knowledge gained from the effort that had been poured into its two predecessors. Since there was no funding approved for the third helicopter, it was largely built from material scrounged from other projects and with a lot of after-hours work. Ship 3 first flew on April 20, 1945. When the Bell management found out about it, they approved of it as a flying testbed only.

"We rationalized the building of that helicopter by saying that it was a testbed to provide additional data to the Bell engi-

Joe Mashman hovers Model 30, Ship 1A configured in its final layout, with wheel pants and a small windshield. Today, it is preserved in the Smithsonian Institution in this form.

neering department, which had been assigned the task of designing the first helicopter that would be marketed by the company," Bart Kelley recalled. "We never looked on Ship 3 as a product." The initial contribution of Ship 3 to the research program was its use by Carlson and Mashman in developing techniques for power-off autorational landings. These landings quickly became routine and were soon being demonstrated to passengers.

Ship 3 quickly showed that it was not only an advanced testbed for helicopter research. It was very nearly a helicopter that could be marketed commercially, and with the addition of a few relatively minor configuration changes, it soon would be.

Reminiscences: Bartram Kelley, chief engineer

I knew Arthur Young from childhood. His family and mine were neighbors and friends of long-standing. But he was about four years or so older than I was, and when you are 10 years old, a boy of 14 seems immensely older and more experienced. Arthur guided me in making crystal radio receiving sets when I was eight or 10. He himself was a ham operator in the early days and could send and receive messages in Morse code. He was sort of a god to me, to see someone who could do that.

After my sophomore year at Harvard, when Arthur had already graduated from Princeton with a degree in mathematics and was starting to do research on the helicopter, I was fascinated by Arthur and his work, just as in the old days of radio. Only this time it was playing with how to make a helicopter work and how to measure the power required to lift so many pounds and much testing of little rotors. At this time he had a model with a large-diameter rotor with little propellers on the tips of each blade. That was in 1931 in the spring, and I worked for him through the summer. And then for 10 years all I did was find out at Christmas time how he was coming and what was happening. I really didn't follow anything, except I knew what he was doing. But I wasn't involved in any way in his work. I graduated from Harvard and taught prep school

for six years.

I went to see Arthur in Philadelphia in June of 1941 -- darkened his door for the first time in 10 years -- and he said "I need you. I'm going to try to go ahead and do something full-scale, and I'm trying to find a backer." So I became his assistant again but in a far different situation now because I knew more than just pushing a slide rule and putting numbers down. But I knew nothing about aerodynamics. Arthur taught me. He taught me many other things such as mechanics. My only arsenal was the practical side of mathematics, which was thin stock at that point as far as what was needed. I also watched him negotiating with other aircraft companies until this sudden meeting with Bell came and that immediately clicked.

We took the train up to Buffalo after the agreement was signed and arrived Nov. 24, 1941. I came along purely as Arthur Young's assistant. I had no contract at all, although Arthur did say to Bell, "I want you to hire my assistant." I was a hanger-on who got into it.

We were put in the office of the chief engineer, Bob Woods, in Buffalo. He was a very talented designer and had designed some very good airplanes. But everybody at Bell thought they would just put Arthur in a drafting room and he would draw the plans for a helicopter and they'd just take it over to the factory and let them make it. They just had no concept of how you develop something. Larry Bell could more or less sympathize with Arthur; but the people around him couldn't at all. They didn't understand that the whole thing was in the doing of it and not just drawing a picture.

It almost got to the point where Arthur was threatening to give up the whole thing and go back to Philadelphia and forget it because he could see that nothing was going to happen. Finally they gave him a shop at the Elmwood Ave. plant in Buffalo to build models in, and they didn't know what to call it. Nobody wanted to say in the middle of a war that we were inventing a helicopter; so they called it Gyro Test. Arthur invented and demonstrated a control system that would work with the stabilizing bar there. We also demonstrated the helicopter model's ability to autorotate with a raw egg aboard and didn't bust the egg. Those were about the only two accomplishments we made in that shop. There was still no sign of anybody being able to make a full-sized helicopter.

Finally, Arthur convinced Larry Bell that they should find a place where he could do the equivalent of what he had been doing in the little shop at his home, but big enough to make a full-scale helicopter. They found a place on Union Road in Gardenville. It was formerly a Chrysler dealership, and after they got it back from us, it was turned back into a Chrysler showroom and is still operating as such to this day.

When we got set up there, we had to be jacks of all trades, and I was only one of several who were there. As an example, we had to learn things such as how to make a fan that would cool the engine in a hover. Also, Arthur had thought that Bell would be very good at transmissions and gears because of their association with Dr. Sharp, but they told him they were not in that field at all. Packard had done all their gearing on the Airacobra. So right away, Arthur turned out to be the best gear expert in Bell. The full-scale transmission we made was really based on just simply drawing up a bigger version of the transmission that had been used on the models. We only added a free-wheeling device, which the model didn't need, and a clutch. We had to learn how to make a clutch. That's typical of how we had to be jacks of all trades.

The most people ever working at Gardenville was approximately 32, and that included the furnace man and the security guard. There was some turnover -- people would come and stay a few months and complete their contribution and then others would come.

When we got ready to design a full-scale helicopter, Arthur said the first thing to do was to select an engine, so we would know what power we had to work with. We decided on a Franklin engine of about 150-hp. Then we did many calculations about rotor diameter and how fast to spin the rotor and how wide the blades should be. [The key was] getting those numbers right, based on literally hundreds of model tests of rotors.

Arthur didn't just make these models to fly; he also did a great deal of testing of those model-sized rotors. We got reams of data on different airfoil sections, how near a stall should you get the blades, the

whole business of studying the rotor. The selecting of these proportions, choice of engine and rotor sizes we began even before we got to Gardenville. On some things we weren't sure; we built two transmissions simultaneously, one with a 9:1 reduction ratio, the next one with a 10.5:1 ratio. We did various control systems, because Larry Bell wanted it to be as much like an automobile as possible.

Just a little over a year after Arthur and I signed on, the helicopter was ready for its first flight test. At that point, we had enough hardware to call it a flying test bed and try to get it running. The first attempts at hovering in tethered flight were made by Arthur. The helicopter at that time had these four legs as landing gear. The trick was to get all four legs off the ground and hover. I remember one fellow from another company who was one of our suppliers saw a flight and got on the phone to his factory in Pennsylvania and told them "It flew -- three feet. But the fourth foot wouldn't fly."

Bart Kelley went to work for Bell officially in November, 1941, although he had worked with Arthur Young on helicopter design previously. He rose to be vice president of engineering in 1949 and retained that position until his retirement in 1974. He is now a consultant to Bell Helicopter Textron and lives in Dallas with his wife, Dorothea.

CHAPTER TWO
Anybody can build a helicopter...

Model 47 and YH-12B helicopters move down the Bell Helicopter production line in Niagara Falls, circa 1947 (center photo). Clockwise from lower right: Bell's Niagara Falls factory, where Bell helicopters were first manufactured; Larry Bell and group showing Army officer Model 30, Ship 2; Larry Bell entering a two-seat (open cockpit) YP-59A for what was to be his first ride in a jet aircraft.

Larry Bell looked out across the airfield at the Niagara Falls plant one day in 1946 and what he saw did not please him. There was Arthur Young, head of his budding helicopter unit, flying a helicopter. And it was not the helicopter that Bell had paid him to develop.

"Get down right now," he yelled up at Young as he ran out on to the landing apron. "I can't risk all the brains in my helicopter program in that thing!"

That thing was a small, twin-rotor coaxial helicopter that Young had designed and built while working on the Model 47 program. It was developed after Young saw Stanley Hiller's coaxial design and thought it intriguing. Young flew his coaxial design only a few times — just to prove it would fly — and then set it aside. Apparently, it came to Texas when Bell Helicopter

Co-axial helicopter developed, built and flown by Arthur Young at Niagara Falls, while the Model 47 was being certificated. The helicopter was flown only by Young for a total of 10 hr.

moved, but then was scrapped.

Larry Bell had a valid point. In truth, few people knew how to build a helicopter in those days; fewer still had the knowledge to design one.

There were, however, those who disputed both contentions. They felt that with their experience and expertise, they could easily learn how to design a helicopter, and building one should be a snap. Some of those who believed this were the leaders in the Bell Aircraft engineering office.

During the years since 1937, they had designed at least seven fighter aircraft, including the first American jet fighter, and one high-speed rocket research aircraft. They had built well over 10,000 of these various aircraft for the U.S. and its allies during World War 2. Designing and building a commercially successful helicopter should be no great challenge, they thought. Furthermore, it appeared then that the days of high-volume fighter production were coming to an end, and they wanted something to keep themselves occupied in the postwar world.

In 1944, the Bell Aircraft engineers convinced Larry Bell to let them take the theoretical knowledge then being developed at Gardenville and add to it their practical experience in order to produce a helicopter that could be mass produced and that would appeal to a wide market. In the latter part of 1944, they began to show up regularly at Gardenville to absorb the knowledge that had been developed there.

The helicopter the Bell engineers intended to build was given the designation Model 42. The design was based largely on a survey which forecast that a major market would be for a helicopter with at least five seats to serve as a downtown-to-airport shuttle.

"They seemed to look on us as distant consultants," Bart Kelley recalled. "And they began designing the Model 42 the same way they designed new fighters, by making production drawings."

Joe Mashman, who had joined the helicopter program in early 1945 as the second

Mockup of the Model 42, which was initially developed by the Bell Aircraft engineering team and later re-developed by the Gardenville team.

Patent for an improved stabilizer bar design. The application was filed by Arthur Young Feb. 18, 1947, and the patent issued to Bell Aircraft July 28, 1953. (bottom)

developmental test pilot after Floyd Carlson, recalled the time as an "interesting environment in which to work." The engineers from Buffalo had a "haughty attitude" toward Arthur Young and his helicopter development team. "It was an environment of almost total non-cooperation," he said, "despite the fact that they had absolutely no helicopter experience."

For quite some time, there were two separate helicopter development programs going on. The Bell Aircraft engineering department in Niagara Falls was designing the Model 42. At Gardenville, Arthur Young and his team were working on Model 30, Ship 3.

Ship 3 quickly demonstrated that its performance capabilities constituted a major improvement over Ship 2. It had such good performance that it immediately became the helicopter in which most of the demonstrations were performed and flights given to visitors. Finally, the decision was made to continue the development of Ship 3 with the goal of producing a certifiable commercial helicopter. Larry Bell decided that the Gardenville develop-

ment site had contributed as much as it could and that a larger helicopter operation was needed to enable the projects to grow and be developed more speedily. On June 24, 1945, the Gardenville team moved to Niagara Falls. The move did not please some of the team members, most notably Arthur Young, who felt that more research was needed and that this could best be done by an isolated development team.

But by and large, Larry Bell's decision proved a wise one. The facilities needed to prepare a helicopter for mass production were there, and adequate space was available. The helicopter team was quickly expanded to approximately 100 engineers and workers, and Larry Bell told them he wanted the first civil certificated helicopter in the world.

The new helicopter that was to grow out of Model 30, Ship 3, was designated the Model 47, and it greatly resembled its parent.

"The Model 47 had irreversible controls to eliminate rotor feedback and a few other internal changes from Ship 3," recalled Bart

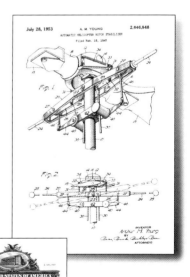

Bell XP-59, the first American-designed and built jet fighter. Glamour programs like this one tended to overshadow the helicopter program.

Kelly, but there was nothing externally obvious that was different. The first Model 47 looked identical to Model 30, Ship 3.

Shortly afterward, however, Ship 3 was modified in a way that improved it and which also gave early Bell helicopters their most distinctive trait. Initially, Ship 3 had two seats like Ship 2, but it had an open cockpit, like Ship 1. Ship 3 was used extensively for demonstrations, and many of the passengers, sitting in the open under the rotor, were uncomfortable.

The helicopter team looked around for a way to enclose the passengers and pilot without losing the visual sensation of sitting "on the edge of a cloud" as the helicopter flew. Eventually, a way was found to

use air pressure to form heated plexiglas into a bubble. When the plexiglas cooled, it was trimmed to size and attached so it covered the two seats.

When this bubble canopy was used on the early Model 47s, it was found that it actually improved performance and even improved visibility. The first 39 Model 47s and Model 47A/YR-13s had it installed. But Larry Bell did not like it, nor did he like the open framework tail boom that was on the first helicopters. A marketing study had told him that helicopters would sell better if they resembled automobiles.

Thus, when the first certificated Model 47s — called Model 47B — were put on the market, they had an enclosed cabin and a covered tail boom. Bell sales representatives noted, however, that among the first thing new owners would do would be to cut the fabric off the tail boom and fly with only the open framework. Arthur Young was unsuccessful in getting the bubble canopy used rather than the automobile-like cabin. He complained that the management wanted the Model 47 "to look like a Buick."

The initial production order for the

Bell X-1 rocket research aircraft at the Niagara Falls plant. Charles E. "Chuck" Yeager flew this aircraft through the sound barrier on Oct. 14, 1947.

Model 47 was for a prototype and 10 test aircraft — 11 helicopters in all. These had the bubble canopy and the open tail boom. In 1946, the Army ordered 28 similar helicopters, designated Model 47A by the company, for test and evaluation. The first one was delivered near the end of December, 1946. Of these, 10 were handed over to the Navy for a similar test program. The Army designated the aircraft the YR-13; the Navy called it the HTL-1.

Developing the Model 47 from the Model 30, Ship 3, took less than five months. The prototype Model 47 rolled out of the Bell factory on December 8, 1945, and later that same day made its first flight with Floyd Carlson as pilot. As soon as it did, Larry Bell told the development team that he wanted it to be the first civil helicopter in the world to receive certification from the Civil Aeronautics Administration, forerunner of the FAA.

Larry Bell's desire to have the helicopter certificated first has usually been said to have been caused by the knowledge that Sikorsky was in the process of certificating a civil version of the military R-5. But some Bell employees who were there at the time say there were other reasons.

"Larry Bell was an impatient man. I think that is largely the reason he got so much accomplished. And he always wanted to be first in everything. But he didn't get the Model 47 certificated just to be ahead of Igor Sikorsky," Bart Kelley recalled. "There was not much rivalry with Sikorsky at that time. They had already produced a couple of hundred R-4s and R-6s for the military, but that [military] market dried up at the end of the war."

The real reason for Larry Bell's desire for quick certification was because he had announced publicly that the company would build an initial lot of 500 Model 47s as a way of keeping the price down. Bell privately told his associates that the number 500 was mostly for public consumption, according to Kelley. However, after

Bell Model 30, Ship 3, the unauthorized helicopter which became the basis for the Model 47, is on the ground at Niagara Falls.

Model 30, Ship 3, slightly modified for this flight, carries seven persons in a demonstration flight. Pilot is Joe Mashman and Arthur Young is standing on far side, facing camera.

Patent for a modified rotor control system issued to Bell Aircraft on May 30, 1950. Arthur Young filed the application on April 5, 1946.

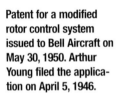

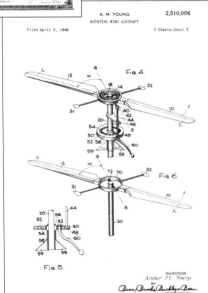

certification was received, he did order 500 Franklin engines as well as forgings and other long-lead time components for 500 helicopters.

Rapid CAA certification was "absolutely necessary" if Bell was to have a chance to sell the 500 machines, Kelley said. In fact, the decision to build the first 11 helicopters on a production line basis dictated that Larry Bell would go for early certification.

And, of course, even if it wasn't the primary reason for getting quick certification, there was always the spectre of Igor Sikorsky and his new commercial helicopter looming large on the horizon.

The CAA, of course, had no experience in rotary-wing aircraft design, operation or maintenance. They had never been called on to certificate a civil helicopter before and had no helicopter pilots on their staff. But they were eager to learn and were helpful in getting the Model 47 certificated rapidly. The CAA sent its chief engineering test pilot, Raymond Malloy, to Buffalo,

where Floyd Carlson taught him to fly in Model 30, Ship 3.

As soon as Malloy mastered the art of rotary-wing flight, Bell and the CAA began a joint program of certification flight testing, which was completed in about three months. The CAA was charged with ensuring safety, both from a design and operational standpoint, and also with promoting aviation generally. Malloy soon realized that attempting to certificate a helicopter according to rules which pertained to fixed-wing aircraft was impossible.

Both the CAA certification team and the Bell Helicopter development team realized that a new basis for certification was needed to accommodate the unique flight characteristics and capabilities of the helicopter, while at the same time making certain that the new type of flying machine would be safe to fly.

One Bell team, consisting of Arthur Young, Bart Kelley and several others from the original design team at Gardenville, worked with CAA engineers on matters such as structures, controls, flight dynamics, vibration and similar subjects. A second team, consisting of Floyd Carlson and Joe Mashman, worked with Malloy, the

CAA pilot, to develop requirements for pilot, training.

A third team, including Charlie Seibel, Roy Coleman and others, established a liaison relationship with the CAA in Washington to ensure that no problems would arise unforeseen and that the CAA officials there would understand what was being done and why. This also permitted a quick response to CAA questions or proposed new requirements.

The certification team from the CAA took a cooperative approach to the effort to certificate the Model 47 and a congenial relationship between the Bell and CAA teams soon developed.

"The whole CAA team wanted to help certify the Model 47 and that led to a friendly attitude from the agency people." From this came a give-and-take on both sides in an effort to establish requirements that the helicopter could meet. The pilot and flight requirements teams required only three days, for example, to informally agree to and write regulations defining what requirements a student pilot would have to

Model 30, Ship 1A, the original Bell helicopter was rebuilt and redesignated after its crash during an autorotational landing in 1943. Floyd Carlson in seated in the helicopter, with Arthur Young to his immediate right, leaning over.

meet to earn a helicopter rating. This was despite the fact that no civil operating data existed and no one had any realistic idea of what the helicopters would be called upon to do.

"Malloy soon realized that using fixed-wing criteria for helicopter certification just was not possible," Joe Mashman said.

When the Model 47 could not meet some of the fixed-wing requirements, the CAA team either revised the rules so that the helicopter could meet them, or it imposed operating restrictions or caution-ary labeling to keep flight in a specific regime safe. For example, fixed-wing regu-lations called for the capability of making a 180-deg. turn at night without reference to instruments or to any lights on the ground. The Model 47 could not meet the fixed-wing requirement, but it could be flown in the maneuver if the requirement was changed slightly. The CAA agreed to this and in such instances, established a heli-copter standard to parallel the airplane standard.

This became the standard procedure for certificating the Model 47. If the heli-copter could not meet a fixed-wing require-ment, either a new requirement was written as the helicopter standard or flight restric-tions were imposed or cautionary placards were required.

Some of the limitations imposed by the CAA were not what the Bell team wanted, but they were accepted on the assumption that growth of helicopter tech-nology would allow them to be withdrawn later. For example, the CAA ended up requiring that the Model 47 had to have a complete overhaul after every 25 hr. of flight time. Although this was soon increased to 50 hr., it probably hindered sales in the beginning.

As the certification program pro-gressed, both Carlson and Mashman were granted instructor pilot ratings, which allowed Bell to open a helicopter flight training school in mid-1946, with Joe Dunne as the first chief instructor. A few months

Model 30, Ship 1A, on the ground at the Gardenville development center. The helicopter's unique "pump-handle" control system is evident.

later, a helicopter mechanics school was added.

The Model 47 successfully made it through the maze of CAA requirements, and on March 8, 1946, the helicopter was awarded the world's first commercial license. Two months later, on May 8, 1946, the CAA awarded Bell Helicopter Type Certificate No. 1, allowing serial production.

While the Model 47 was being designed, built, tested and certificated, work on the Model 42 plodded on. Larry Bell, who had been told that helicopters would sell better if they looked like automobiles, brought in a car stylist from Detroit to shape the fuselage exterior and outfit the interior. The helicopter even had automobile-type doors.

"The problem really was that the Bell management didn't understand the need to develop things logically," Bart Kelley said. "They always wanted to take the 'big leap.' But you have to see if things work before you can do that. The Model 42 was a terrific bite out of the cake."

The Bell engineering team paid more attention to chrome trim, leather upholstery and ashtrays than they did to

the rotor system, several members of Arthur Young's design team commented. Bart Kelley noted that the first time he saw the Model 42, he pulled the collective control up, only to see the rotor angle pitch down.

Larry Bell could not afford a lengthy development program. Bell Aircraft was losing money — $657,000 in 1946 alone — in the wake of the cancellation of the wartime fighter contracts. So as soon as the Model 47 certification was completed, he asked Arthur Young and his team to take over the program and make the Model 42 into a saleable helicopter.

"About the only thing on the Model 42 that didn't give us problems was the main transmission," Dick Ledwin recalled. "It had been made by Borg-Warner."

There was also a major problem with rotor instability which led to control difficulties. "They had tried a lot of different rotor designs and none of them worked," Ledwin said. "Finally, they went to Charlie Seibel and asked him how long it would take him to design a new rotor that would not have all the instability they had encountered. Charlie thought a minute and then told them, 'I can do it in about a week if you'll leave me alone.'"

After making major changes in the Model 42 controls, rotor system and fuselage — one story has it that only the engine mount was not modified to some degree — the Gardenville team, as it was still called, got the Model 42 to fly. The helicopter was publicly demonstrated at the Cleveland Air Show late in 1946. But none were ever sold, and all three of the prototypes either crashed or were severely damaged in accidents on the ground.

"One of the Model 42 prototypes turned over in a high wind right in front of the experimental hangar where we worked," Ledwin said. Joe Mashman, Arthur Young and a mechanic named Kenny Angel were on board. "The first we knew of it was when a piece of the rotor came through the hangar door and lodged

The famous bubble canopy was developed for the early Model 47 helicopters. Despite Larry Bell's dislike, it became the most familiar trademark of Bell helicopters.

Floyd Carlson holds his hands up while hovering an early Model 47 at Niagara Falls to demonstrate the design's stability.

Purportedly there were two NC1H. This photograph supposedly depicts the rarely seen first which was destroyed in an accident.

The Bell Helicopter team which successfully obtained the first commercial helicopter license on March 8, 1946, and the first helicopter type certificate on May 8, 1946, pose in front of the first certificated helicopter, NC-1H.

Reminiscences: Harry Finagan, mechanic and crew chief

In early 1942, I had never heard of a helicopter. Didn't know what one was or what it was supposed to do. But a friend told me that this company in Gardenville, N.Y., was hiring mechanics. He didn't know what the company was doing, just that it was a 'project' of some sort. At the time, I was working as an arc welder for a railroad. Much of the work was outside, and in Buffalo, that can mean it's pretty cold. Arc welding was fun when it started, but I lost interest pretty quick.

So I drove down to Gardenville, found the company in an old automobile garage and showroom and went in and applied for a job. Art Young interviewed me and told me that they were going to build a helicopter. At first, I thought that was an automobile brand name, like Hupmobile or Pierce-Arrow. I asked Art what it was supposed to do, and he said it was supposed to fly.

"You mean like an airplane?" I asked and he replied, "No, like a helicopter." Then he took me in the back and showed me what they had in the way of helicopter models he had built and I got real interested. This looked like a challenge, and I like challenges.

My first job was helping to assemble the model helicopters they used for flight research. They would take them out and fly them, and when they cracked up, I put them together again. At first, these were only a couple of feet in diameter, but later on they grew to be pretty close to 48 in. I guess we worked at that for three or four months and Art got a lot of information out of them. [Most of the models built at this time had 60-in. rotor diameters -- Ed.]

Then we went to work on a full-size helicopter about the middle of '42. We had a couple of machinists in the little machine shop there to make the parts, and the Bell Company sent a couple of sheet metal workers down from Buffalo to help make the tail boom and the center fuselage. I worked on assembling the transmission. Bart Kelley did a lot of the designing of it. About this time Floyd Carlson, the test pilot, was assigned to the project and helped develop the control system.

Gardenville village at that time was very small -- maybe only 150 people -- and way out in the sticks. There was a gas station and the garage where we worked, and right across the street there was a restaurant called Smeltzes or Smaltzes, something like that. [It actually was called Schmalch's Bar and Restaurant. -- Ed.]. It was run, as I recall, by an Italian lady. Anyway, the food was pretty good, and we'd go over there for lunch or after work and all sit together around a big round table. We'd talk about whatever problems we were having at the time, and pretty soon Art Young would start to draw on the white tablecloth. And when we got through with lunch, he'd have them clear the table, and then he'd take the tablecloth off and tell the owner we were going to "borrow" it for a while and would send it back later. Then we'd take it back across the street and copy what was on it off onto paper. A lot of problems were solved around that table at Smeltzes.

When we got the full-scale helicopter complete, we put long spider legs on it and put it all on a tie-down out in the little yard back of the building. It was a single-seat helicopter, and Carlson would get in and start it up and test the controls for a minute. Then he would try to lift it off the ground, and some of us would hold it down with a rope and pulley system. As he got the feel of it better, we'd let him have a little more rope so he could go higher, a few inches at a time. At first, we had three men on the rope, but later we decided we could hold the helicopter down with only two of us. [The tie-down described is the second of two that were used with the Model 30. The first consisted only of two ropes tied to the machine above the center of gravity.--Ed.] If it looked like things were getting away from him, we'd pull him back on the ground. Then they'd make some adjustments on the swash plate or the controls -- whatever he thought was needed -- and he'd try again. Art Young was there all the time and they'd talk out the problems. After a while, Carlson got to where he could hold it steady at eight or nine feet off the ground.

Carlson taught himself to fly the machine, and when he felt he was ready, we took if off the tiedown and he hovered it without a rope. And it wasn't too long before they would ease out into the field out in back of the building and fly around there. It was, as I recall, about eight or ten acres in size, so we had plenty of room to fly around.

One of the big advantages we had at Gardenville was that you could do things quick. There wasn't any of this production control or any of that. The engineers would tell the machinists what we needed, and they could push it out fast. And I would take and assemble it and put it together. Another thing, I don't think any of us ever punched a time clock there. We'd just come and work -- eight, ten, sometimes twelve hours a day.

We found out that there was a lot of vibration from the main rotor because it wasn't stiff enough. So we had to figure out some way to put a stop to that, and Floyd Carlson came up with an idea for a thing to make the rotor stiffer. We called it the "Swedish Yoke," because he had Swedish ancestry. Then we made it and tried it out on the tie-down first, and it seemed to limit the vibration.

After a while we took the spider gear off and put a real landing gear on the helicopter, with a tail wheel and a wheel on each side of the fuselage. Then we took it down to a larger field down the road about a mile, and we flew it around there. Now, we'd never made an autorotation landing and we didn't know what would happen. So he [Carlson] got to flying around the field and it was just beautiful. And he was at about 300 ft., approximately, and he went into an autorotation and was coming down very nicely. But as soon as he hit the ground, the main rotor went back and hit the tail boom. And it made toothpicks out of all the rotor, because we had wooden blades. Fortunately, nobody got hurt and the ship wasn't damaged very much, just the tail boom was dented.

Later, we built Ship 2, which was designed for people to ride in and it had a cabin on it and a different type of landing gear. And that was a very successful helicopter. We flew it quite a bit. It's the one Joe Mashman flew a lot of demonstrations in after he came down from Buffalo. I never got to fly in it, although I did a lot of flying in Model 47s later. Larry Bell flew in Ship 2, and he was sold on it and always wanted to show it off. He was a terrific man.

We flew Ship 2 in the armory in Buffalo [in its first public demonstration, May 10, 1944]. Floyd Carlson was the pilot and, of course, I was crew chief. I tell you I thought we were nuts [to fly it there] because it was an experimental aircraft. We went in and did a test flight in the armory the day before, and then I went all through that machine with a fine tooth comb, checking everything. Our control system bellcranks and so forth were just sheet metal riveted together. I was real scared, myself, about what could happen with these rotor blades so close to all those people around. But Carlson, he didn't seem to have a nerve in his body. He was a terrific man when he was flying. He hovered it, and I just wanted him to set her back down and get the heck out of there. But he took her off and flew her around again.

We were there in Gardenville about three years and moved to Buffalo right after the war. I've never gone back, even for a visit.

Harry Finagan retired in 1978 after 36 years with Bell Helicopter Textron and its predecessors. He still lives near the factory in Fort Worth.

Bell Helicopter production line at Niagara Falls in 1947. At right are Model 47Bs with automobile-like styling. Bubble canopy machines at left are U.S. Army YR-13s.

in the roof. We looked outside and there was the Model 42 on its side with gasoline gushing out of the tank. Everybody was running like hell to get away from it before it blew up, except Arthur Young. I ran up to the helicopter and yelled at Arthur to get out. 'I can't,' he said, 'I'm looking for my fountain pen...'"

Several military helicopters were developed from the Model 42 as revised by Art Young and his team. The first of them was the Model 48, which was designated the R-12 by the Army. Two prototypes of the five-place helicopter were ordered and tested. The Army initially ordered a production run of 34, but canceled the order in 1947 before any were actually built. One of the prototype R-12s, however, did set a world's speed record for helicopters of 133.9 mph.

The Army then ordered a test quantity of a stretched version of the Model 48, which it designated the R-12B. This helicopter could carry two crew and eight passengers. After taking delivery of the order for 11 evaluation helicopters, the Army ordered no more.

The third helicopter developed at this time was the Model 54, which was more akin to the Model 47 than to the Model 42.

Bell entered it in an Army competition for a new liaison helicopter and finished second. Despite this, the Army ordered three Model 54s, which it designated the R-15 and used for test purposes until about 1950, but the service never ordered more.

But there was a silver lining in these apparent dark clouds. The Model 42 and its successors were failures in the sense that no great production orders came from the effort put into them. But they were successes in that they gave the designers valuable experience which made a big difference in only a few years.

"The Model 42 and its successors gave us a lot of experience in designing larger helicopters," Bart Kelley noted. "They gave us an entree into machines the size of the Huey. Bell's experience in the Model's 42 and 48 paid off. The Huey's later success tracks from these early efforts."

Certification of the Model 47 and the redesign of the Model 42 led Arthur Young to the conclusion that his work at Bell was complete. He had no interest in marketing the designs and he felt that those who had worked with him were capable of continuing development without him. He wrote a letter of resignation to Larry Bell,

Eight of the first 28 YR-13s ordered by the U.S. Army are lined up on the Niagara Falls ramp ready for delivery. Company designation was Model 47A.

unfortunately while Bell was out of the country. Upon his return, Bell was miffed by the note, which seemed to him to be an attempt by Young to avoid his responsibilities, if not his contractual obligations.

Bell insisted that Young stay on, which he did until late 1947, but the relationship between the two was strained after the incident. After he finally left Bell, Young returned to his native Paoli, Penn., and resumed research work into futuristic concepts of rotary wing flight.

"Art Young got shoved into a big bureaucratic organization," Charles Seibel said. "He couldn't do things the way he had done previously, and he didn't like it. They should have left him to do his own research and development work."

The Model 47, although it moved slowly into production in 1946-47, was a design that had a lot of growth in it. The 11 Model 47 test aircraft were retained by Bell for training, research and development. The Model 47A, with a bubble canopy, was delivered to the military as the YR13/HTL-1, with the first delivery being made in late December, 1946.

The first civil helicopter to be sold by Bell was the Model 47B, a design which delighted Larry Bell, but not the customers.

It had a stylish automobile-like enclosed fuselage with car-like doors on each side and it seated a pilot and a passenger side by side. The Model 47B had a four-wheel landing gear and could accept an optional nylon float landing gear for operation on water. Only 78 were built, all in 1946-47, and were sold in ones and twos to various operators around the nation. The first commercial delivery was made on Dec. 31, 1946.

The Model 47B's most notable early success was in agriculture, and it was superseded in 1947 by a specially designed version, the 47B-3, for use in agricultural work. The 47B-3 had an open cockpit and could carry up to 400 lb. of pesticide dust.

The Model 47B was followed quickly by the Model 47D, which entered production in early 1948. It reverted to the bubble

Army YR-12B helicopter hovers during development testing. The R-12B was an enlarged version of the Model 48/R-12, which, in turn, was a development of the Model 42.

Prototype Model 42 hovers at Niagara Falls. Only three prototypes of the unsuccessful design were built, but the experience paved the way for the later Huey designs.

Model 48/XR-12 prototype hovers with floats attached. The Army ordered 34 of the helicopters, but canceled the order in 1947 before any were delivered.

Model 54/XR-15 finished second in an Army competition, but was ordered anyway. The Army took delivery of three prototypes, but never ordered the helicopter into production.

canopy which the original Model 47s had used, had an open-frame tail boom and the four-wheel landing gear which all Model 47s had until the early 1950s.

Early Model 47D helicopters featured a split bubble canopy, in which the upper part of the bubble and the doors could be removed and replaced by a small windshield. The Model 47D became the early standard among light helicopters, forming the basis for the H-13B military helicopter and later the H-13D. However, it was while the Model 47D was in production that Bell first felt the impact of competition.

Stanley Hiller had developed a small coaxial twin-rotor helicopter while still a teen-age student. This machine gave him

such prominence that when he later visited the Bell factory in Buffalo, Larry Bell let him tour the facility, had Joe Mashman fly him around in a Model 47 and sold him a complete Model 47 rotor system. Bell told Joe Mashman that what was needed in the helicopter field was competition in order to make everyone better.

Hiller's new single-rotor helicopter, the Hiller Model 360, was the first to give the Model 47 serious competition in the light helicopter field. It could carry three persons, versus the Model 47's limit of two, and it embodied, in some ways, more advanced manufacturing techniques.

Bell's immediate response was a lightweight version of the Model 47D, designated the Model 47D-1. This version of the Model 47 was about 1,000 lb. lighter than the original and could seat three persons. The decreased weight improved its performance noticeably. Payload increased by up to 35% over the Model 47D.

A version of the Model 47D-1–with an improved transmission, gear box and some modified structural members and an uprated engine–was purchased by the Army as the H-13E. More than 490 of this type were sold to the Army. They gained fame as the medevac helicopters of the Korean War.

Reminiscences:
Frank (Chick) LaJudice,
mechanic

In July, 1941, I went to work as a mechanic at the Bell Aircraft factory in Buffalo, N.Y., working on P-39 Airacobra fighters, and eventually worked my way up to crew chief on the flight line.

One day in the early fall of 1941, I was working in the hangar at Buffalo and the foreman came by and told us all to stop what we were doing and help push airplanes out of the way to clear some room for some sort of demonstration. Then Arthur Young came in with a little electric model helicopter and demonstrated that it could fly right there in the hangar.

The helicopter work later went down to Gardenville, but I stayed in Buffalo until I went into the Marine Corps in 1944. When I came back in 1945, I went to work in the experimental hangar at the new plant in Niagara Falls, and they had brought the helicopter operation there by then. We started a school to train helicopter mechanics and another to train pilots.

There was plenty of room for everything in the aircraft bays at Niagara Falls, where airplanes had been built during the war, and the helicopter division took them over. There was just a small production area in one bay at first, but after the military orders came, we set up the first real production line in 1948 and had 15 or 20 ships on the line at one time.

I helped in the certification of the Model 47. Everything was experimental then, and several of us helped build the throttle system for the helicopter. We devised the cam that made the throttle work and made the first one with a hacksaw and a file. Then we had them make up the production drawings from that.

When the first production Model 47 came off the line, I got to travel all over on demonstration tours. We went down to Louisiana to show how we could fly crews into the oil rigs that were out in the swamp then. And we went up to Canada and Alaska to demonstrate how we could do geological surveys. We went up into the Adirondacks to spray the black flies that were bad up there, and we found we could control them real good. The Hollywood Hotel, which was a big resort, was able to open a month earlier than it had been.

I went all over the U.S. -- Florida, Tennessee, Oklahoma, Illinois, New York. We demonstrated flying the mail in Chicago and crop dusting in New York. On all these demonstrations in 1946, '47 and '48, we had to show how to use a helicopter, because the potential customers usually didn't know how. And it was important to have a mechanic along. In 1948, I think it was, I went down to Argentina with Joe Mashman to demonstrate what the Model 47 could do, and I had to rebuild eight or nine helicopters during the eight months we were there.

In the fall of 1950, we were told the helicopter operation was moving to Fort Worth, and a group of five of us arrived here on Jan. 6, 1951. The first pilot came in the following week. We went to work in the old Globe plant and started an assembly line for the Model 47 in January and February, 1951. We moved over to the present factory in late 1952 or early 1953.

I worked on every Bell helicopter from the Model 47 on. The Huey was my favorite, and I helped build and install the first transmission on that helicopter. I also helped do the ground runs on the first tilt-rotor, the XV-3, and later spent five months down at Arlington Airport working on the XV-15.

Frank (Chick) LaJudice retired in 1989 after a 48 year career at Bell Aircraft and Bell Helicopter. He and his wife reside today near the Bell factory in Ft. Worth.

CHAPTER THREE

...But why would anybody want to buy one?

Army H-13Gs lined up for delivery at the Fort Worth factory circa 1953. Some 265 of this model were delivered to the Army. Clockwise from upper right: Model 30, Ship 1A, rolled into Buffalo's Civic Stadium for a public demonstration in 1944; Oil exploration work with a Model 47D; Agricultural chemicals being loaded into a Model 47D hopper.

51

Joe Mashman came to work one day in 1946 with bags of Pillsbury's Flour in his car. He didn't know for sure, but he thought they might help Bell launch itself into the world of commercial helicopter marketing.

With a certificated helicopter ready to market, Bell was in the position of having to invent something that the helicopter could do better than a fixed-wing aircraft in order to get any civil sales at all.

One of the first things that was suggested was dusting or spraying agricultural fields. Mashman had noted that the rotor downwash seemed to be particularly good at getting under things, mainly women's skirts. He thought perhaps a helicopter might be more efficient at getting pesticide on the underside of plant leaves than conventional fixed-wing crop dusters.

A couple of dust dispenser bins were rigged up on each side of Model 30, Ship 1A — the original Bell helicopter — and Mashman loaded them with the flour. He used the flour to perfect his aerial application technique on the airport at Niagara Falls. It worked so well that a short motion picture was made and used as a sales tool.

The first civil Model 47 was purchased by a Yakima, Washington, undertaker who was an aviation enthusiast and came up with the idea of using helicopters to dust apple and cherry orchards in the Pacific Northwest. Herman Poulin came to Buffalo, saw the film of Mashman 'dusting' the airport, and on the strength of that, purchased a Model 47B. His purchase led to the Model 47 being the first helicopter certificated for aerial application of pesticides to crops.

But it was evident that sales of the Model 47 to a few crop dusters were not going to keep the helicopter in production, so Larry Bell launched a vigorous campaign to get the helicopter noticed by the general public and potential users.

The first thing he did was select Joe Mashman as the company's demonstration pilot. In 1946, Bell employed only a handful of helicopter test pilots. Floyd Carlson had been first, in 1943, and was joined in early 1945 by Joe Mashman, after all the other test pilots in the fixed-wing group turned the job down.

"I was the junior pilot in the group, but when no one else volunteered, I stuck my hand up. And I got razzed by the others because I had volunteered to go," Mashman recalled.

Mashman was taught to fly helicopters by Carlson, and the two cooperated in testing the Model 30s for a time. But Mashman was quickly singled out by Larry Bell as the pilot to give demonstrations to prospective customers.

A frequently recounted story of the selection of Mashman as Bell's chief demonstration pilot says that one day Mashman was flying the Model 30 at Niagara Falls, attempting to find out just how much maneuverability the helicopter had, when Larry Bell came up and pointed, and without knowing who was flying the machine said, "I want that man to

Model 30, Ship 2, being readied for the first ever public demonstration of a Bell Helicopter inside Buffalo's 65th Regiment Armory. Floyd Carlson, in cockpit, is talking to Arhtur Young, standing.

Model 30, Ship 1A, the original Bell helicopter, was fitted with this experimental agricultural spray rig for early aerial application tests.

demonstrate my helicopters!"

It's a good story — but it's not true.

Certainly, Mashman had a flair both for helicopter flying and for making friends with those he met. Arthur Young commented "Mashman makes it [flying a helicopter] seem easy, no matter what the configuration."

"When we certificated the first helicopter," Mashman recalled, "Larry Bell came to Art Young and Bart Kelley and said 'Floyd Carlson is an excellent experimental test pilot, and your man Mashman appears to be the kind of pilot we want doing our demonstrations.' So I was appointed Bell's ambassador and was sent all over the country demonstrating helicopters, trying to convince people they were a success. And I continued doing this until I retired from active flying in the 1970s."

At first, I remained a member of the development engineering team, but I devoted a lot of time to being a demonstration pilot," Mashman said. "A lot of the early demo flights were given to Larry Bell's friends — Col. Frank McCormick, who owned *The Chicago Tribune*, and Juan Trippe, president of Pan American Airways. I always tried to show how easy it was to fly a helicopter and how stable it was. I learned to move my body slightly to compensate for any instability and would fly with my hands off the controls

to impress the passenger."

Larry Bell understood that the only way to sell helicopters was to educate the public to their utility. He often flew to local meetings around Buffalo in one of the Model 30s, both to impress potential customers and to let people see that the helicopter did have some real utility. At least once , while enroute to a meeting in one of the Model 30s, he was forced down by a mechanical problem. In that instance, Floyd Carlson made a safe autorotational landing, and Bell called his office and ordered Joe Mashman to get the other Model 30 and fly him the rest of the way to the meeting.

An early Model 47B equipped with floats gives a flight demonstration at the Bell Aircraft factory in Niagara Falls.

An early export sale of the Model 47B was to Ostermanns, a Swedish helicopter operator.

As the helicopter operation grew, additional pilots were added to the flight department. The third pilot hired was Frank H. "Bud" Kelley and four or five others had been added to the staff by late 1946. These included Owen Niehaus, Frank Drake, Harlan Hosler, and Joe Dunne, who headed up the Bell pilot school.

One tragic addition to the staff was Milt Carlson, Floyd's older brother and the person who had originally taught Floyd to fly. He was working on building up time in one of the pre-production Model 47s in order to demonstrate the helicopter's endurance capability. In August, 1946, his helicopter crashed and he was killed. No reason for the crash was ever determined, although a fatigue failure was suspected. The accident so affected Floyd Carlson that he was taken off flight status for a time.

Flight demonstrations continued even when the Model 47 was in the midst of certification work.

"I'd take the prototype out on the weekends after a full week of experimental flight test work and fly demonstrations wherever I could," Mashman said. "I'd take an engineer along and we'd go demonstrate at some Army base. We were trying to get them to outline some sort of mission that could lead to a design specification."

After certification of the Model 47, Mashman was put to work doing demonstrations before large groups, even if they were not particularly aviation oriented. One such demonstration was embodied in the Olson and Johnson vaudeville act at a fair in Toronto in 1946. Ole Olson would be delivered to the open air stage each night by helicopter. It got a lot of attention.

Civil sales were slow, but there were enough to show that the helicopter could do some things better than other types of aircraft. By late 1947, there were about 30 Model 47s engaged in crop dusting in the U.S. A few others were purchased by charter operators, corporations and one newspaper. The newspaper, the Portland, Ore., *Oregonian,* used the helicopter largely as a flying photo platform. In the days before electronic photo transmission, the paper could photograph an event miles away, fly the film to the roof of the printing plant, and have it in print hours before the opposition.

However, sales were nowhere near the 500 helicopters that Larry Bell had envisioned when he invested in 500 Franklin engines and other components. Due to a lack of storage space at Buffalo, many of the engines were stored on a balcony at the plant, where some of them sat, literally, for years. In fact, when the Korean War came in 1950, and the government placed orders with both Bell and Hiller for light helicopters, Larry Bell sent some of the engines to Hiller so that both companies could meet the military's delivery deadlines.

A few Model 47s were sold to international customers earlier, but the first really large foreign sale was to Argentina in 1947. A private company there bought 13 Model 47s, with government assistance, to help fight a locust plague that was devastating parts of the nation. Larry Bell sent Joe Mashman to Argentina to head a team of Bell pilots and mechanics which would train their Argentinean counterparts, while at the same time demonstrating how the helicopter could defeat the locusts. In his spare time, Mashman was told to give sales demonstration flights around the continent.

It took more than a year and a demonstration tour of most of South America, but the effort resulted in a few sales and a lot of exposure for Bell Helicopter.

In early 1948, Stuart Symington, secretary of the Air Force, asked Larry Bell if he could provide a helicopter to a friend of his in Texas who was seeking election to the U.S. Senate. Bell, seeing a chance for more public exposure, agreed and sent Mashman to Texas to meet with then-Rep. Lyndon Johnson. Johnson wanted to use the helicopter on a campaign tour of the state.

"At that time, it was the law that a manufacturer had to be paid in cash for services to politicians," Mashman recounted. "I didn't know exactly what arrangements had been made between Symington, Johnson and Larry Bell, but I felt it was a pretty dicey situation. Fortunately, no one asked any questions."

Mashman and Bill Diehl, a Bell service representative and mechanic, flew a Model 47D to Texas to carry Johnson around the state as he campaigned in the Democratic primary. Johnson had a large loudspeaker system fitted to the helicopter, so he could talk to the people in small towns as he passed over. The weight of this, plus

Joe Mashman demonstrates an Army H-13B, one of 65 ordered by the Army in 1949, before delivery.

Johnson and Mashman, meant that the two-place helicopter was frequently operating near or at its maximum weight.

However, only once did the helicopter fail to get Johnson to a scheduled appearance. The tour, conducted in hot, often dusty conditions far from maintenance facilities, showed that the Model 47 was a more rugged and dependable helicopter than most people had believed. The tour lasted almost a month in the summer heat of Texas. How much effect it had on the outcome of the election is debatable. Johnson finished second in the first round of the primary election by using a helicopter, but won the final round, when he did not use a helicopter.

By 1950, Model 47s were operating in Europe, South America and several other areas of the world and were being used for such widely varying jobs as mail transportation and fire fighting in North America. But sales were still far below projections, and Larry Bell decided to see if more military orders could be generated.

The Army was just as much in the dark on how to use helicopters as anyone else. The Army had operated several hundred helicopters during World War 2 — mostly in the U.S. although a few saw service in the Pacific. But the service had never developed any sort of doctrine or tactics for their use. When Bell had the Model 47 flying and nearing civil certification, the Army placed an order for 28 Model 47As, the first Bell helicopters to be built on a production-line basis. The Army designated them the YR-13.

These helicopters had bubble canopies, covered tail booms and four-wheel landing gear with bungee-cord shock absorbers to cushion the landings. Of the 28 helicopters purchased, the Army transferred 10 to the Navy, which designated them the HTL-1. Three more were modified for cold weather testing in Alaska, and redesignated the YR-13A. The rest were used for test and evaluation work and eventually sent to San Marcos, Texas, where military helicopter training was being carried out by the Air Force for all the services.

The very first Army helicopter pilots were trained by Bell in Buffalo, at first individually and later in the Bell flight school which opened in mid-1946. Two of the early students at this school in Buffalo were Hugh Gaddis and Jack Marionelli, both of whom were in the fourth class to graduate, in the spring of 1947. Both of them later rose to be generals and head of Army Aviation.

One of the pilots trained at San Marcos in early 1948 was a young Army officer named Cliff Kalista, who was just back from a tour as a military advisor to the South Korean government. In later years, he rose to be vice president of international sales for Bell Helicopter. But in 1948 Kalista was an Army fixed-wing pilot who had been selected to get his helicopter rating before going on to a desk job at Fifth Army headquarters in Chicago.

"I checked out in a Bell YR-13 after 25 hr. of instruction in 28 days," Kalista recalled. "That was the total program. I only had five-and-a-half hours dual before I was soloed. I didn't think I was ready, but they had other students, and you had to keep moving along. Among other things, I never did an autorotation to touchdown at the school because the Air Force instructors didn't believe in doing them.

"The YR-13s I trained in had a 175-hp. Franklin engine, a wheeled landing gear, covered tail and they had to have a complete overhaul every 25 hr. of flying time," Kalista recalled. "Some months later, two

Patent for skid landing gear was issued to Bell on June 9, 1953, following the initial application on Sept. 27, 1951.

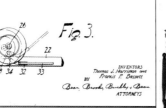

An early Model 47D demonstrates an experimental spray bar developed to extend the coverage swath.

of us were detailed to fly two H-13Bs, equipped with float landing gear, from Warner-Robins air base in Georgia, to Alaska. We never made it. It took 17 days to get to Colorado, including the time we spent at Ft. Sill, Okla., getting the 25-hr. overhaul. When we got to Fort Carson, the temperature was 95 deg. Fahrenheit, there was no wind and the airfield was at an altitude of 6,300 ft. With floats we couldn't make a run-on landing. So we came in and made a big, high flare to kill off speed, then just dumped it in on the ramp. The tower called and asked us to move to allow other traffic past and I told them to call a crane, because that H-13B could not get off the ground."

Model 47B-3 lays chemical dust while being operated by Helicopter Aircraft Services of Syracuse, N.Y. The helicopter, serial number B-55, was sold June 11, 1947.

An experimental dust hopper was tested on this Model 47D-1 in 1952. The helicopter had earlier been converted from a Model 47B-3.

The H-13Bs were part of the Army's second order for Bell helicopters. These were similar to the civil Model 47D, but were powered with a 200-hp. Franklin engine. The service ordered 65 of them in 1948. They retained the bubble canopy and wheeled landing gear and they were the last Bell helicopters ordered by the military prior to the outbreak of the Korean War.

After the Korean War began, the Army ordered another 85 H-13Ds, which were delivered in 1951, just before the company moved to Fort Worth. These helicopters were the first to have skid landing gear in place of the four wheels on earlier models. They also had the covering removed from the tail boom. The landing skid was developed by Bell on a modified H-13B, which was the only helicopter to be redesignated as an H-13C.

When these helicopters began to be deployed to Korea four or five months after the war broke out, there was still little concept of what they could do. Initially, they were thought to be a somewhat more versatile replacement for the Stinson L-5 liaison aircraft that had been the standard Army liaison airplane since World War 2. It was some time before someone had the idea of lifting wounded troops directly from the front line to the rear area hospitals. Even with a very limited number of helicopters assigned to this mission, hundreds of wounded were successfully recovered in the first few months of this type of operation.

The discovery of this capability prompted the Army to order hundreds more H-13s in the next several years.

The Korean War also produced the first attempts at an armed attack helicopter. The results were good, but military thinking had not progressed to the point where a specification could be written to describe what was needed for such a mission.

The first attempt came in 1951, after Hans Weichsel and Joe Mashman were told by Marine Corps officers about the problems that Russian-built T-34 tanks were giving U.S. forces in Korea. The only weapon the U.S. infantry had to combat tanks was the Bazooka, a tube which was held on the soldiers' shoulder and launched a short-range rocket with a warhead.

The Bazookas were often not available at the place where the Russian tanks were encountered. So the idea came about to put a Bazooka on a helicopter, increasing mobility and making the helicopter into a good anti-tank weapon.

Most of the existing Bazookas were either in or on their way to Korea, when Bell wanted to test the concept. But Mashman and Weichsel went to the Pentagon and got the Navy to loan them one. The only Bazooka that could be located was in a display case in the Pentagon hallway. It was taken out of the case and given to the two Bell representatives who took it back to Buffalo on a scheduled Capitol Airlines flight.

"The thing came apart into two pieces and we tied them together with tape and string and just carried them on

Movie makers quickly saw the potential of helicopter camera platforms. A camera installation is being fitted to this Model 47B-3 in 1949.

like carry-on luggage," Mashman recalled. "Part way to Buffalo the stewardess came over and asked what the pieces of pipe were for and we told her they were a rocket launcher used to destroy tanks. We showed her how it worked and even let her look through the sight. She wasn't alarmed and no one else on the aircraft exhibited any fear. It was like it was just an everyday occurrence. Can you imagine carrying a rocket launcher on an airliner today?"

Back at Buffalo, the helicopter engineers developed a mount to hold the Bazooka onto the helicopter's landing skid. They also made a device which allowed the pilot to aim the Bazooka rocket, which was unguided, by lining up a rear sight in the cabin with a mark on

the canopy. There were no Bazooka rocket rounds to be had through any official source, but through friends in the Marine Corps experimental section at Quantico, Va., a few rounds were obtained. There are persistent reports, which no one will confirm (or deny), that a couple of cases of Scotch whiskey were later discovered at the experimental section headquarters.

Before making a demonstration at the Quantico firing range, Weichsel and Mashman performed an impromptu test to see if firing the rocket would damage the tail boom or tail rotor. Balsa wood sticks were fastened to the tail boom and tail rotor, which was made of glass fiber-covered balsa wood. A Bazooka round was fired while the helicopter was sitting on the ground. Despite the blast from the rocket motor, the

The H-13 rapidly became the symbol of Army aviation, and the bubble canopy recognizable world-wide.

Forestry protection was another job performed by early versions of the Model 47. Here, a Model 47B-3 sprays an evergreen forest.

balsa wood strips were virtually undamaged.

With a Marine Corps colonel on board as official observer, Mashman flew the H-13 to the gunnery range and came into a hover a little over 300 yards from the target, which was a big, square board with a dot painted in the middle.

"I had no real idea of how to aim the Bazooka, high, low or dead center on the target, so when I got the sights lined up the way I thought they ought to be, I just closed my eyes and squeezed the trigger," Mashman said. "I opened them just in time to see the rocket hit the target almost dead center.

"I asked the colonel, 'Does that convince you of its accuracy?' and flew him back to the field," Mashman added. "He seemed impressed and I felt pretty good, hitting the target the first time with no prac-

tice, although I knew it was mainly luck. I thought the Marines might really adopt the idea."

The Marines at Quantico were impressed, but the idea was killed at higher headquarters. The argument against arming the H-13 with Bazookas was that to do so would give the enemy a valid reason to try to shoot the helicopters down and thus would put at greater risk the H-13s carrying wounded.

The development of rocket-firing helicopters was delayed until a later war.

Some time later, Dick Stansbury, a Bell test pilot, flew the HSL-1, which had been designed as the Navy's anti-submarine helicopter, to Ft. Rucker, Ala., to demonstrate it to the Army Aviation Board. Bell was trying to sell the aircraft to the Army as a troop and cargo transport.

"We gave them a pretty good show," Stansbury said. "I did an autorotational landing with 5,000 lb. of lead on board."

Later, Stansbury was standing with the Aviation Board officers when a young captain came up and introduced himself. "If you have a few minutes, I'd like to show you something," the officer said. Stansbury followed him to a nearby hangar, where a guard was posted. Inside, the captain showed Stansbury an H-13 with two .30-cal machine guns mounted on the skids.

"He asked me if I thought it would work, and I told him that I thought the first time they fired it, they would blow the bubble off the helicopter," Stansbury said.

"Besides," Stansbury told the captain, "we're rescue people, we're not gun people."

An Army YR-13 hovers at the Bell factory in Buffalo in 1947. Early training of Army pilots was done in Buffalo.

An H-13B hovers at Fort Sill, Okla., in 1948. The Army based its helicopter aviation program there before later moving it to Ft. Rucker, Ala.

Bazooka mount for a Model 47 was developed at Bell's Niagara Falls facility before being demonstrated to Marine Corps officers at Quantico, Va.

One of the first 10 HTL-1 helicopters delivered to the U.S. Navy in 1947 is on the ramp at Niagara Falls. The HTL-1s were identical to the Army's YR-13.

Joe Mashman: 'Bell's Ambassador to the World'

In 1946 and 1947, the [Bell] prototypes often would get only a week or so of flight testing by experimental pilots before I would take the helicopter out on a demonstration tour.

By doing this, I quickly got a keen understanding of the capabilities and the deficiencies of the helicopter which I would discover during demonstration tours. I also had the opportunity, by inviting our competitors' demonstration pilots to fly our prototypes, to fly their aircraft and I was able to determine the pluses and minuses of their aircraft.

I wasn't concerned with them flying our prototypes, because once an aircraft becomes a prototype, it's already had a number of years of development. In my eyes, it was already becoming obsolete. But I was able to provide valuable information to engineering as far as correcting existing designs and improving prototypes. So throughout the years, in addition to being a demonstration pilot, I was also a member of the engineering team.

Most of the time, I worked for Hans Weichsel, who came to Bell, I believe, in 1947. We became a pilot - engineer team with the responsibility of demonstrating the helicopter to our military forces and creating military requirements.

Back in those days, the military didn't know enough about helicopters to come up with a design spec. So it was Hans Weichsel's ingenuity, in figuring out what the military would be responsive to, that gave engineering an insight into what sort of design we needed or what to improve. And he was responsible for a lot of the designs -- many of which were improvements on early production helicopters -- some of which were based on my observations.

Joe Mashman was Bell's second helicopter pilot and undoubtedly its most famous. He began flying helicopters in 1945 and continued until the late 1970s. Mashman retired from Bell in 1981. He died in 1994, shortly after being interviewed for this book.

Bell Model 47D, center, was the first version of the helicopter design to be produced in significant numbers, initially at Niagara Falls, pictured here, and later at Fort Worth. Lower left, This Model 47B was among the early Bell helicopters used in commercial service. It was operated by the Metropolitan Aviation Corp. of New York. Lower left, Floyd Carlson hovers NC-1H, the first Bell Model 47, hands off to demonstrate its stability in flight. This photo was taken at Niagara Falls, probably in early 1946.

CHAPTER FOUR
The Awl Bidness

I n 1943, a U.S. bomber was hit by flak over a Japanese base in New Guinea and made it only part way back to its home airfield. The aircraft crash landed in a huge mangrove swamp, where it floated, stuck in an impenetrable, water-logged hell. The crew climbed out on top of their downed bomber, but could not leave it without sinking in the ooze and slime.

Dick Stansbury was a U.S. Army Air Force C-47 transport pilot at that time, flying military supplies and troops between Allied bases in New Guinea. After the downed bomber was located, he and others in his unit were given the task of getting supplies to the downed airmen. Rafts were dropped in hopes that the crew could float out, but that did not work. Australian paratroops, familiar with the area, looked at the site from the air and refused to jump, claiming it was suicide to do so.

"I had heard that there were a couple of experimental helicopters being used to fly mail between several islands, and I tried to get them down to help rescue the men, but they claimed they didn't have the range," Stansbury recalled. "Finally, we lost that crew but I'm positive that if we had gotten the helicopters, we would have saved them. Anyway, that episode stuck in my mind, and I decided that after the war, I'd get into helicopters."

The third Model 47 manufactured was used as a structural drop test airframe during certification work at Niagara Falls. This photo was taken on Feb. 13, 1946.

After the war, Stansbury did just that. He enrolled in the Bell helicopter pilot training school in 1946 on the strength of a promise from the Bendix Helicopter Co. to hire him as a test pilot when he completed the course.

"The Bell school was the only one there was in those days," Stansbury said. "Sikorsky didn't have one, and none of the other helicopter companies were big enough to support one, so it was Bell or nothing." Stansbury completed the course, but by the time he did, Bendix had gone belly up.

"I was fortunate," he said. "Floyd Carlson checked me out in NC-1H and then hired me as an instructor pilot. I had 2,000 hr. in fixed-wing aircraft, but only 30 hr. in helicopters. I was in Class 6F at the Bell school, which had three pilots from customer companies and me. I received Civil Aeronautics Administration (CAA) helicopter license No. 10."

NC-1H, the first certified Bell helicopter, was among the craft used for pilot training at the Bell school, and it was wrecked sometime during this period. "Students were always using it to practice autorotations and one day one of them misjudged his height," Ed Unwin recalled. As they were picking up the pieces, Unwin ran out and unscrewed the name plate off the helicopter, Years later, he donated it to the Bell Hall of Heritage in Fort Worth.

At the time Stansbury was in the Bell school, there were two instructor pilots, Joe Dunn and Harlan Hosler. But Floyd Carlson gave every student his final check ride, because he was the only pilot at the school licensed as a CAA check pilot and had to sign off on each student. Joe Mashman also held a check pilot rating, but he spent most of his time on demonstration work.

"Floyd liked to give each student a little problem on the check ride to see how they handled the unexpected," Stansbury said. "With me, he waited till we were returning to the field. When we were low, right over a hangar, he chopped the throttle, turned to me and said 'Where you gonna put her?' I said, 'On the ramp,' and did, which seemed to satisfy him."

Stansbury went to work as an instructor in January, 1947. The first group he taught was Class 10F, which had 10 students, of whom four were U.S. Army pilots from Ft. Sill, Okla. Ft. Sill was the home of Army Aviation at the time, but there were no pilot training facilities there yet, so new

Army helicopter pilots were trained by Bell for a time. Two of the four Army pilots in that class -- Hugh Gaddis and Jack Marionelli – went on to head the Army's aviation program. The Army subsequently adopted the Bell flight and mechanic training curriculums at its own training facilities when these were opened. Bell provided both free of charge.

While the Bell training facilities were being developed, Larry Bell was continuing to see what markets existed or could be created. He knew that in order to sell more helicopters he had to create different markets.

"Somebody pointed out to Larry Bell that the oil companies had a lot of money and were using marsh buggies for their exploration work in the Louisiana swamps," Ed Unwin recalled. Unwin, the safety inspector at Gardenville, had become a service engineer and was traveling the country making certain that Bell operators knew how to maintain their machines. Larry Bell decided that helicopters might be able to replace the swamp buggies.

At this time, there were only about 25 civil Model 47s in existence, Stansbury recalled. "That's all that had been built. I recall flying Nos. 14 and 15 frequently."

Meanwhile, by early 1947, Alva "Tex" Johnson – the same Tex Johnson who later became famous for slow-rolling the Boeing 707 prototype during a demonstration at Seattle – had become chief pilot of Bell Aircraft. Larry Bell told Tex to take the company's private P-63 Kingcobra fighter and go see what he could drum up in the way of oil industry contracts. He was to get some helicopter business from the major oil companies, use a helicopter to perform them, find out what the problems of oil field work were and write a report to Larry Bell. The oil industry was, after agriculture, the first to feel the impact of the helicopter's unique capabilities.

Johnson flew to Houston and set up shop in a hotel there. With his nickname, his noticeable western apparel and his flair for publicity, Johnson soon was talking to the senior officials of several major oil companies, moguls of what was universally known in Texas as the "awl bidness."

Near the end of July, 1947, Johnson came to Stansbury and told him to take a helicopter to Houston and demonstrate it to the oil company officials. Stansbury and a mechanic flew N-103B, originally designed for agricultural spraying. The helicopter was the third machine built which had been designed and equipped for crop spraying. Johnson had arranged demonstrations for officials of Shell, Humble and Texaco to show how helpful a helicopter could be in oil exploration work.

"For the next two or three months, I flew with a gravity meter in the machine, demonstrating the helicopter's usefulness to the oil company officials," Stansbury said. "We worked over a marsh near Galveston and not only showed the oil company people what we could do, but I learned how to get around in a swamp.

Newspapers quickly found uses for helicopters. This one, shown in front of the Bell Aircraft administrative offices in Buffalo, was delivered to the Chicago Tribune.

An early Model 47B hovers with floatation landing gear laced on to metal frames. These were then attached to the axles which normally held the wheels. Body of water is believed to be Lake Erie.

Soon we had contracts with Shell and Humble and, by the end of the year, we were operating three helicopters in the Louisiana swamps."

Side view of this Model 47-B3 shows the rear fuselage design of the early helicopters. This craft is registered NX-131B, indicating it was used for experimental purposes.

A subsidiary company of Bell Aircraft, called Bell Aircraft Supply Co., or BASCO, was formed to perform the work, pretty soon it had more business than it could handle.

In December, Johnson called Larry Bell from Louisiana and asked if he could send a fourth Model 47 down to handle the grow-

ing effort. "Larry was so pleased that he sent the company's Twin Beech airplane down to bring us all back to Buffalo for Christmas," Stansbury recalled.

In January, 1948, the Bell workers began to overhaul the helicopters, since the exploration crews did not work during the winter. During January and February, the helicopters were essentially rebuilt. In spring, the Bell crews began to fly in support of seismic geologic work for the first time.

"This meant we had to be able to lay out 1,500 ft. of cable and explosives," Stansbury recalled, "and then move the cable from one site to the next." Tubs large enough to carry all the equipment needed for the seismic work were designed and built. They were then mounted on the supports from which dusting hoppers were originally slung. A jacking device that was on the agricultural Model 47 to lift the loaded crop-dusting hoppers up into place under the helicopter was used to lift the tubs up and hold them between the twin floats under the Model 47.

"In this way, we were able to move all the equipment needed for the geologi-

cal operations right along with the helicopters," Stansbury said. "After we got everything in position and laid out the 1,500 ft. cables, the geologists would fire their explosive charges. Then we would fly the helicopter sideways, dragging the cable along to the next site they wanted to test. We did this for a couple of years until the marsh was completely surveyed."

Ed Unwin had arrived to help maintain the helicopters operating in Louisiana and he and the others devised a way to attach the 1,500-ft. cables to the helicopter engine mounts, which were on the helicopter's center of gravity, and pull the cables along while flying sideways.

"It worked pretty well," Unwin said, "But there was one time when Bill Quinlan, one of the pilots, forgot about the cable and straightened the helicopter out. The tail rotor hit the cable and he lost it. They called me in to see what could be done, and we worked out a way of putting the helicopter on wheels and towing it back to the base at Chalmette to repair it."

Another incident occurred when an oil worker stepped into an area of deep ooze and began to sink. One Bell pilot tried to rescue him by hovering low and having the man grab the helicopter floats. But when the pilot tried to lift the stuck worker, he found the man was holding on so far off the center of gravity that the control system could not hold the helicopter upright and it rolled over and crashed. Neither man was injured, but the helicopter had to be rebuilt.

Unwin was present when the idea of using helicopters to support offshore oil rigs was born – of necessity.

"One day this pickup truck raced up, with a Humble Oil driller in it. He had a small tool that they had to get out to a rig

Kerr-McGee was operating eight or 10 miles off shore. The rig was shut down until they got the tool. He wanted to know, 'Could we fly it out there?'," Unwin said. "Al Danner, the pilot, looked at the part and decided we could carry it in the cabin of a Model 47, so we took it out to the rig. As far as I know, that was the first delivery to an off-shore oil rig."

In early 1949, two Louisiana companies, American Exploration and Offshore Navigation, agreed to jointly form a new company and buy the oil exploration operation from Bell. They had been watching with interest the Bell experiment, but the incident that drove them to move into the helicopter field was a nature preserve in Louisiana which refused to allow their swamp buggies to pass through while doing oil exploration work. They were afraid the swamp buggies would cause the spread of marsh grass.

The Navy's second order for Bell helicopters consisted of 12 Model 47Ds, designated the HTL-2. Deliveries were made in 1949.

An Army H-13B disperses dust from an agricultural hopper attached to the side of the fuselage. No reason is known for the use of a military helicopter in agricultural experiments.

The two companies agreed to buy the Bell interests only on several conditions. Bell had to provide most of the employees, including all of the pilots, and the new company had to be permitted to use the Bell name to show that it had stability and was supported by the manufacturer.

Larry Bell agreed, and Petroleum Bell Helicopters came into being. The four principals were Jack Lee and Larry Gussman, who had operated American Exploration, and Bob Suggs and Maurice "Dookie" Bayon, who had owned Offshore Navigation. Both Suggs and Bayon had been colonels in the Army during World War 2. Bayon was from an old New Orleans family that owned the *Times-Picayune* newspaper.

Stansbury, possibly at Larry Bell's suggestion, also was permitted to invest some money in the enterprise and was named general manager. "I think I was supposed to act as a go-between and peacemaker between the two partnerships," Stansbury said. Four Bell pilots -- Stansbury, Leonard McConley, Quinlan and

Elton Smith – went on the Petroleum Bell payroll, and Bell Aircraft sent four mechanics to keep the helicopters operating. Stansbury flew his pregnant wife, Carolyn, from Buffalo to Lafayette in a Model 47 in the spring of 1949 to begin his new job. She was the first woman to make an extended cross-country flight in a helicopter. When the baby was born, Stansbury got the infant a logbook and carefully noted that the child had 17 1/2 hr. of cross-country dual flight time.

"We quickly had more work than the four helicopters that Petroleum Bell owned could handle,' remembered Stansbury, "but we couldn't afford to buy any more right then. So Larry Bell sent three more machines down to operate alongside ours and pilots to fly them. Bell retained ownership of the three helicopters, and they stayed on the opposite side of the hangar from Petroleum Bell, but it was essentially one operation. "By the end of 1949, Petroleum Bell had a net profit of more than $30,000, which was more than all of us had originally invested," Stansbury recalled. "But we had a problem. We had planned to take January and February of 1950 and overhaul the helicopters, as we had done the previous year, and both Jack Lee and Larry Gussman agreed. But Bob Suggs and Dookie Bayon wanted to shut the operation down until spring and lay off all the employees to save costs."

Stansbury, with a minimal investment, suddenly held controlling interest in Petroleum Bell. But that condition didn't last long. "Bob Suggs said he was going to settle the argument in one day and he got

Jack Lee to go to Shagg's restaurant and they stayed there and apparently argued it out all one night," Stansbury said. "Next morning, Suggs showed up at the office and said he had bought out Lee and Gussman and he wanted to buy my shares, too. So I sold out and went back to Bell in Buffalo. Virtually all the old Bell employees left, also. McConley was the only pilot who stayed."

After the ownership changed hands, the Bell name was dropped and the company became simply Petroleum Helicopters, Inc. (PHI) which it remains to this day. Petroleum Helicopters used only Bell machines in the early days, despite intensive efforts of other companies to sell their helicopters to PHI. "But they were satisfied with the Model 47 and didn't change," Stansbury said.

C.L.Tisdale, who joined PHI in mid-1950 as a mechanic and rose to be the company's maintenance chief, recalled the problems encountered at PHI in operating the early Model 47s.

"We had all Model 47Ds at first, but some were converted to 47D-1s. The main problem we had at first was the very short overhaul life. In mid-1950, the overhaul life of the Model 47 transmission was something like 100 hr.," Tisdale said. "But before long, they changed the planetary gear arrangement [in the helicopter's transmission] and the overhaul life went up sharply to about 600 hr."

The PHI maintenance shop devised a way to lubricate the tail rotor drive shaft bearings without having to remove the entire shaft. Also, the PHI maintenance people convinced Bell that the electrical generator should be moved from the underside of the vertically mounted engine, up to the top.

"The rotor blades were wooden and had surprisingly good durability," Tisdale said. "We could repair them in the field by just putting an insert in to replace any damaged section. They stood up a lot better

than you might think."

Tail rotor gear boxes were a problem at first, he added, because light castings were used in an effort to keep the helicopter's weight down. But the gears made of lighter castings just didn't mesh well, and things got better only when Bell shifted to heavier metal castings.

"The electrical system was a first-class pain," Tisdale added. "It had an old vibrator voltage control like the cars had then. We changed it to include a modified voltage control used by the military, and it worked a lot better. The fan belts were hard to install, and their life expectancy was not very good. I saw belts that failed in as little as 25 min. Also, the wire cores in the belts tended to rust or corrode in the wet Louisiana atmosphere, and the belt would break."

The Model 47G, which came along in the mid-1950s, was the first to have metal rotor blades. Tisdale said the improvement was not as great has he had anticipated. "We got longer blade life, but they were not repairable in the field," he recalled. "The main thing they did was put less stress on the engine."

Tisdale praised the original Bell maintenance and operations manual for the

Many of the original 28 YR-13s ordered by the Army eventually found their way to the helicopter pilot training program. This one is a Fort Sill, Okla., in 1947.

The Navy also used the first Bell helicopters it operated in the training role. This HTL-2 is in flight at NAS Patuxent River, Md., in 1949.

Model 47, calling it "probably the best manual ever published. It had to be, as many mechanics became acquainted with the helicopter in this manner."

Another pilot familiar with the early Model 47s was Stan Clay, who flew aircraft during World War 2 and learned to fly helicopters at the Bell school in 1948. He came to work for PHI in mid-1950 and rose to be chief pilot before retiring in 1982.

"The very early Model 47s were tiring to fly because they had a mechanical irreversible control system, which didn't filter out all the feedback from the rotors," he said. "The hydraulic damper system was a lot better. Also, the wooden rotors were always getting out of balance or out of track, and that caused more feedback from the rotor.

"Another problem we had," Clay continued, "was a lot of moisture in the air, which condensed on the rotors and rotor heads at night. At first, we covered the rotor hub every night with a canvas cover, but pretty soon we found out that all that did was hold the moisture in," he said.

"One thing which always bothered me on the early Model 47s was the very short throttle throw, which was only about a quarter turn or so from idle to full power," Clay said. "If you flew for very long, it would get tiring and even painful to have to make a lot of very small and precise throttle changes. One day I made 365 takeoffs and landings while laying out a geophone line in lengths of 12 ft. at a time. That night I really hurt."

Around 1953, PHI did its first work involving off-shore oil rigs. Up until that time, the helicopters had been pretty much limited to oil exploration work in the marshes of Louisiana.

"At that time, most oil rigs weren't more than about a mile off shore, and the exploration companies had to use boats to run small parts out to them. The most frequently needed were batteries to run the navigation and obstruction lights on the rigs. Someone got the idea that it would be a lot cheaper and faster if they were flown out by helicopter," Clay recalled. "After we began to take parts out, someone wanted us to take supervisors out and then other important workers."

The Model 47 was not large enough to move entire crews, however, and their transportation to and from the rigs was not begun until larger helicopters became available.

Early operators like PHI gave Bell tremendous feedback on the minor as well as the major problems they encountered with the early Model 47s, and this was the beginning of Bell's "partnership" arrange-

Reminiscences:
Ed Unwin, safety inspector

I first met Bob Stanley, Bell Aircraft chief pilot and later chief engineer, when he was flying gliders at a glider club in Elmira, N.Y. back about 1935. I was a kid and worked there on weekends and during my other free time. Stanley had a mind of his own. Once he decided to see what it was like inside a thunderstorm, so he flew his glider into one at 1,500 ft. and came out a few seconds later at 15,000 ft.

So when, in early 1943, he went to Gardenville and tried to fly the Model 30 without having any helicopter experience, and wrecked it, they asked for a safety inspector to go down and look at the wreck and report back on what had happened. My boss at Niagara Falls was offered the job and turned it down, but I wanted to get in with helicopters, so I took it.

It was obvious what had caused the accident. The Model 30 had no seat belt and the aircraft pitched Stanley up through the rotor, where he was lucky to survive with only a broken arm.

Aside from that, however, I found a lot of safety needs. For example, they hadn't used cotter pins on any of their latches or fastener joints. It was interesting work, so I stayed on. I became the inspector at Gardenville and also worked as a mechanic and turned into the liaison man to keep contact with the safety and inspection offices back at Niagara Falls.

As the program progressed, the space at the Gardenville factory was too small for the kind of flight test work we had to do. There was an airport about a half mile away, but we didn't want to fly over there because we would have to fly over a populated area. So I got my old Studebaker and we put Ship 1 on a trailer, hitched it up and I towed the helicopter to the airport.

We started doing our flight test work at Gardenville Airport, and Larry Bell laid down a strict rule: "Don't start the engine until the camera is running."

Because we were safety conscious, we tried to figure out a way to get down if the engine quit. Floyd Carlson devised the piloting technique for an autorotational landing. I was standing right beside the camera when he landed. When the tail wheel hit, a bolt sheared and the tail cone and the rotor collided.

My main concern was Floyd. I saw him bounce in his seat when the helicopter crashed, and I took off for the wreck. I think I was the first one there, and I found Floyd sitting there. He didn't have a scratch, but he was madder than hell.

Ed Unwin retired from Bell in 1981. Ed and his wife, Mariam, live in Fort Worth.

An early model Bell helicopter, probably a Model 47D, is operated in Italian navy markings. Location is believed to be Niagara Falls.

ment with its customers.

By the early 1990s, PHI had purchased or leased nearly 800 Bell helicopters, out of a total of nearly 1,100 that it had operated. The company had completed well over seven million flight hours and had individual Bell helicopters in its fleet which were approaching 20,000 hr. of safe flying.

"The engineers at Bell designed a pretty good piece of equipment," Tisdale said. "But it took us operators to show them how to really maintain a helicopter."

Reminiscences:
Betty Hunter, secretary

I came to work for Bell Aircraft in 1943, during the war, and stayed until 1945. Then I quit for a time and came back in June of 1946. I was secretary to Bob Wolf, one of the engineers on the P-59 jet fighter, after he moved into helicopter design. Later I worked for Bart Kelley for three years in Buffalo and I was one of the three women transferred to Fort Worth from Buffalo.

A lot of people came down from Buffalo during the first half of 1952, and when the weather began to get hot, they were unhappy. So Mr. Bell said to go out and buy the largest air conditioners -- the old squirrel-cage kind -- and sell them to the employees at cost in an effort to keep them here.

I tried to revive the custom of the secretaries' Christmas party. In Buffalo each year the senior secretaries had a Christmas party, and their bosses -- vice president and division heads -- gave each of them a small gift. There was some opposition to doing this here, because we usually had champagne or wine, but mostly the secretaries hired here just didn't know what it was. Anyway, we got it going and it was held every year.

At the 1955 Christmas party, Mr. Gaylord came to me and said, "The board of directors would like for you to be my secretary." I always wanted him to say, "I asked for you to be my secretary," but he never did. Mr. Gaylord was a very nice man, but he was very proper. I always thought of him as a Princetonian Easterner.

After I came to work for him, I shared an office with Mr. Ducayet's secretary. This office was between Mr. Ducayet's office and Mr. Gaylord's office and had a door into each. Mr. Ducayet got a new secretary once and we got to chatting and found out that we had both studied ballet in our earlier years. We got to talking about various steps and I asked, "Did you ever learn this one?" Then I did this step and misjudged my distance. I flew right through Mr. Gaylord's office door and landed in a graceful position with my arms outstretched in front of his desk. He was sitting there working on some papers, and I don't know if he saw me or not. He never looked up, and I beat it out of there in a hurry.

I left Bell in 1958 and as I was cleaning out my desk, Bart Kelley came in to say goodbye. We chatted for a while and then I said, 'You know, Mr. Kelley, I think the years I've spent at Bell have been the best years of my life.' And he looked at me for a moment and replied, 'Betty, they've been the best years of all of our lives.'

Betty Hunter now works for the Frontiers of Flight Museum of aviation at Love Field and lives in Dallas.

The first helicopters built in the present Fort Worth plant were HSL-1s for the Navy (center). Approximately 30 of the 50 HSL-1's manufactured are visible on the production line. Left, top to bottom: An HSL-1 is used in a ship-towing test; the Globe factory was Bell's first Fort Worth facility; Float-equipped Model 47G lands on a wheeled dolly for easy ground movement.

CHAPTER FIVE
You Gotta Become a Texan

"Larry Bell looked at me and said, 'Well, if we hire you as our public relations man in Fort Worth, what is the first advice you'd give me? "Jim Fuller recalled. "I thought a minute and said, 'Mr. Bell, the most salient advice I can give you is that when you move to Texas, you've gotta become Texans.

"He had his whole staff there, and he hit his desk with his fist and said, 'I want everybody in this room to listen to that. When we went down to Marietta, [Ga., to build B-29 bombers during World War 2] we thought we were God's gift to the South. And we couldn't put window panes in fast enough because they were throwing bricks through them.

"Then he said, 'You're hired. I've got another meeting.' and left. That was in October of 1951."

A year earlier, in 1950, the announcement had been made that Bell Aircraft's tiny helicopter operation was moving from Buffalo – to the Wild, Wild, West, as many employees saw it – a place called Fort Worth, Texas, wherever that was.

Rumors started flying in the Buffalo plant in late 1949 and they intensified in 1950. Something was up, but no one seemed to know just what. What it was turned out to be a search for a new site for the helicopter operation.

Larry Bell's decision to move the helicopter operation out of the relatively new Niagara Falls plant was based on a variety of reasons.

First, there had been friction between the helicopter development team and the main Bell engineering organization ever since 1944. While the tension had been partially alleviated by 1949, it had led Larry Bell to believe that the helicopter organization needed to get away from the older, aircraft-oriented operation if it was ever to achieve its full potential.

"The helicopter operation at this time was small. It was stuck way over in a corner of the Bell Aircraft experimental hangar," Jim Atkins, former Bell Helicopter president, recalled. "And it was competing with a lot of much larger programs within the company.

"We had the X-1 and X-2 [high-speed research aircraft] programs out there, both big and very glamorous. We had the Rascal missile and the Tarzon [guided] bomb, and we built engine pods for the Convair B-36 [strategic bomber].

"You have to understand, the helicopter operation at this time was just sitting there, not building much of anything – it was just existing," Atkins recalled. "On the other hand, the guys in Buffalo didn't want to give up their domains, whether it be engineering or administration or whatever. Larry Bell could see that there were too many activities at Buffalo and that the helicopter was not going to get the recognition or the resources it needed to grow and develop there. And Larry had been receiving a lot of flak for

his decision to develop the helicopter during World War 2. Most of this came from his own people." As Larry Bell himself put it, "I want an organization that thinks helicopters morning, noon and night."

Secondly, there had been a long and extremely bitter strike at the Bell factory in 1949. "Larry Bell never believed his workers, some of whom had been with him since before the war, would ever do something like that to him," Roy Coleman, who became Bell Helicopter vice president of manufacturing, recalled. Bell was looking for a place with an adequate labor pool and a history of stable labor relations when he went seeking a new plant site.

Finally, there was interservice rivalry. In 1949, the U.S. Navy had asked for proposals from industry for a helicopter capable of operating from ships and carrying a sonar system which could detect submarines while the helicopter hovered over the water. Bell, which had no experience in the type of larger helicopter which seemed to be called for to meet this need, originally refrained from bidding for the design work. But two factors changed the company's decision.

Larry Bell wanted to broaden the company's military market base. If Bell was perceived as being allied with a single service, it was likely to harm later

The Model 47G was the first helicopter model designed and developed entirely in Fort Worth. The two-piece bubble on the Model 47D was replaced with a single-piece bubble.

Ground-breaking for the present Hurst factory was held on May 21, 1951, with Divisional Vice President Harvey Gaylord presiding. The ceremony was delayed by the late arrival of Amon G. Carter.

efforts to sell helicopters to other military users. The Navy was considered unlikely to purchase very many Model 47/HTL type helicopters, so a new design was needed.

In addition, some of the helicopter engineers were interested in carrying forward work begun by Arthur Young, before his departure from Bell, of a twin-rotor helicopter. While still at Bell, Young had built and flown small models with twin, overlapping rotors. These early model tests seemed to indicate that such a configuration was feasible, using two standard two-bladed rotors with stabilizing bars and a conventional control system.

"It was a 'let's try the tandem and see what we get' sort of approach," Bart Kelley recalled.

Work on the Bell Model 61 began immediately, but Bell was considered an underdog against its competitors, Sikorsky and Piasecki, both of whom had large helicopter experience. Moreover, Piasecki had extensive experience in helicopter designs using twin, overlapping rotors. In light of

this, it was a bit surprising that Bell was named winner of the competition for what the Navy designated the HSL-1. The award was made in mid-June, 1950, and Bell immediately began work at Niagara Falls on the first prototype.

But there was a catch to the Navy's selection of Bell. Bell's main factory at Niagara Falls was government-owned and was managed by the Air Force. The Air Force and the Navy were then locked in a very bitter and public battle over the money available in the limited Defense budget of the pre-Korean War period. Navy officials passed the word to Larry Bell that they didn't want their new helicopter to be built in an Air Force-managed facility. They had suggested that a new plant site at least 100 mi. from Niagara Falls would greatly aid Bell in winning the HSL-1 competition.

"The helicopter side of the house needed its own home. So Larry Bell found in the HSL-1 program the opportunity he needed to get the entire helicopter unit out

of Buffalo," Jim Atkins said.

Bell began a search for a new site for the helicopter operation. After a short time, three site finalists were selected – Fort Worth; Westfield, Mass., and a site in California.

The California site was quickly eliminated, but Westfield, Mass., was a different story. It had a solid aviation support infrastructure already in place – small machine shops, specialty houses and other businesses which could supply most of the high-technology components Bell would require. It was near enough to Sikorsky's Stratford, Connecticut, factory, so that workers with helicopter experience might be found.

Bart Kelley, for one, openly lobbied for Bell to move to the Westfield site, because it had the machine shops and other support facilities he knew would be vitally important in the manufacture of large numbers of helicopters.

Fort Worth, in contrast, did not have such a large support industry. Although it was an aviation center, most of the work in the area consisted of designing, assembling or test flying aircraft. The Convair Division of General Dynamics (now Lockheed Ft. Worth Co.), the Chance Vought Division of United Aircraft (now Vought Aircraft Corp.) and a number of smaller companies formed the core of the local industry.

But Fort Worth had some advantages not present in other locations.

"Fort Worth had good weather, which was important to Larry Bell," Jim Fuller recalled, "and he got a very good reception here, particularly from Amon Carter." Carter, publisher of the *Fort Worth Star-Telegram* and the leading promoter of the city, worked hard to get Larry Bell to move his helicopter operation to Texas. Fort Worth, with its rough and ready "Where the West Begins" image, impressed Bell as having the sort of frontier environment which could readily accept new ideas and new technology.

Finally, the Defense Department at that time was urging defense contractors to locate well inland, if possible, to increase the distance from a potential Russian attack from the sea. This gave Fort Worth an edge over both California and Massachusetts.

Bell and Carter met and liked each other, which smoothed the path for Bell's selection of Fort Worth. Carter suggested several sites for the new factory, including one south of the city on what is now Interstate 35W and another north of town near the site of a World War 1 flight training base, Hicks Field.

"Larry Bell said, 'Thank you very much, Amon, but we'd like to select our own site,'" Jim Fuller recalled. "He picked the

The Hurst factory is shown in its original form, top, with 165,000 sq. ft. of production floor and 40,000 sq. ft. of office space. Below, the site during the initial phases of construction. The two-lane highway visible in both photos was then Texas Highway 183, now renamed Texas Highway 10, and was the main highway link between Fort Worth and Dallas.

Hurst area particularly because it had lots of flying area over empty fields and a railroad behind the plant site. At that time, [Texas Highway] 183 was the main artery between Fort Worth and Dallas. [The section which runs in front of the Bell factory has since been redesignated Texas Highway 10].

"So he bought about 40 acres [Actually, it was 55 acres – Ed.] of land fronting on the highway from the Duskey family. And they had a little home on part of it and they wanted to stay living there and Larry said, 'That's fine.'"

There was a second reason for selecting the Hurst site, according to Roy Coleman. "The highway came out of Dallas and ran straight to Hurst, then it turned and ran straight to Fort Worth," he said. "And Larry Bell had a vision of this great big sign saying 'Bell Aircraft' right there at that turn where it would become a landmark on the road between the two cities."

The move to Fort Worth caused some major changes in the management structure of the helicopter organization. It became the Texas Division of Bell Aircraft. Harvey Gaylord was named vice president to head it up, get everything moved to Texas, build a new factory and not miss any

production deadlines for military helicopters while all this was going on.

Gaylord was a good choice. Although not an engineer, he knew how to select a good staff and he had the confidence to rely on them. Also, he had a flair for public relations and he impressed the people he met. He had been in the financial side of Bell for some years and had been credited with saving the company once when dissident stockholders staged a revolt and tried to remove Larry Bell and wrest control of the company from his associates. Gaylord raised additional capital on Wall Street and played a major role in beating back the rebels.

Several people who were there at the time suggested that Gaylord was sent to Texas as a move by jealous executive rivals to get rid of him. If that was their reasoning, it backfired badly. "Mr. Gaylord came down here and made Bell Helicopter a success, when a lot of people were hoping he wouldn't," Betty Hunter, Gaylord's secretary, recalled.

Gaylord's chief assistant was Edward J. Ducayet, an engineer who originally had come to Bell from Curtiss-Wright. He was the first man to move into the new Fort Worth factory and later succeeded Gaylord as the company's president.

Bell paid the Duskey family $1,000 per acre for the land on March 22, 1951. Two months later, on May 21, 1951, ground was broken for the new factory. It was designed to have a 165,000-sq.-ft. manufacturing area and a two-story administration building providing 40,000 sq. ft. of office space.

"Larry Bell came down to see the area, and I picked him up at the airport and drove him out to the new plant site," Jim Fuller remembered. "He was the kindest man I have ever known. He said 'Jim, we're about to come roaring in to this little town where people are accustomed to walking across the street without looking. If we ever killed a dog, it would really hurt me; if we killed a child, it would kill me. You do something about it.'"

In response to this request, Fuller

Test pilots Floyd Carlson (left), E.J. Smith (center) and Joe Dunne discuss the HSL-1 during test work about 1953. Smith and Dunne served as chief test pilots under chief pilot Carlson.

instituted a safety program which required each person who came to work for Bell to sign a pledge they would never exceed the speed limit, even if it meant being late for work. Decals were put on windshields of all the employees' automobiles: "I will not exceed the speed limit through Hurst."

Even before ground was broken for the new plant, Bell established a production line for the Model 47D and 47D-1 at a factory it leased near Saginaw, Texas, a Fort Worth suburb. It was known locally as the Globe Plant, after the company which had operated it during World War 2.

The first Bell workers moved in there in early January, 1951, and began to set up a production line for the Model 47D, which was the only product Bell Helicopter had at that time. Rapid installation of the Model 47 manufacturing operation into the Globe plant while the rest of the Bell operation was moving from Buffalo was imperative. The Korean War had broken out in mid-1950. Bell was beginning to receive a flood of orders for military helicopters and could not afford a break in production, even to move its factory halfway across the country. Into the Globe facility went all the Model 47 tooling, some of which was shipped from Buffalo by train and some of which came by air.

"We planned to move flight test first, then assembly, then sub-assembly and manufacturing," Roy Coleman said. "Through friends in the Air Force, we got the use of a large transport aircraft and moved the sub-assembly work over one weekend. That included the fixtures and everything. We sent six employees down to start the plant up and immediately hired 10 mechanics locally, so the operation had a majority of Texans almost from the start. We knew we needed Texans on the payroll and that it would be very advantageous to have a majority of the employees be Texans."

There was hardly a ripple in the production of the helicopter.

Only 388 helicopters of all types had been built in Buffalo between the time work began there in 1946 and the end of production in 1951. The large majority of them were Model 47Ds.

After the new factory was complet-

Model 47G is demonstrated on floats, possibly as a prelude to off-shore oil rig support operations. Body of water is probably the Gulf of Mexico.

Arthur Godfrey, radio and television star of the 1940s and 1950s, and a Navy reservist, poses in front of a Navy HTL-1/Model 47B.

Two Model 47Gs carry a section of radio mast to demonstrate their effectiveness in construction work.

ed, the Globe plant continued to turn out components for the Model 47 and, later, other Bell helicopter models. These included the famous bubble canopies, which Larry Bell had so resisted, but which had, in time, become a highly visible and well-known trademark for the company.

Getting a new plant in Fort Worth was only half the battle. Bell couldn't build

helicopters without the skilled engineers, technicians and workers who had been developed in the years at Gardenville and Niagara Falls. About 300 key workers and officials were identified as critical to the success of the operation, and the company set about getting them to agree to accept a transfer to Texas.

Most of them had never been to Texas and those who had had either made brief visits or had been in the state during World War 2, when they might not have seen the best parts. Many of those who had visited the state did so under conditions that did not necessarily make them want to come back. Joe Mashman, who came to Texas for a few weeks in the summer of 1948 to fly Lyndon Johnson around, was typical of those with a negative attitude. Texas was hot and dusty during his visit – one of the most uncomfortable episodes in his life. "I was ready to leave when the job was done," Mashman said, "and I promised myself I'd never come back."

The first need was to show the workers what it was really like in Texas and what they could expect. "After I was hired, I came back to Fort Worth and started to make a color movie of the area through which we could tell the Bell employees in Buffalo everything they would need to know to move to Texas," Jim Fuller recalled. "But as luck would have it, there was a terrible drought that year and there wasn't anything green around the area to photograph."

Fuller went back to Buffalo with the film, lacking in color though it was, and started showing the movie to the families of the 300 key people Bell wanted to transfer to Texas. For six weeks, he met with them in small groups, showed the picture and then answered any questions.

"We hired a young fellow whose sole job it was to find homes for all the people who accepted a transfer," Fuller said. "Most of them had little frame houses in Buffalo, and they could sell them for about $7,500, which was a lot of money in

in 1951. Then they would come down here and find that for that amount they could buy a three-bedroom brick house on a half acre with all the amenities, which they never could have afforded in Buffalo, and they were absolutely elated.

"That helped a lot, because the wives became happy in a hurry," Fuller added. "We took the ones with school-age children around to see the schools. Most of the people who came moved either to Fort Worth or Dallas. Very few settled in the mid-cities area because there was just nothing there in 1951."

When Jim Fuller came back to Fort Worth after showing movies in Buffalo for six weeks, Ed Ducayet, Harvey Gaylord's top assistant, came down with him. The original management staff was small to start. There was Harvey Gaylord, vice president in charge of the Texas Division, and his assistant, Ducayet. Also on the man-

agement team were Roy Coleman, who headed manufacturing; Matt Barcelona who ran industrial engineering; John Finn, who was in charge of industrial relations; Bart Kelley, head of engineering; Bill Humphrey, who was responsible for quality control; and Fuller in public relations. All were directors. Except for Harvey Gaylord, there weren't any vice presidents.

Fort Worth's lack of an industrial infrastructure capable of supporting Bell's manufacturing work turned out to be a plus, rather than a minus.

"There was a kind of electric spark in the air when we first came to Fort Worth," Bart Kelley recalled. "The people around the area showed they wanted us. But there were a lot of skeptics within Bell who felt that we could not teach 'cowboys' to build helicopters, with all their intricately machined components.

Test rig built at Hurst was used to evaluate the HSL-1 at various pitch angles. Foundation of the rig still existed in 1995.

Petroleum Helicopters, Inc. (PHI), a major user of Bell helicopters for oil field support, was founded as Petroleum Bell by Bell Aircraft seeking more commercial use of its machines, including this Model 47G

Pratt & Whitney R-2800 engine, shown here mounted in the helicopter, powered the HSL-1. The 2,400-hp. piston engine proved too noisy to permit efficient sonar operation.

But, in the long run, the lack of machining capability in the Fort Worth area became a great advantage to us."

First of all, he noted, the "cowboys" proved adept at learning the machining trades, some of which involved new technologies back in the early 1950s.

"Secondly, we learned how to do this work correctly because we had no one else to rely on," Kelley said. "Back in Buffalo, we had built some of our own gears and had learned how to make a successful transmission. We found that the existing support industry in Fort Worth could not do this, and neither could the major aircraft manufacturers in the area. We had some terrible troubles at times, but we learned how to make the machined parts on which the helicopter relies. Later on, when we farmed out some of our gear and transmission work, we knew what to look for and how to tell whether the subcontractors were doing quality work.

"This proved to be a great advantage to us over some of our competitors, who had

relied on subcontractors right from the start," he added. The same was true, he said, of rotor blade manufacturing. When subcontractors began working on rotor blades for Bell's helicopters, the company had the knowledge in-house to know how things should be done and to maintain tight quality control.

Until the new factory in Fort Worth was completed, development of the Bell Model 61, the Navy's HSL-1 anti-submarine helicopter, continued at Buffalo. The first several of the twin-rotor aircraft were built at the Niagara Falls factory and later shipped to Fort Worth. Fuselage sections continued to be built at Niagara Falls for some time after that.

"Pretty quickly there developed a sort of rivalry between the Bell workers in Buffalo and those in Fort Worth," Betty Hunter, recalled. Betty was one of only three women employees transferred to Texas. She later became Harvey Gaylord's secretary. "At that time, Ford was building cars in Texas and putting a sticker in the rear window that said, 'Built in Texas by Texans.' When the first HSL-1 fuselage left Buffalo, it had a big sign painted on the side which read 'Built in Buffalo by Buffalos.' But somebody found out about

it, and the company stopped the train enroute and washed the sign off."

The development of the HSL-1 formed the basis for the construction of the Fort Worth factory, and much of the initial manufacturing equipment in the new plant was purchased with Navy funds. Development and, later, production of the HSL-1 covered the overhead expenses of the new factory for some time.

In early December, 1951, just over six months after ground was broken for the new factory, the first employee moved in. Ed Ducayet, Gaylord's assistant, put his desk in the office building even before the administration part of the facility was complete. Construction workers on the night shift would move his desk so they could do their work. Consequently, each morning Ducayet would have to search for it before he could get down to business. He finally had a telephone installed with a very long cord so he could have it on his desk,

regardless of where the desk was that day.

Adjacent to the new factory, there was an old farmhouse which initially was used to house the flight department, because it was located right next to the factory heliport. Later, because it had a separate entrance which allowed job applicants to enter it without going into the plant's secure area, it was used as the employment office. Job applicants could reach it without going through a rigorous security process, but could not go further without company permission.

The new Texas Division immediately had two major tasks when it opened for business, aside from the production of the

Bell XHSL-1, prototype of the Navy's HSL-1 anti-submarine helicopter, made its first flight March 4, 1953, at the Hurst plant.

The HSL-2, shown here as a three-view, was never built. It was to have had saddlebag-type fuel tanks to increase endurance.

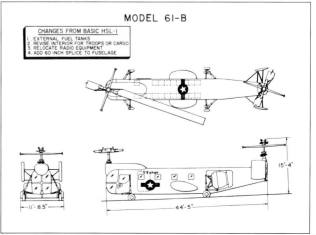

MODEL 61-B

CHANGES FROM BASIC HSL-1
1. EXTERNAL FUEL TANKS
2. REVISE INTERIOR FOR TROOPS OR CARGO
3. RELOCATE RADIO EQUIPMENT
4. ADD 60 INCH SPLICE TO FUSELAGE

15'-4"

11'-8.5"

44'-5"

Model 47G cockpit had an instrument panel centered to permit maximum visibility through the bubble.

Model 47D/H-13. The first of these was the completion of development of the HSL-1 and its production under a Navy contract calling for an initial production run of 78 helicopters.

The second was a redesign of the basic Model 47, incorporating all of the improvements which had been identified in the five years the helicopter had been operational. The result of this work was the Model 47G.

The development of the HSL-1 was slow and difficult. The helicopter was plagued with control and vibration problems. Its single Pratt & Whitney R2800 engine was too noisy for the sonar operators to hear the sonar's various high-frequency noises which located and identified submerged submarines in the vicinity.

And after the HSL-1 began shipboard tests with the Navy, it was found that even by folding its rotors, the craft could not be made to fit on the flight deck elevator of the escort carriers which had been designated to carry the helicopter.

Some Bell engineers who worked on the program believe the successful development of the HSL-1, and particularly its control system, was simply beyond the state of the art at the time.

"We tried to use the same see-saw rotor system that we had used on the Model 47 on the 50-ft. diameter HSL-1 rotor and it just wasn't able to do what we wanted it to do," Bob Wheelock, then senior flight test engineer, remembered. "If only we had had the underslung feathering axis hub at that time, the HSL-1 would probably have been a success." The UFA, however, had not been developed at that time.

The prototype XHSL-1 made its first flight on March 4, 1953, with Floyd Carlson at the controls. "Floyd flew all of the new models on their first flight," Dick Stansbury recalled. Stansbury later became the HSL-1 project test pilot.

Development flight test work later was moved out to Hicks Field where the HSL-1 was housed in an old wooden hangar, thought to have been built as a World War 1 maintenance hangar for training aircraft. But due to delays in the

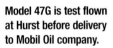

Model 47G is test flown at Hurst before delivery to Mobil Oil company.

Reminiscences:
Dick Stansbury, test pilot

The day they broke ground for the new plant in Hurst there was a big party. They had a big tent for the hundreds of visitors, Walter Jetton came out and catered a barbecue lunch, and there were several helicopters on hand to give 10-minute rides to various important people. They brought one man over to my helicopter, helped him in and told me he was Amon Carter and said to show him around. I had heard that he was Mr. Fort Worth, so I said, 'Where would you like to go, Mr. Carter?' He said "Let's go east so I can see where they are going to build our new municipal airport, Amon Carter Field."

So we took off and flew southeast toward the site of the airport and I was amused because Mr. Carter kept saying, "Oh, my, this is just great. You can see everything from up here."

Pretty soon, Mr. Carter said fly over this way a little, then fly over that way some. He kept directing me to various places and then on to someplace else, so finally I asked him if he owned some land around here. "Yes," Mr. Carter replied, "I've got a little over here and some over there and a little more over yonder." He had gotten me to take him on a tour of all his property in the area so he could check up on it and see how things were going. We were away from the factory site for about an hour instead of the normal 10-minute flight, and I knew they would be worrying about us, but I wasn't about to tell Mr. Carter we had to land unless we were getting low on fuel. Finally, he said he had enough, and we returned to the factory site.

I saw Harvey Gaylord, who was vice president in charge of the new Texas Division of Bell Aircraft, head toward my helicopter, and I knew we had problems. Mr. Gaylord had been a boxer in his younger days, and when he was mad, he would hunch up his shoulders and walk up on his toes, like he was in the ring. He was coming toward us with his shoulders up around his ears. I told Mr. Carter that we were in trouble because we had been gone so long that we had delayed the groundbreaking ceremony and that I was probably going to get fired.

Mr. Carter didn't say anything until Mr. Gaylord opened the cabin door. Before he could say a word, Mr. Carter unloaded.

"Harvey, that helicopter ride was the best thing I have ever done and this boy is the greatest helicopter pilot in the world. He has done me and Bell Helicopter a real service." He had his arm around me when he said this. Then he and Mr. Gaylord walked away, with Mr. Carter still talking. Mr. Gaylord never got in a single word.

That was the only time I ever met Amon Carter.

Dick Stansbury joined Bell in 1947 as an instructor pilot after getting his initial training at the Bell helicopter school in Niagara Falls. He is retired and lives in Fort Worth.

Navy HSL-1 hovers near the Hurst factory while demonstrating the helicopter's rescue capability. Twin vertical fins distinguish the production helicopter from the prototype.

development program, the initial 78-helicopter order, which included 18 HSL-1s for the British Royal Navy, was cut back only 50 machines, all for the U.S. Navy. The first of these was delivered to the Navy in January, 1957. A follow-on contract for 18 more was canceled.

"A lot of these ships came off the production line and went straight to the boneyard," Bob Wheelock said.

Actually, some few were operated in their original role as anti-submarine helicopters for a short time, but the major use

found for the HSL-1 was as a development craft for helicopter towing and aerial minesweeping. Such studies involving the helicopter continued until late 1960 or early 1961, with about 15 HSL-1s involved. The remainder of the production run was cannibalized for spare parts.

The Army also looked at the HSL-1 as a potential troop carrier. During these evaluations, the HSL-1 set a world's time-to-climb record at a high gross weight. But Piasecki got the troop transport contract.

Developed in parallel with the HSL-1,

Jim Fuller, public relations director

In 1951, I was the sports editor of the [now defunct] Fort Worth Press and Larry Bell was looking for a public relations guy in Fort Worth, or as he liked to say, "somebody to dip snuff with the natives." Francis Dunn, who was the Bell Aircraft public relations director in Buffalo, wrote some letters to other public relations directors and I got a recommendation. Harvey Gaylord and Ed Ducayet had me out to lunch and tried me on for size, and then I was asked up to Buffalo to talk to Mr. Bell.

Before Bell moved down from Buffalo, there were only 128 families in the mid-cities area -- total. We inventoried them from the air. We felt that because of the helicopter being a different animal, it might frighten them an awful lot, and we wanted to know the places to stay away from to avoid problems. And if anyone called in with a problem, I wanted to get out and see them. One farmer called in and said, "Your helicopter came over and killed ten of my best chickens." I went out to see him and said, 'Now you tell me how much you think those chickens were worth and I'll see that a check is sent to you immediately.' And he said "Aw, to tell the truth, my wife went and dressed them right away and they are all in the ice box. You don't owe me nothin'.'"

Later on, as people started to move in, the Hurst-Euless-Bedford school district was building a new school and each of the three cities wanted it named after their town. So I called up a friend of mine on the school board and asked him how the new school was coming. He said fine. Then I asked him how the library was coming along, and he said they were a little short on money for the library. So I asked him how he would like to get 4,000 books. Later that day, I called Larry Bell and told him that he'd just given the new high school a library and he said "Fine." 'And,' I said, 'they're going to name the school after you.' "Great," he said, "give them some television sets, too."

[Television had only reached the Fort Worth - Dallas area a few years before this and was still considered a new and rare phenomenon.]

Incidentally, all 300 families from Buffalo came to Fort Worth, and only one family went back after moving here. Some went back after they retired, but only one left early. They all became Texans, and their children and grandchildren are still here and are still Texans.

Jim Fuller directed Bell Helicopter's public relations program until his retirement in 1980. He lives in Fort Worth with his wife, Wilma.

Initial development work on the HSL-1, shown here in mockup form, was begun in Buffalo and later transferred to Fort Worth.

the Model 47G was much more successful. It remained in production in both civil and military versions until well into the 1970s.

While the 47G was being developed, an older Model 47D set an astounding record for that era. Test Pilot Elton J. Smith set a world's distance record for the class by flying non-stop from the Hurst factory site to the Bell Aircraft headquarters in Buffalo. The distance was just over 1,217 miles, which he covered in 12 hr. 57 min. The helicopter used in the record flight, N167, later was used as a test vehicle in the development of a number of new technologies for helicopters.

The 47G embodied all of the improvements which had been developed from earlier Model 47 operations, much as the Model 30 Ship 3 had utilized all the knowledge gained from Ships 1 and 2.

"The Model 47G was the first helicopter designed and built at Fort Worth," Bart Kelley recalled. The helicopter had saddle tanks which gave a much improved center of gravity tolerance. The craft had a stabilizer that was located near the end of the tail boom and which was geared to move with the cyclic control. The Model 47G retained the irreversible control system first developed for the Model 47A, however. This helicopter was the first Model 47 type to be produced under license outside the U.S., with Agusta of Italy beginning manufacture in 1954.

Follow-on versions came rapidly. The Model 47G-2 and -G2A had hydraulically boosted controls replacing the original irreversible control system. "This was really a big thing," Bob Wheelock recalled. "Flying became something you could enjoy."

These two versions also were the first to use Lycoming engines, rather than the Franklin powerplants which had been used in previous models. These variants also were manufactured internationally both in Italy by Agusta and in Japan by Kawasaki, as were most succeeding versions of the -47G.

The Model 47G-3 had a more powerful Franklin and the -3B and -3B-1 had an even higher-rated Lycoming powerplants. The -3B-2 had a supercharged Lycoming engine for improved high-altitude performance, and a revamped cabin which was widened by about 8 in.

Development of the Model 47G continued through the -5A version, but the basic design also was evolved into the Model 47H and H-1, which were deluxe versions with a soundproofed cabin, upholstered furnishings, and a baggage compartment.

A number of special test versions of the Model 47 were built in the 1950s and early 1960s. Prominent among these was the Model 201, designated the XH-13F by the military, had a Turbomeca Artouste turboshaft engine, license-built in the U.S. by Continental. This was Bell's first turbine-powered helicopter, and tests with it paved the way for the use of the Lycoming T53 engine in the UH-1 Huey. Another variant was a winged version of the Model 47G. It was called the Wing Ding and was intended to permit the helicopter to carry loads heavier than it could lift from a hover. A Model 47 also was used in the early 1960s to test a four-bladed rigid rotor concept.

Meanwhile a new version, the Model 47J, was being developed as an enlarged and improved version of the -H and -H1.

"We wanted to sell a helicopter to the White House as a Presidential transport, but the Secret Service wanted a twin-engine machine," Joe Mashman recalled. "We needed a helicopter that the President could use, but the Model 47H was too small. We needed at least a four-place helicopter."

So Mashman and a group of engineers were given a Model 47 and told to develop it into a four-place version within a budget of $25,000. The primary problem encountered was that of cooling the engine, which tended to overheat badly with the cabin extended to carry four persons.

"When we started, we had to change the engine every 50 hr.," Mashman said. The engine cooling problem was solved within the budgetary limit – but that wasn't what sold the helicopter to the White House.

"The first president to fly in a single-engine aircraft was Eisenhower, and the Secret Service finally approved his flying in the single-engine Model 47J helicopter after we showed them the exceptional power-off and autorotational flight characteristics it had," Mashman said. "And that was because Arthur Young and Bart Kelley had insisted right from the start that the rotor had to be a high-inertia design so it could store up the power needed to cushion the landing."

There was another reason, too, added Robert Duppstadt. "Joe flew John Foster Dulles, Eisenhower's secretary of state, and his wife in the Model 47J and later took Mrs. Dulles for a second flight by herself. She was an avid naturalist, and Joe found an eagle's nest in the top of a tall tree and flew the helicopter in a tight circle above the nest so she could see what was in it. She raved about the helicopter, and John Foster Dulles said if it was safe enough for his wife, it was safe enough for the President. So he recommended to Eisenhower that he get one."

UH-1D Hueys crowd the Fort Worth production floor in 1965, at the height of the Vietnam War production surge. At the peak rate of production, Bell was building in excess of 150 Hueys per month. Clockwise from top right; Artouste turbine engine is mounted on Model 47 airframe prior to flight test; Presidents Harry Truman, left, and Lyndon Johnson, right, shake hands with Warren G. Woodward, a Johnson Aide, with a Huey in the rear; troops jump from a Huey "slick" during Vietnam combat in 1968..

CHAPTER SIX

Huey: Mainstay of the Helicopter War

The fate of the Bell UH-1 Huey and all its future derivatives and descendants was decided by one man, so Perry Craddock's story goes.

He was not an engineer, nor a pilot, nor a corporate official nor an Army officer. Rather, he has been described as "a politician up to his eyes." And he knew absolutely nothing about helicopters.

Wilbur Brucker had been governor of Michigan before he became Secretary of the Army in the Eisenhower administration and, most of the people he worked with still called him 'Governor.'

In an effort to get initial production of a new, turbine-powered helicopter, the Army held the competition for a new medical evacuation helicopter, to take over the

Navy HTL-5, one of 36 delivered in 1951/52, hovers. The Navy used the HTL-5 for pilot training. This version of the Model 47D-1 continued to use a wheel landing gear.'

role that the Model 47/H-13 had filled so brilliantly during the Korean conflict. The HU-1 had been designed with its fuselage sized to enable it to carry four litters crosswise in the cabin, although there were those at Bell who saw its ultimate role as a troop carrier and a liaison helicopter.

In order to get some new turbine-powered helicopters into the inventory, the Army conceived the idea of using the only money it had immediately available to fund the competition for the medevac helicopter. The other finalist was the Kaman H-43, turbine-powered helicopter with twin, intermeshing rotors.

Because of various inter-service agreements, the Army did not, at that time, perform the technical evaluation of the aircraft — whether fixed- or rotary-wing — that it bought. Instead, either the Air Force or the Navy provided this function and qualitatively rated competing aircraft against the specifications which the Army had prepared.

In the case of the medevac competition between the HU-1 and the H-43, the Air Force was the service which scored the two competitors. The result was, for all practical purposes, a dead heat. Air Force officials hesitated to make a selection in a contest where the two competitors had finished with scores so nearly identical. Instead, they tossed the hot potato to the Secretary of the Army. Their rationale in doing so was based on the belief that it would not be wise on their part to let some Army general decide this extremely important and close competition. The H-43 already was in the Air Force inventory and increased production would help lower the Air Force's unit costs. The Air Force may have felt that they would have a better chance to influence the decision at the political level of the Army rather than within the military section.

Secretary Brucker at first declined to even hear a briefing on the matter, but at the last minute changed his mind. After sitting through a bewildering assortment of numbers and technical items, he said to the briefers, "Bell — aren't they the ones who built that little bubble helicopter that saved so many of our boys in Korea?"

Briefing officials confirmed this. "And what did this other company build that we used in Korea?" When told that Kaman had no helicopters in Korea, Brucker asked once more, "And I can pick either one of

these helicopters without going against any of the tests you have made?"

Again assured this was so, he said, "Well, then, I'm going with the company that did something for our boys in Korea."

And life was breathed into the Huey.

Craddock witnessed these events as an Army officer stationed in the Pentagon. He retired in 1965 and later came to Bell to work in the government sales area.

The story of the Huey really began in the winter of 1950-51 in Korea. The Korean conflict was the first war in which helicopters had been extensively involved. Most military planners then saw them only

Army H-13E with side-mounted litter carriers. This version of the Model 47 first made the helicopter famous as the "Bell" rescue ship in Korea.

Bell Model 201/XH-13F, a modified H-13D re-engined with a 250-shp. Continental/Turbomeca XT51 turbine engine hovers at Hurst in 1955. The craft was the first turbine-powered helicopter to fly in the United States.

as a replacement for the light fixed-wing aircraft that had been the Army's chief liaison vehicle since World War 2.

The military, although they had operated a small number of helicopters since 1942, had never come to understand the capabilities that enabled the helicopter to do much more than any fixed-wing aircraft could ever do.

One general, before the outbreak of the Korean War, told Larry Bell that if he really wanted to make his helicopter useful, he should find a way to power the wheels, "so that after you land, you could drive right up to the field headquarters." This suggestion drew the predictable outburst from Larry Bell.

However, all the outbursts in the world could not and had not convinced military planners that the helicopter had a real role to play in warfare. But the crucible of war quickly forced the battlefield commanders to find out just what the capabilities of helicopters really were.

The first Bell H-13s did not arrive in Korea until late in 1950, just about the time that the allied U.S. and United Nations forces were hit by a large-scale Communist Chinese offensive. As the Allies fell back, in bitter cold and heavy snow, there were instances in which units were cut off and forced to either hold a position until they could be relieved, or, more often, fight their way out. In either case, wounded men suffered greatly. They also were a burden to the remaining troops in their unit, who had to carry them on the retreat and care for them along the way.

It quickly became obvious that the H-13 could get into very small areas. The helicopters were used to bring in food, ammunition and other supplies. Then these craft would carry out the wounded, getting them to safety rapidly and relieving the combat unit of the need to care for them.

Through 1950, all of the H-13Bs and H-13Ds in the Army inventory were equipped with a four-wheel landing gear. Bell had developed the skid gear, and Joe Mashman had demonstrated it to Army officials in November, 1950, but the initial operations in Korea were performed by H-13s with wheels. By early 1951, most of the Army's helicopter crews in Korea had been decorated for their efforts. A few months later, the Army officially recognized the superb job the helicopter was doing in evacuating wounded.

As Bell began work on its move to Fort Worth, large orders were received for the H-13E, which was an upgraded version of the Model 47D-1. It had dual controls, three seats, a 200-hp. Franklin engine, improved transmission system and rotor gear box, a new design tail boom and skid landing gear.

Eventually, the Army would order 500 of the H-13Es with two externally-mounted litter supports. The aircraft's work in Korea would make it famous as the first successful medevac helicopter in history. "Ducayet and I negotiated that 500-ship contract with the Army, and we felt like we were sitting on top of the world," Jim Atkins, former president of Bell, remembered.

Although the Army designated the H-13 as the 'Sioux' in keeping with its policy of naming helicopters after American Indian tribes, the name never really caught on. In Korea, the helicopter was called simply "the Bell" and the cry of "here come the Bells" was a welcome indication that help was on the way.

Larry Bell went to Korea during the latter stages of the war to see the H-13 in

Model 47G-3, modified with low-drag landing skids, set a number of world's helicopter speed records in early 1961.

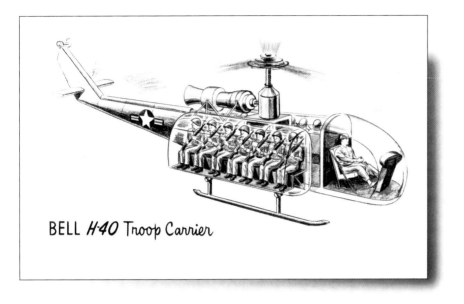

BELL *H-40* Troop Carrier

The need to carry up to 14 troops in a single helicopter prompted Bell to explore several concepts. Top, the H-40 Troop Carrier had a single pilot, with troops carried in two external pods. Bottom, the proposed UH-1C would have been a standard Huey A/B with troops facing outward and seated under a folding door/awning.

action, and actually flew along on several medical evacuation missions. He became ill on this trip — a manifestation of the heart ailment which eventually caused his death — and never fully recovered.

"He saw a lot of the top officers in Korea and talked with them about the helicopter and what it could do," Hans Weichsel recalled. "His interest in finding out what was really needed made Bell Helicopter tops with the Army officers in Korea."

Although records are, in some cases, sketchy, indications are that the H-13 rescued about 25,000 persons in Korea. This includes both wounded troops and injured Korean civilians, the majority of whom would probably have died if they had been forced to rely on surface transportation to reach a hospital. The popular television series *M.A.S.H.*, in which Bell Model 47Gs portrayed their older brothers, the Model 47D, never gave the helicopter much verbal credit. But the visual opening of the show really said it all. Two helicopters arrive, drop off their wounded passengers very near the hospital and head back for more wounded. Overall, about 80% of all the helicopters flown in Korea by the United Nations forces were Bell designs, and more than 80% of all the wounded rescued by air were saved by Bell helicopters.

There were problems with the H-13

in Korea, of course, but most were solved by Bell and Army technicians. Some weren't because they were inherent in the design. The 200-hp. Franklin engine did not produce enough power for the high-alti-

tude conditions in which the helicopter was often called on to fly. "There was a lot of spark plug fouling, and there was not enough capacity for fuel, which created range problems. And the fuel tanks were in a poor location, which gave us a center-of-gravity problem," Hans Weichsel recalled. "And there were just a lot of maintenance problems."

A spares shortage developed, further increasing the difficulty of keeping the Bell helicopters in Korea in operation. Harvey Gaylord assigned Ed Ducayet, his top assistant, to set up a support system

Mockup of the first Model 204/XH-40 takes shape in the Fort Worth factory in the early 1950s. The XH-40 first flew in 1956.

One of the first three XH-40s built is loaded into USAF Douglas C-124 at Fort Worth in November, 1956, for transportation to Wright-Patterson AFB, Ohio, for tests.

that could be relied on by the military in Korea. The system devised by Ducayet and his team not only solved the spares shortage in Korea, it became the basis for Bell's worldwide support network, which over the past four decades has kept both military and civil Bell helicopters flying around the world.

The H-13s did a lot more in Korea than just rescue the wounded, but that is how these particular helicopters were remembered by Secretary Brucker in 1955 and by the public today. And that capability apparently was what most impressed the Army, for immediately after the Korean War, the Army began to develop the specifications for a new medical evacuation helicopter. This one was to be designed specifically for that mission — and it was to be powered by a gas turbine engine.

The Army had sponsored development of the Lycoming XT53 engine for several years, with the intent of using it to power a helicopter and possibly other vehicles which needed a small, light, yet powerful engine. In 1955 Bell had taken an H-13D and re-engined it with a French-designed Turbomeca Artouste turbine engine, built in the U.S. under license by Continental

Motors as the XT-51. The Artouste provided 280 shp., about 80 hp. more than the original Franklin engine in the H-13D. The test aircraft, designated the Model 201 by Bell and the XH-13F by the Army, provided baseline data on turbine engine operation to assist in mating the T53 to the Huey. It was the first turbine-powered helicopter to fly in the United States.

"The Army came up with about 10 areas in which they thought major improvements could be made in a new medevac helicopter," Hans Weichsel recalled. But successful development of a turbine-powered helicopter required more than just sticking a turbine engine in a helicopter fuselage. The two had to be properly matched. Bell's studies determined the proper crossover point between the weight of the engine and the amount of fuel required. "With these studies, we found an area in which the turbine engine was best suited," Weichsel said.

The next requirement was to get the engine manufacturer to tailor the new engine to the needs of helicopters generally and Bell's proposal specifically. "We found out that Lycoming had a team of German engineers working on the development of the T53. Bart Kelley spoke pretty good German, so he went to Lycoming and worked directly with the design team," Weichsel said. "He told them what characteristics a helicopter needed from its engine and got the T53 largely developed to meet Bell's needs."

The Army's specifications for its new medevac helicopter called for a machine with an 8,000-lb. gross weight, a mission radius of 100 naut. mi. at 100-kt. speed and a service ceiling of 6,000 ft. out of ground effect. As modest as these requirements may seem today, in 1955 they spelled out the need for a helicopter on the cutting edge of technology. The new helicopter was to have secondary duties as an instrument trainer and general liaison helicopter, but was not expected to serve as a troop transport.

"There were about four groups within the Army, each trying to get different

requirements met," Weichsel said. "Bell, in fact, proposed five different versions of its helicopter design for Wright Field's evaluation. The Air Force favored another design, but there were a lot of people in the Army who had seen Bell 47s in operation in Korea and who strongly favored the Bell design. One of them was Maj. Hugh Gaddis [who had graduated as one of the first Army pilots trained at the Bell school in Niagara Falls and who later became chief of Army Aviation]. Another group which favored the Bell design were the Army medics.

"In the end, Bell got the medevac helicopter award, and that award made Bell Helicopter," Weichsel said.

The original order planned by the Army was for 200 medevac versions and about 100 trainer versions of the new helicopter. But the initial order Bell received was for three prototypes under a contract awarded in February, 1955. The helicopter was designated the

A YH-40, one of six built for test purposes, hovers outside the Hurst Plant about 1957.

Hubert Humphrey (center), Jim Wright (left) and and Bell president Ed Ducayet view the UH-1 in 1959.

Then Vice President Lyndon Johnson waves from a Model 47J, in which he frequently traveled. Pilot is Joe Mashman. The date was 1963.

XH-40 by the Army. Bell called it the Model 204. The 700-shp XT53 engine which powered it made the XH-40 the first turbine-powered aircraft ordered by the Army.

The XT53 engine powered a 44-ft., two-bladed rotor which retained Arthur Young's weighted-tip bar as the means of stabilization. The XH-40 also had a stabilizer linked to the cyclic control for better pitch stability and control. The original cabin in the XH-40 could not only carry four litter patients inside — double the load of the H-13 — but it also provided space for a medical attendant, something no previous medevac helicopter had done.

The first XH-40 prototype was completed and ready for flight in the fall of 1956, only about 16 months after design work began. The new helicopter made its first flight, with Floyd Carlson at the controls, on Oct. 20, 1956, a day which was both joyous and sad. The Huey prototype flew, and Larry Bell, founder of Bell Aircraft and Bell Helicopter, died.

Larry Bell had been ill for several years with coronary artery disease and had been forced to relinquish his position as general manager of Bell Aircraft in October, 1954. He spent an increasing amount of time in the hospital during this period, but still remained active as president of Bell. On May 24, 1956,

he suffered a stroke, which temporarily blinded him. Although he soon regained his sight, he was increasingly unable to travel, even to local events. On Sept. 18, 1956, Larry Bell resigned as president of Bell Aircraft and was elected Chairman of the Board. But on Oct. 10, he suffered a heart attack and died 10 days later.

On the day of Larry Bell's passing, Bell's Texas Division had yet to build its 2,000th helicopter. The first thousand mark had been passed only in 1953. The helicopter operation was still small, but it was growing, and its most phenomenal growth was near at hand. That growth would be centered around the helicopter that first flew on the day Larry Bell passed from the scene.

Without Larry Bell and his ability to see what the future needed, there would certainly have been no Bell Helicopter. Without his enthusiastic support of the early development program, the effort would likely have died aborning. And without his decision to move the operation to Texas and to support it there while it took root, it probably would have been strangled in its Buffalo crib.

Larry Bell left behind him two great monuments to his life. One is the great number of lives which have been saved by the helicopters he fostered and sustained, a fact of which he was immensely proud. The second is the family of people at Bell Helicopter, who still, today, in many ways mirror the personality of the man whose name graces the helicopters they build.

Even before the first XH-40 flew, the Army had ordered another six as service test aircraft. These YH-40s were all completed by mid-1958, and already they were significantly changed from the first three. The T53 engine had grown from 700 to 770 shp., and the helicopter's fuselage had been lengthened by a foot and the crew doors widened.

While these aircraft were being readied, the Army changed its aircraft designation system. The XH-40s and YH-40s became XHU-1s and YHU-1s, respectively. This HU designator eventually gave the helicopter its familiar nickname of Huey. The Army's official name of Iroquois, like the Sioux designation of the H-13, was consigned largely to official histories of the aircraft. In 1962, the military designation system was again changed, making the HU-1 into the UH-1. But the Huey nickname stuck.

The next order for Hueys provided for nine pre-production models of the HU-1, powered by the improved, 860-shp. Lycoming T53-L-1A. While these helicopters were being delivered, an initial production order was placed by the Army in March, 1959, for the HU-1A. This initial production version of the Huey was powered by the 860-shp. T53-L-1A, which was derated to 770 shp. for service use. The engine turned a 44-ft. rotor with a chord of 14 in. A number of other changes were made to the craft as a result of service tests, but the most noticeable one was a shortened rotor mast.

The order for HU-1As called for production of 173 helicopters and this was completed in March, 1961. Fourteen of the craft had dual controls and went to the Army Aviation flight training school as instrument trainers. One more was modified for a more lethal role. It became a test bed to see which different types of armament could be effectively used on a helicopter. This was done well before Vietnam

blossomed into a conflict — even before more than a handful of U.S. military advisors arrived there — and it showed that the Army was seriously studying the possibility of making its helicopters into combat aircraft.

"In 1959, a group of us took a pre-production Huey to visit the 101st Airborne Division at Ft. Campbell, Ky.," Phil Norwine recalled. Norwine had joined Bell a year earlier after service as a helicopter pilot in the Navy and a short stint as a structural engineer at Boeing. He started as a sales

This armed Huey used in Vietnam in 1968 was armed with a quad M-60 machine gun mount and two seven-round rocket pods. The door gunner is firing a hand-held M-60 machine gun to the rear.

Initial studies in rapelling from a helicopter were carried out by Army troops from this UH-1B.

engineer working for Hans Weichsel marketing the Huey and rose to be a vice president.

"The first thing they did there was to tell us to take the litters out of the Huey and see how many troops we could get strapped down in the ship. We finally settled on nine. We also showed them how the Huey could be a mile away 60 sec. after the pilot got in the cockpit. And we demonstrated how, with the right radios on board, the Huey could be made into a pretty good airborne command post. They began to feel that the HU-1 might make a good assault aircraft."

Bell people also saw the possibility of a wider use for the Huey. In 1960 a group from the company went to talk to Gen. Hamilton Howze, who at that time was propounding the idea that the capability of an Army infantry division could be greatly increased if the unit's transportation requirements were met by helicopters rather that trucks.

"The Huey at this time was strictly a medevac helicopter," Norwine recalled. "The infantry still had only piston-engined helicopters, and only a few of these were capable of transporting a sizeable number of troops. Gen. Howze used the Huey to demonstrate how easy it would be to move an infantry company across a river. He argued that the Army's two airborne divisions — the 82nd and the 101st — needed this capability. Eventually the Army formed the 11th Air Assault Div. to test his ideas."

The effort to get the Army to adopt helicopter mobility was long and difficult, and not the least of these difficulties were caused by opposition to the concept from within the Army itself.

"The effort to get the Huey into the infantry units was driven by the Army's need for greater speed and capacity increases in its helicopters," Norwine said. "What they needed most was a helicopter big enough to permit them to maintain the integrity of a rifle squad, which at that time consisted of 13 men. The HU-1A could carry about nine sol-

Troops leap from a Huey "slick" during combat operations in Vietnam. Slicks were unarmed troop transports as opposed to the armed gunship Hueys.

diers, and because the Army's logistics system and other service organizations were keyed to a 13-man squad, they couldn't easily change the size of the squad."

"We thought a lot about how to get 13 men into the Huey even though at the time there was no official requirement for this. On one flight back from Washington, Hans Weichsel pulled a barf bag out of the seat pocket and began to sketch a version of the Huey that had two benches facing outward outside the fuselage," Norwine related. "It had an awning-like roof over the benches and it could carry the required number of troops. We got back to Fort Worth and built a mockup of this arrangement, which we called the HU-1C. It had accordion doors that folded up."

There was an immediate adverse reaction from the Army Transportation Corps, Norwine said, which saw the proposed version as a threat rather than a solution. That corps was then in charge of all transportation, and if the individual units got their own helicopters, which was part of Howze's air mobility plan, it could jeopardize the Transportation Corps' mission assignment, which they desperately wanted to keep in their own hands.

"So they killed our HU-1C with kindness," Norwine said. "They kept adding more and more equipment to the required list until finally the helicopter couldn't meet the performance requirements."

But both the Army and Bell continued with full development of the Huey. Three months after the production order for the HU-1A, the Army ordered four prototypes of the next version of the Huey, the YHU-1B. The B models were powered initially by the T53-L-5 engine, with a power rating of 960 shp. Later versions had the -L-9 or -L-11 versions, which gave the Huey B more than 1,000 shp. The rotor chord was increased from 14 in. to 21 in.

The HU-1B had an enlarged cabin to permit it to carry up to five wounded plus a medical attendant or nominally seven equipped troops. Tests showed it could carry nine, although that was not the number in the manual. The HU-1B was the first version of the Huey to really be built in large numbers. Production began in March, 1961 and extended into 1965, with an overall total of just over 1,000 being manufactured for the Army.

A variety of armament packages were developed for the B Model Huey, designed to provide standard weaponry for

President Eisenhower sits in a Model 47J, the first helicopter used by the White House for presidential travel. Photo was taken in 1957.

Ammunition boxes are dropped from a hovering UH-1D near Kontum, South Vietnam, in support of the U.S. Army's 4th Infantry Division in late April, 1968. The Hueys made possible the operation of isolated bases and troop movements into areas far from their bases.

The Huey also served as a trainer. This TH-1L of the U.S. Navy, shown in flight near its Florida base in 1974, was one of 89 such trainer helicopters delivered to the service.

the helicopter, in place of the variety of field-installed weapons which were proliferating in Vietnam as U.S. involvement there increased.

The first Hueys to operate in Vietnam were medevac HU-1As, although the early model Hueys were deployed to Panama, Korea, Alaska and Europe before they went to Vietnam. The first Hueys in Vietnam arrived there in April, 1962, before the U.S. became officially involved in the conflict. They were used to support the South Vietnamese army, flying its wounded soldiers to rear area hospitals. These helicopters were operated by U.S. Army crews, not South Vietnamese.

Later that year, in October, the first armed Hueys entered service in Vietnam. These were HU-1As which were equipped with 2.75-in. rocket launchers and .30-cal machine guns. This armament package was installed in Okinawa, and the helicopters were used in Vietnam to escort piston-engined transport helicopters. In November, the first Huey B models arrived, this time carrying armament installed in the U.S. These helicopters carried the M-6 quad machine gun system, which became the standard armament of the Huey for much of the war.

As U.S. involvement in Vietnam increased, so did the number of Hueys. By the end of 1964, there were more than 300 Huey A and B models operating in the country, used primarily as medevac and transport aircraft, with a secondary employment as armed escort helicopters.

While the Army's use of the Huey in Vietnam was growing, other users began to order and operate it. In March, 1962, the U.S. Marine Corps selected the Huey to be its next-generation assault support helicopter. This version was designated the UH-1E and was basically similar to the Huey B, except for different avionics systems and a few other minor changes. A few UH-1Bs were ordered for test purposes, and deliveries of the UH-1E to the Marines began in early 1964. By November of that year, the Marines were seeking a standard armament package to fit on their Hueys. The first armament put on the Marine Hueys consisted of .30-cal machine guns and 2.75-in. rocket pods.

Marine Hueys first arrived in Vietnam in May, 1965, and it was not long before they were in combat, both transporting troops and flying escort missions. And it was not very long before the Marines began to complain about shoddy workmanship in their Hueys, although the Army had never registered such complaints. Specifically, the Marines complained that the engine cowlings on their helicopters did not fit snugly.

There were gaps of up to an inch between the cowling and the main fuselage, they said.

"We knew damn well that those helicopters were alright when they left the factory, and nobody could come up with any explanation for the Marines' complaints," Phil Norwine recalled. "Finally, Elton Smith [a senior test pilot by this time] was sent out to work with the Marine combat units and see what the cause of the problem was. He looked over their maintenance procedures, operational manuals, everything, and couldn't find a reason. Finally he asked if he could fly along on a combat mission and see if he could locate the problem there.

"The Marines were happy to oblige. They took Smitty along on a support mission and pretty soon made a gunnery run on a target," Norwine related. "Now the normal redline speed on a UH-1E was 140 kt., but on this run, the Marine pilot came in at 165 kt., firing all his weapons and then made as steep and as hard a pull-up as he could. When they got back to base, Smitty had them pull off the access panels, and he looked at the structural beams in the fuselage. They were bent. The Marines were actually pulling so many g's in combat that they were structurally bending the airframes,which showed up as poorly fitting engine cowls.

"When Smitty got back with his report, we all looked at the problem and nobody could think of a way to correct it except to tell the Marines to slow down, which we knew they weren't going to do," Norwine said. "So we ended up telling them not to worry about it, just tie the cowlings down firmly and keep on doing

what they were doing."

The Army also had its problems with the Huey. After a new helicopter had been in use for several weeks, it would seem to lose power, although there was nothing showing on the engine instruments to confirm this.

"The Army operated its helicopters very aggressively," Norwine related. "We found that when they would take troops into a flooded area, of which there were a lot, they would often set the Huey right down on its skids. Every time a Huey would land in a rice paddy like this, it would pick up a hundred or so pounds of

Cold-weather testing of the Huey by the Army included this icing spray work in 1959.

A number of alternate missions were proposed for the Huey. This UH-1B, despite Army markings, is equipped for anti-sub-marine warfare work, with depth charges slung underneath the fuselage.

Remote control flight of the UH-1 was developed to enable the helicopter to serve as a target vehicle for anti-aircraft missile development.

water in the lower part of the cabin, under the floor. After doing this for a time, we found that the Huey would have 200 or 300 lb. of dirt, silt, water and what-have-you inside, under the cabin floor, which made it seem as if power had been lost.

"But they kept on flying. There is an actual recorded instance when a Huey took off from a rice paddy with 25 troops on board. This and other events gave the Huey a reputation as a rugged combat helicopter," Norwine added. "One Huey came back from a mission with a hole in the rotor big enough for the pilot to stick his head through. The Huey earned the respect of the troops."

The Air Force also ordered the Huey. In June, 1963, the Air Force selected a modi-fied version of the Huey as the support heli-copter for its ballistic missile launch sites. Initially identified as the XH-48A, the craft was later called the UH-1F. It was powered by the 1,300-shp. General Electric T58 engine, rather than the T53, which was used in all other Huey models. The new engine required a new transmission and engine housing to be designed. The UH-1F also had the Model 540 door-hinge 48-ft.-dia. rotor with the first underslung feathering axis rotor hub. The rotor blades were designed with a stall-resistant 27-in. rotor chord, which gave the UH-1F increased speed and maneuverability over earlier versions of the Huey. One hundred nineteen of these Huey versions were made between 1964 and 1967.

"One day back about 1955, Bart Kelley came to me with this rotor head he had designed," Dick Stansbury, Bell test pilot, said. "He said to me, 'I think this thing has about five hours of life. Would you be willing to test it in flight?' It was the first underslung feathering axis hub. We put it on our test vehicle, a Model 47 with the registration N-167. I ran it up on the ramp and it seemed OK, so I hovered with it and finally took it over the fence. There was no problem. It later went on the Huey."

The Army upgraded the UH-1B to the UH-1C. This was not the same as the pro-posed 13-troop version with the side-mount-ed benches. Instead, it was a straight-for-ward development of the existing UH-1B, incorporating the same Model 540 door-hinge rotor as the Air Force's UH-1F, which increased both speed and maneuverability. But it retained the Lycoming T53-L-11 engine. Later, virtually all 750 of these heli-copters were re-engined with the 1,400-shp. T53-L-13 powerplant and redesignated the UH-1M.

A total of eighteen other nations also acquired the UH-1A/B/C/M Huey for military use.

Even before the Huey was involved in the Vietnam War, thoughts at Bell had turned toward improving the helicopter's lift capability. One idea was to install two engines in the Huey, which was later done.

However, first priority was given to improving the single-engine Huey. It had become apparent that the helicopter did not have enough high altitude/hot day capability. Several instances were recorded where the Huey could not lift off the ground on very hot days. A major improvement seemed to be in order. To accomplish this, the Model 205 was designed and proposed to the Army, which issued a contract for seven of the aircraft in July, 1960. The Army designation of the craft was the YHU-1D.

The Model 205 or UH-1D was still a Huey, but it was much improved over any previous Huey. The fuselage was stretched 3 ft. 5 in., and gross takeoff weight jumped to 10,500 lb. The helicopter's fuel tanks were relocated to increase interior cabin space to 220 cu. ft. This permitted six litter patients and a medical attendant to be carried, or up to 13 fully equipped troops. The problem of carrying a full squad had been solved.

A new 48-ft. diameter rotor with a 21-in. chord was developed for the D model Huey, and the tail boom had to be lengthened to accommodate the new rotor. Actually, the first UH-1Ds had the same 44-ft. rotor as the earlier A/B/C versions had and the same length tail boom.

When the first 48-ft. rotor was readied, a B model was modified with a longer tail boom to act as a demonstrator aircraft. The aircraft also had a modified transmission which could handle increased power. After seeing the demonstration, the Army accepted the 48-ft. rotor.

"The D models delivered with the 44-ft. rotors, and the short tail booms were modified in the field with kits Bell produced," Norwine said. "In late 1964 or early 1965 we began delivering, direct from the factory, D models with the 48-ft. rotor and the Lycoming T53-L-11."

Unfortunately, the 1,100-shp. Lycoming T53-L-11 engine was retained, which meant that the early D Models remained underpowered and still lacked the high/hot capability that the Army wanted. Despite this, the Huey D went into production in 1963 and became the most numerous version of the Huey built by the time production of it ceased in 1967. More than 2,000 D models were built for the U.S. Army. The first of these were delivered to the Army in August, 1963, and by the end

Most numerous version of the Huey was the UH-1H, shown here in a cutaway drawing. More than 4,900 of this version alone were produced. Powerplant was the 1,400-shp. Lycoming T53-L-13. Thousands are still in service with the U.S. military.

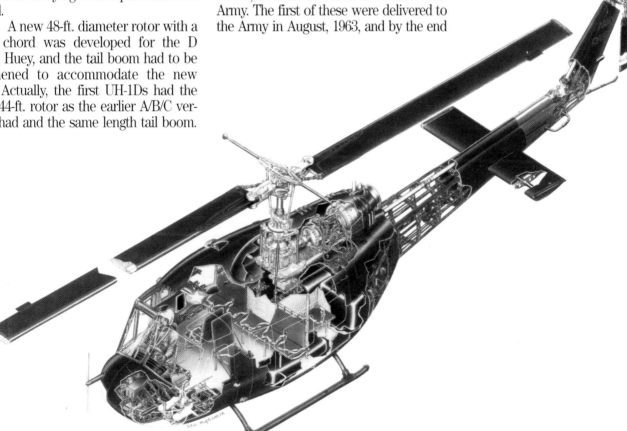

Civil version of the advanced Huey, the Model 205, was used around the world. Here a 205A lands on an oil drilling rig in Prudhoe Bay, Alaska.

Reminiscences:
Roy Coleman,
manufacturing director

The Air Corps sent me down to Marietta, Georgia, in 1944 to help speed up production at the Bell Aircraft factory there, which was building Boeing B-29s. After the war, I was about to return to my civilian job as an airline inspector with the Civil Aeronautics Administration, where I had worked since 1941. They had told me they were going to send me to London. But Larry Bell invited me to come up to Niagara Falls and look around the place.

Bell Aircraft had built thousands of aircraft, but it had never certificated one. All the previous aircraft were military, and they didn't need certification. Bell had developed this helicopter, and the company was planning to get it certificated so they could sell it.

Larry Bell talked me into coming to work for Bell, and we moved to Niagara Falls in the autumn of 1945. I was on the team that was to get type certification for the Model 47. I knew virtually everybody in the CAA, which was small then compared with today, and that helped a lot. Charlie Seibel and I would ride the train down to Washington about every

week to work with the CAA. It took us about six months to get the certification.

We wrote the CAA's manual -- the guide to certifying a helicopter -- because the CAA had no experience whatsoever in helicopters. When we took it to the Government Printing Office to get it printed up, we were told that it would be at least six months before they could get around to it, so I took it back to Niagara Falls and had it printed there in a few days.

When we finally got the certificate, I walked into Larry Bell's office and tossed it on his desk. Now, in those days, the CAA just took registration numbers in sequence and I think ours was NC-70 something. But Larry Bell wanted it to be NC-1H. So I had to go back to Washington and talk the CAA into changing their whole registration system just so we could get the registration number that Larry Bell wanted.

And when that was finally done, I took the registration papers for NC-1H back to Larry Bell and he just said, "Now, why didn't you do that the first time?"

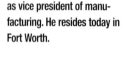

Roy Coleman retired in 1978 as vice president of manufacturing. He resides today in Fort Worth.

of that year, more than 300 were in Vietnam. There, they took over the medevac and troop transport roles, while the earlier B and C models were used as armed escorts.

The D Models eventually were devoted exclusively to transport duties, as the later UH-1H versions arrived and took over the medevac duties. The H Models were nearly identical to the Ds, with the exception that they were powered by the 1,400-shp. Lycoming T53-L-13, which finally gave the Huey the power to perform virtually any mission it was assigned in Vietnam. Eventually, more H Models were built than any other Huey version. The Army accepted more than 3,500 of the type, and another 1,300 UH-1D/H aircraft were exported to the armed forces of 34 other nations. Germany, which acquired more than 300, was the largest international operator.

As the conflict in Vietnam increased in intensity in the late 1960s and early 1970s, Bell Helicopter was faced with the problem of meeting increasingly difficult delivery dates for a rapidly growing number of Army orders.

"One time, an assistant secretary of the Army came down to see how we were doing, and I got a car and driver and went to the airport to meet him. Duke [Ed Ducayet] was out of the country at the time," Jim Atkins recalled. "We were building about 75 Hueys a month at that time and having to work pretty hard to stay on schedule. I met the Army official and as soon as we got in the car, he asked me how long it would take to double production to 150 Hueys a month.

"I knew we couldn't do it with the transmission facilities we had then, and we had subcontracted all the other transmis-

sions builders in the country. So I told him we'd need another transmission factory because the capability to build more transmissions than we now were getting just didn't exist in the country," Atkins said. "'If you'll build it, we'll equip it,' he told me. And this was before we even got out of the airport parking lot."

Even as the production rate for Hueys soared to meet the need in Vietnam, the company met every schedule laid down by the Army. In fact, Bell never missed a delivery deadline either during the Korean conflict or the Vietnam war, according to Roy Coleman, who was vice president of production. "In the 16 years I headed up production, we never missed any schedule, even when there were substantial production rate increases. And we kept all of the production in house. But it was difficult sometimes.

"We had to go to three shifts, both during Korea and Vietnam, to keep up with the Army's needs," Coleman said. "We had to keep the production lines moving to keep with the schedule. If we got behind, we were sunk, because there simply wasn't

This UH-1D was among those delivered to the armed forces of Indonesia. More than 45 nations operate or have operated the Model 205/UH-1D.

Turkish air force and army operate both UH-1D/H models, shown here, and Agusta- built Model AB 205s.

any way to catch up, especially when we already had three shifts working. We just didn't have enough tooling to provide for catch-up production."

Like all families, Bell had its internal problems, which sometimes got in the way of meeting important military delivery schedules.

"Ever since the bitter strike at Buffalo in 1949, we had tried to be very sensitive about labor relations and problems," Coleman added. But, he said, sometimes priorities had to be established.

"We had problems in the plant area where tail booms were manufactured, and although we tried to soothe things, we heard there was going to be a one-day strike, starting at noon one day and going to the next noon," Coleman recalled. "Sure enough, at noon on that day, all the workers in that department walked out. And we were desperate. We had to have those tail booms to enable us to meet delivery schedules."

Coleman had taken the initiative to seek out an alternative production site for the booms. As soon as the strikers left the plant floor, workers were on hand to remove all the manufacturing jigs and other components and truck them over to the subcontractor in Garland. "The workers there were represent-ed by the same union as the Bell workers, but the union said it was OK with them [for us to move tail boom production], so we moved everything. And we told the subcontractor that he would get all the business for that entire production run of helicopters. We weren't just going to move in and then move out on him. When the Bell workers came back the next day, all that was in the shop was their tool kits."

Bell had to face problems with sub-contractors, also. Their work in manufacturing components often was critical to Bell meeting its schedules. Bell had huge order backlogs during this period, and there was a lot of political pressure being brought to bear on the company to let other aircraft manu-facturers build some of these helicopters. If a critical contractor failed to meet his schedule and caused Bell to miss one of its delivery dates, this pressure was sure to intensify. So the company wound up paying close attention to and providing a lot of help for its sub-contractors.

"Subcontracting during World War 2 had been easy," Coleman said. "Later on it was not so good. Many subcontractors believed that the military business just wouldn't come back, so they shifted to pro-duction of civilian needs, which were felt to be both more certain and more profitable. It was a heck of a problem. Subcontractors who could do the work, wouldn't. And those who wanted to do the work sometimes didn't have either the manufacturing or business expertise to do it."

The Bell industrial engineering department would calculate the number of man-hours that should be needed to make a particular component. If the Bell factory was not able to meet this limit, then Bell would begin to seek out a subcontractor who could.

"This procedure tended to keep our employment level pretty steady," Coleman recalled. "The company had a reputation around the Fort Worth area of not hiring and then laying off. People who were hired could usually expect to be kept on for the long haul."

One of the initial problems in finding subcontractors was the need to get companies which could offer low bids on very limited production runs. "A lot of our orders to subcontractors in the early days would be for parts for 25 or 50 helicopters," Coleman said. "This led us to use subcontractors who had overhead costs low enough to make a profit on a small order. Later on, when we would order parts for 250 or 500 helicopters, these guys couldn't handle that volume, so we had to find other subs who could. Sometimes in order to meet our schedules, we would get two subcontractors to build the same part under different contracts. Then the military auditors wouldn't understand why some of the same parts cost more than others."

Bell also had to keep the flow from subcontractors coming, even when the subcontractors were shut down for long periods or even went out of business. In one instance, a supplier went into bankruptcy, and the com-pany's factory was seized with material vital to Bell inside. Bell officials were told that to get their material out, they would have to put up a cash deposit, equal to the value of the property Bell wanted. This was on a Saturday. "Somehow, Jim Atkins got a bank in Fort Worth to issue him a $50,000 cashier's check on Sunday morning and had it flown to me and we got the material out," Coleman said. "On Monday morning, we had another subcontractor working on it. We didn't miss our schedule, but it was close.

"There was a way around every problem," Coleman added. "In one instance, a supplier went bankrupt and had in the factory a lot of material for which Bell had already paid. A guard was posted outside, and the local officials were adamant that

Another unusual mission proposed for the Huey was as an airborne radar station. This EH-1H carries a rotating radar antenna beneath the fuselage and was one of several electronic warfare versions of the Huey. The skid gear was designed to retract to clear the radar's line of sight.

Latest version of the Huey is the Huey II developed for countries needing improved hot day/high altitude capabilities. It is based on the UH-1D/H airframe.

nothing would be moved out of the factory until a judge allowed it. We couldn't wait. When the sun went down, a sheriff's deputy was guarding the locked plant with our property inside. When the sun came up, a sheriff's deputy was guarding a locked plant. Some distance away, a new subcontractor was starting work with our material."

The peak production rate achieved by Bell during the Vietnam War was about 150 Hueys per month, plus approximately more than 50 other helicopters.

The total number of UH-1H helicopters manufactured, including those made in Italy, Germany, Taiwan and Japan under license, was nearly 5,500. Production of the UH-1H stopped at Bell's Fort Worth plant in 1980 but was restarted later to fulfill export orders. Production finally ended in 1987. The helicopter continues to be a mainstay of the U.S. Army's transportation and liaison helicopter force and will remain in service with the Army, the Army National Guard and Army Reserves well into the 21st Century.

A new version of the Model 205, the Huey II, now is being marketed by Bell internationally. It consists of a UH-1D/H airframe with a more powerful T53 engine, modern avionics and subsystems and other improvements. Bell has designed it to be a modification of the original Hueys, rather than a new production aircraft.

More than 16,000 Hueys, including the Huey Cobra gunship variant, have been manufactured to date, and production is continuing at a low rate . This total makes the U/AH-1 the U. S. aircraft with the second largest number of units produced. Only the Consolidated B-24 Liberator of World War 2 fame, which also was built in Fort Worth, has been built in greater quantities.

But the Huey is gaining.

Reminiscences: Robert "Duppie" Duppstadt—development engineer

I worked for Curtiss in Buffalo during the war and I met Larry Bell when he gave a talk at the Aero Club of Buffalo. The war was about over and all the engineers were fearful that they'd soon be out of a job as the military production ceased.

Larry Bell, though, said he felt there would be ample work for professional engineers after the war. So I took him at his word and applied for a job by telephone. A friend had given me the proper name and number to call at Bell. They called back pretty soon and hired me. I went in and told my boss I was quitting to go to Bell and he didn't say much. When I got to Bell, he was there also -- he'd quit Curtiss at the same time I did. About that time I would guess that 20 or 30 engineers came to Bell from Curtiss. I was the 96th person to be hired by the Bell Helicopter division.

When I went to work the first day at Bell, no one told me what to do, so I was just standing around, watching. Art Young was up on top of the Model 42 and he looked down at me and asked me something that I normally wouldn't have known. But for some reason I did and told him and from then on I had it made at Bell.

I stayed at Bell for about a year; then went to another job for a year; then came back. When I got back, there was a big dispute going on about what type of control boost the helicopters needed. Arthur Young had devised a little test to give to prospective engineers and Bart Kelley usually gave the test.

Bob Stanley wanted a mechanical control booster and Bart Kelley wanted something else, so as not to destroy the feel in the stick for the pilot. Neither one could convince the other. Finally, Stanley hired an engineer with gear experience to 'help' Kelley. Kelley took him back in the back and gave him Art Young's test. That's the last we saw of him. Then Kelley brought me in to help with the control boost and I think we made a big improvement.

Bob Stanley was a genius, but he wanted to take over the marketing side of the business and that eventually cost him his job. He later started the Stanley Seat company and we used his seat designs in the early model Hueys.

Robert Duppstadt joined Bell Aircraft shortly after the end of World War 2 and worked in the Niagara Falls facility before moving to Fort Worth. He and his wife live in retirement in Bedford.

Reminiscences:
Arthur Young — Inventor

Back in the 1930s, when I was first working on the concept of a helicopter, people kept asking me what good would a helicopter be? What could it do? I heard this so often that I finally began telling them that it would be indispensable for oiling weathervanes. That may seem outlandish, but the first real work that one of the Bell helicopters did was to blow the dew off the cherries so they wouldn't burst before they were picked. That's even more outlandish; I would never have thought of that work as something a helicopter would be useful for.

I didn't anticipate all the things a helicopter would prove itself capable of doing and I didn't worry at the time about the future of the helicopter industry. I did tell Larry Bell, when he announced in 1946 that he would build 500 helicopters a year, that we couldn't do it. I told him we'd be lucky to make 100 a year and it turned out we didn't even do that. But he told me that the 500 number was just a public relations gimmick to call attention to the helicopter and not to worry. Eventually, it took more than 10 years to soundly establish a helicopter market. It wasn't until the time of the Vietnam war that the helicopter really took off and I was out of it by then. I am glad of this, because I really did not like to see the helicopter used so much for military purposes.

The helicopter when we first developed it was in the same situation an automobile would have been in about 1800. It might have worked fine, but in 1800 there were no roads, no gasoline or repair stations and nobody would have understood what it would be capable of doing.

In 1941, I had gone as far as I could go with the limited resources available to me. I knew it was time to find a financial backer to enable me to proceed further, but the war [World War 2] had made everything uncertain. I went to Wright Field and they promised me a contract, which kept me out of the draft, but it never came through.

When I signed the agreement with Larry Bell, I had been ready for six months to move past the model stage and into the development of a full-sized helicopter. That agreement gave me a budget of $250,000 to build two man-carrying helicopters and we stayed within that budget. But the when the budget came through, it called for drawing two helicopters and I have never liked drawing things. The drafting they were doing at Bell involved sheet metal aircraft panels. It had nothing to do with gears or transmissions. Finally, I went to Russ Creighton, who was head of production at Bell Aircraft. I was making things and he was making things and we talked the same language. Russ signed the budget to allow us to make two helicopters, rat her than just draw them.

Things were scattered all over at the Bell plant in Buffalo. Engineering was one place, drafting another and machining a third. I wrote a memo to Larry Bell, saying that we needed a place to experiment where everything could be together and where we could have an open field for preliminary flights. That's when we went to Gardenville. They wanted to set up a drafting room there with 20 or more tables, but I got them to cut that down to two or three draftsmen. Ed Cook, who had been a professional baseball player in a previous career, was chief draftsman at Gardenville. I had no experience with drawing when I had him draw a gear design I wanted. It took him about a week. Then I took it to the company which made our gears. The man in charge there said he couldn't make it because he didn't have a 10-pitch hob. I thought we'd have to wait another week for Ed to redraw the design, but the man took the drawing and made a note "8-pitch," on it which made it unnecessary to change the drawing and alleviated what I had perceived to be a major problem. Before we left Buffalo for Gardenville, I designed and built a new helicopter model which had provision for pilot control, rather than remote control. This is what we later scaled up six times to build the first helicopter. To build the model, I needed a lathe, vice and a drill press. Rather than go through all the red tape of getting them approved by the company, I just bought them with my own money. This later upset the Bell accountants because they couldn't determine who the tools belonged to. I also got help in making the new model from John Pozda, a top machinist. I then asked to have Pozda come to Gardenville when we moved. When word got around that he was coming to Gardenville, two other top machinists requested transfers to Gardenville, so we got three of best machinists in the Bell organization.

John Pozda, incidentally, was a full-blood Iroquois Indian. Years later, I attended a talk by a distinguished American Indian shaman named Mad Bear. He was in his full Indian regalia with all the feathers. He was a very educated and distinguished man. He spoke four languages and had traveled around the world. I found out he was also an Iroquois and I asked him if had ever met John Pozda. "Oh, yes, I knew old John," he said. "When we was down with you in Gardenville, I was a fifteen-year-old boy working in the rivet department at Bell Aircraft and trying to look like I was sixteen so I could keep my job."

At Gardenville, we moved right along. We had a wonderful team there and we got along very well. There were no memos; if someone had a problem they talked to everyone about it until someone solved it. The Bell people kept asking me to draw up an organizational chart, but I never did. In fact, when we moved back to Niagara Falls, a man came to see me , offering to introduce me to the workers – the same people I had been working with for two years!

After we began to fly the first helicopter, the only major aerodynamic problem we ran into was in July of 1943. It consisted of a two-per-rev vibration that limited the helicopter's forward speed to about 25 mph. We studied the situation for about a week and, using data derived by a French inventor named Etienne Oemichen, we identified the problem as coming from a differential downdraft effect. We solved it by stiffening the rotor and, on July 30, we made some spectacular flights and achieved 70 mph. We couldn't keep up with the helicopter in a car. Later, we experienced some other mechanical problems, but that was the only aerodynamic problem.

Once we got to Niagara Falls, we experienced a different sort of problem. They were more bureaucratic and seniority centered. For example, we trained an inspector to check the gears that we made for the helicopters. The dimensions were critical to safe operation. But after the man was trained, the inspection department found he didn't have enough seniority, so they sent someone else to do the job.

The engineering and weight control departments were independent. We designed the rotors to have a certain mass and weight so they would not cone upward. But the weight department insisted that they be made lighter because they looked at the problem from a fixed-wing point of view. We explained to them what we had done and why. But later, after I left, they designed another rotor with the same flaw in it.

When we certificated the Model 47, the government people were very cooperative and helped a great deal. Larry Bell was, I think, very smart to get that first commercial certification because it enabled him to get ahead of Sikorsky, who really had developed a helicopter long before we did. About a month after we got the certification, the hub on a Model 47 broke. No one then called for the certification to be revoked or the helicopter grounded. I don't know why, but they didn't. We performed vibratory testing on the hub and found out exactly where the stresses were.

I considered my job done after the helicopter received its certification and entered production. I was always interested in philosophy and I took up the helicopter problem as an apprenticeship in how to do things — sort of a 'how does nature work' effort.

The helicopter was a bit like the answers they used to have in the back of school books. I could use its success to determine if I really was learning how nature works.

Arthur Young, inventor of the Bell helicopter, left the company in late 1947 to pursue further aeronautical and later philosophical studies. He currently divides his time between residences in California and Pennsylvania.

CHAPTER SEVEN

Tilting at Rotors

Bell Boeing V-22 Osprey, the first tilt-rotor aircraft to have operational military capabilities, hovers during its first flight at Arlington Municipal Airport on March 19, 1989. Clockwise from upper right: The Bell XV-3, the first tilt-rotor aircraft to fly; the Bell XV-15, the design which solved the problem of tilt-rotor flight; Arthur Young's original patent, filed January 8, 1941, for a combination helicopter airplane. The patent was granted on August 14, 1945.

Arthur Young, way back before he ever joined forces with Larry Bell and Bell Aircraft, devised and patented an innovative concept — a machine that combined the best features of the helicopter and the airplane.

Later on, while he was still working to complete development of the Model 30 at Gardenville, he built a small model and flew it to test his concept.

"It was a tail-sitter with a tripod landing gear," Bob Wheelock, who went on to become Bell's chief flight test engineer, recalled. "It had a rotor blade on top, and a wing behind that and some sort of control surfaces on the tail. The wings were made out of balsa and tissue paper, just like a kid's model, and had about a three-foot span and an eight-inch chord.

"Art Young would lift it off and then tilt the whole thing forward very quickly by remote control to let the wing pick up the lift. Because the rotor generated a lot of thrust, the model accelerated very quickly," Wheelock remembered. "It was spectacular to watch because it went like hell."

Young established a project to develop what was designated then as the Model 50

Convert-O-Plane, but left the company before anything substantive was accomplished.

The idea of a convertible helicopter lived on, however, and Larry Bell was a strong proponent of the concept. Even before the Model 47 was certificated, he was preaching the value of such a machine. "The convertiplane will open new avenues of aerial transportation that no one dares to dream of now," he was quoted as saying.

Work on such a design continued in Buffalo and some sketches survive which show a concept similar to the later XV-3 and XV-15. In 1949, Larry Bell hired Robert Lichten, who had already designed the rotor and transmission system for a convertible helicopter for another company. But that company went bankrupt before a flying version could be built. Lichten had been studying convertible helicopters since his days at MIT and was considered by many to be the top expert in that field.

Lichten continued the efforts toward solving the problems of designing a convertible helicopter before the Bell helicopter operation moved to Texas. The Bell development team, which included Lichten, Bart

The XV-3 research tilt-rotor aircraft is unveiled at the Fort Worth factory on February 10, 1955.

Kelley, and others, began to see the possibilities of a tilt-rotor aircraft, although that was not the only concept which was pursued. Among the other ideas was a variable-diameter rotor concept from Art Young. Young, no longer directly involved with Bell, had moved back to his home in Pennsylvania and continued to study advanced concepts. He submitted to the company his design, which received considerable development and test work before being dropped in favor of the tilt-rotor aircraft.

The tilt-rotor machine could fly like a helicopter when its rotors were in the upright position. It then could tilt the rotors forward and use them like propellers to pull the aircraft forward, with the lift being produced by a fixed wing. The basic concept was appealing, but there were a lot of unknowns that would be expensive to research.

The beginning of the Korean conflict forced the military to begin looking seriously at the long-term future of rotorcraft. In August, 1950, the Army announced a competition for a practical convertible aircraft which would combine the best features of the helicopter and fixed-wing aircraft. Bell's earlier interest and work on such a machine now paid dividends, and 10 months later, Bell was selected as one of the companies to receive a Phase 1 study contract from the Army. After Phase 1 was completed, the Army selected three finalists — Bell, McDonnell and Sikorsky — to construct and test a flying prototype.

Bell's convertible aircraft was given the company designation of Model 200 and the military designation of XH-33, which later was changed to the XV-3. The aircraft consisted of a airplane fuselage, tail and wings, with three-bladed rotors mounted on each wing-tip. The XV-3 was powered by a single Pratt & Whitney R-985 engine mounted in the fuselage behind the cockpit. This 450-hp. engine drove both rotors through an angled gearbox and power transmission shafts located in the wings.

The rotors were tilted by electric motors, which were housed in small pods at the base of the rotor masts. This system permitted the pilot to rotate the rotors back to the helicopter position for an autorotative landing if the engine failed while the craft was in the airplane mode. A gearshift arrangement permitted the pilot to reduce the rotor speed during forward flight.

Bell had a full-sized mockup of the aircraft ready for inspection by the Army in June, 1952, along with a smaller wind-tunnel model. Wind tunnel work

Fuselage of the first XV-3 is loaded into a C-130 at Fort Worth's Meacham Field in April 1959. It was headed to NASA's Ames Research Center for wind tunnel tests.

The XV-3, in its early configuration with three-bladed rotor hubs, is run up on the ground on July 15, 1955 at the Fort Worth plant.

began that same month and was completed in November, 1952. Results of these tests gave the Army confidence to award Bell, in October, 1953, a contract for two flying prototypes.

The first of these prototypes was completed in January, 1955, and immediately began whirl testing of the rotors and static ground tests. These tests lasted through November of that year. The second prototype was finished in April, 1955.

The distinction of making the first flight in the XV-3 fell to Chief Pilot Floyd Carlson, the same test pilot who had taught himself to fly in the Model 30 back in 1943. On August 11, 1955, Carlson hovered the XV-3 at an altitude of about 20 ft. above the main heli-

port at the Fort Worth plant and maneuvered forward, backward, and to each side. No attempt to convert to forward flight was made during this first hovering test. An instability problem was encountered on this test and resulted in a hurried landing. No one knew exactly what was causing the instability, but work began immediately to define the problem and solve it.

In late 1955, Dick Stansbury was given the job of development test pilot for the XV-3 program, freeing Carlson for other work.

"We called Floyd Carlson 'Iron Man,'" Stansbury recalled. "He was a big, strong man with massive shoulders and arms. He had done his early helicopter flying in the

Model 30, which had no irreversible system in the controls. Consequently, there was a lot of feedback of rotor forces through the control system. But once Floyd got hold of them, nothing ever disturbed the control levers. In fact, one of his constant complaints was that other pilots didn't put enough friction into the controls, especially after we got to boosted controls, and he was always screwing it up to the maximum."

Carlson notified Stansbury, who was then chief experimental test pilot, that he was to take over as the XV-3 project pilot. Carlson said he would check Stansbury out in the operation of the aircraft before Stansbury began flight test work on his own.

"We worked out of the Globe plant then, and the ground crew took all of the test equipment out of where the rear seat of the XV-3 was located so I could get in. Floyd got in the front seat," Stansbury said. "We got everything started and I felt the collective lever start to come up. And it kept on going up and up. Finally, it hit the upper stop and we were still sitting on the ground. Floyd moved the cyclic to the right until the left skid eased off the ground. Then he moved it left until the right skid lifted a little. Then he shut everything down and got out. 'You won't have any trouble,'" he told me. "That was my checkout. I never got off the ground."

Stansbury took over the test flying in late 1955 and quickly learned some of the XV-3's foibles. "The engine was a rebuilt R-985, which had previously powered a trainer aircraft — I think it was a BT-13," he said. "We never had any excess power, and there were times when I was not sure we had all of the 450 hp. we were supposed to have."

Stansbury flew the aircraft for a few hours during the winter of 1955-56 to test modifications that were made in an effort to correct the instability. Much of early 1956 was spent with the XV-3 on a tie-down struc-

ture where it was run in various configurations to see if they improved things. "We made many fixes to the rotor mast, the mast mounting and the rotor system itself," Stansbury said, "and after each one was on the ship, we would run a conversion flight on the tie-down stand."

The three-bladed rotor system was found to have an oscillation problem, and a shield of quarter-inch iron plate was placed around the cockpit to keep the pilot safe if the rotor came off. "It would start to oscillate, and by the second oscillation it was going divergent. By the third oscillation, the rotor was gone," Stansbury recalled.

"With the shield on, I felt a lot safer, because while I could still see the rotor, it couldn't get to me." The pylons which housed the tilting mechanism and the rotor masts were redesigned in an effort to solve the oscillation problem, and a number of other modifications were developed to combat the instability characteristics of the XV-3.

"We added struts to hold the wings down, all sorts of dampers and tried half-a-dozen different length masts," Stansbury said. "Finally, we thought we had it."

Flight test work began again at the Globe plant and Stansbury recalled flying "quite a bit. We did autorotations and pushed the aircraft out toward the edge of the flight envelope. We would start with the rotors in the vertical position and then tilt them forward a degree or so and fly around like that. After about 17 hours of flight, I got to where I could fly with the rotor tilted forward as

much as 20 deg."

But the problems had not been solved. On the afternoon of August 23, 1956, while Stansbury was making the XV-3's second flight with the rotors forward 20 deg., disaster struck.

"I was on the northeast side of Globe field at about 200 ft. when I felt a little nibble," Stansbury recalled. "I was heading back to the field and was ready to pull the pylon back to the vertical, when a vibration hit that was so violent that I actually blacked out. I started to radio to my chase [pilot] that I was in trouble, but all I ever got out was 'I'm . . .' I remember lowering the collective, and the only thought in my mind at that time was 'get it on the ground.'"

Stansbury tried to reduce his forward speed before the XV-3 hit the ground, and flared the aircraft to slow it. "Bill Cruikshank, who was flying a Model 47 chase helicopter, said I flared at the right time, but there just wasn't any noticeable effect. There was no rotor lift available.

"The one smart thing I did was to remember that the XV-3 was equipped with an oscillograph recorder, which was activated by the radio transmit switch on the cyclic, if you moved it the other way from the transmit position," Stansbury said. "I moved it out of the transmit position just as I was trying to tell them I was in trouble, which is why my radio call ended after one word. This allowed the recorder to save data from the flight for the period just before the crash."

Stansbury was seriously injured in

The modified XV-3 hovers at the Globe Plant on February 18, 1959, about two months after the first conversion to wing-borne flight was achieved.

the accident and was rushed to a Fort Worth hospital. "I was afraid they wouldn't realize that I had recorded all this data and I remember yelling 'oscillograph' over and over as they rolled me into the emergency room. Some people thought I was delirious, but Bill Quinlan realized what I was trying to tell them, and he called back to Globe and saved the data."

Quinlan later succeeded Stansbury, whose flying career was ended by the accident, as Bell's chief experimental test pilot. Later, when Floyd Carlson retired, he became Bell Helicopter's chief pilot. It was Quinlan who later made the first complete transition from rotor-borne to wing-borne flight in the XV-3, but that was more than two years after the accident.

Damage to the first XV-3 caused the flight program to be delayed until a new, two-bladed rotor could be designed and tested. Test work on the rotor occupied most of 1957, and it was installed on the second XV-3 prototype in early 1958.

Full-scale wind tunnel tests were run on the new configuration before flight test was resumed in late 1958. Quinlan made the first complete transition to wing-borne flight on December 18, 1958, a maneuver which he termed "smooth and comfortable."

The XV-3 then went to Edwards Air Force Base in California for evaluation by the services. The service test pilots found the XV-3 capable of flying in both modes while operating in a wide range of conditions and air speeds. However, they reported continuing instability problems. At lower airspeeds — under about 35 mph — the aircraft exhibited both static and dynamic instability. Further, because it was underpowered, it was affected by air recirculation while hovering and was less stable than desired.

Meanwhile, flight test work continued at Bell. In April, 1959, the first conversion and gearshift to lower the rotor speed was accomplished. During about 250 test flights in this period, the XV-3 completed about 110 full conversions under control of a number of different pilots, several of whom

made a successful conversion on their first flight in the craft. Additional problems with the craft were identified in these tests and associated wind-tunnel testing. These included a continuing rotor instability problem.

Flight test work was halted in 1962, but theoretical work continued and occasional wind tunnel tests were conducted in NASA's 40 x 80 ft. tunnel at Ames Research Center. Unfortunately, during one of these tests, the left rotor pylon mount failed and the XV-3 was damaged too severely to be of further use.

The XV-3 instrument panel contained two rotor position gauges (near center of panel) and clutch oil pressure and temperature dials at bottom.

It was the XV-3 program that first proved that the tilt-rotor concept was practical. But it also showed there was still a lot of work to be done. Bob Lichten, for his work in developing the aircraft, won the Dr. Alexander Klemin Award. After the XV-3 passed from the scene, there was no flying by any tilt-rotor aircraft for more than a decade. Lichten and other Bell engineers continued to study the problem, however, using data developed from the XV-3 flight test program. Tragically, Lichten died a few years later in an automobile accident.

In 1964, shortly before the XV-3 full-scale test program ended, Kenneth Wernicke joined the tilt-rotor development team. He had worked on the XH-40 program, later on the YH-40 and finally on the UH-1 development program. "I thought the Huey development program was very slow," he said, "but actually it went very fast compared to all the other programs I worked on." Later, Wernicke worked on air cushion vehicle programs, spending nearly a year at Bell Aerosystems in Buffalo as part of the development. But no

Joe Humphress (left), superintendent of the HEB independent School District, and Harvey Gaylord dedicate a memorial to Larry Bell at L.D. Bell High School in Hurst, on March 3, 1957.

The modified XV-3 in wing-borne flight with rotors fully forward. This photo was taken during test flights at Ames Research Center.

The XV-15 is loaded into an Air Force C-5 at Carswell AFB, Fort Worth, on March 27, 1978. The craft was bound for wind tunnel tests at NASA Ames Research Center, California, before its first flight.

commercial or military program resulted from the effort.

"In 1964, I went to work for Bob Lichten and we looked at all sorts of ways to combine the helicopter and the fixed-wing aircraft," Wernicke said. "We looked at slowed rotors, stopped rotors and folding rotors. To my mind, they were all garbage. We also looked at the variable-diameter rotor which turned out to be too complex. The tilt rotor was the only feasible way to go."

During this time, Michael Payne, who incidentally was Arthur Young's stepson, began working on a model which could be used to explain the XV-3's rotor instability. Another engineer, Charlie Davis, in a separate effort, began working on solving the aircraft's dynamic stability problems. He began wind tunnel experiments to devise some fixes which might be incorporated in the XV-3.

"Finally," Wernicke recalled, "Michael Payne built a bird-cage model, so-called because it had a lot of wires surrounding it. With it, he was able to duplicate the instability that the XV-3 had exhibited in wind tunnel tests. Earl Hall ran an analytical program and found he could also duplicate the XV-3's instability.

"We decided we needed more than the birdcage model and analytical testing," Wernicke said, "so we got the research lab to build a high-Q model, which consisted of a wing and rotor system and a swash plate tilt mechanism. This model combined the earlier configuration work with an analytical solution to the instability program. It was verified by more wind tunnel tests, and we developed additional computer programs to spell out the problem and solution."

In 1965, the Army announced a competition for a large, vertical-rising aircraft. It was to have been an aircraft in the 28,000-lb. gross weight range, and Bell's proposal of a tilt-rotor design was selected as one of two finalists in the competition. However, the increasing cost of the Vietnam conflict forced the Army to curtail its research and development budget, and no final award was ever made.

From that time until about 1968, Bell continued wind tunnel work, but did not attempt to build a tilt-rotor aircraft or make any of the hardware that would be needed for one.

By 1968, Wernicke said, there were beginning to be serious concerns within Bell about the company's ability to maintain its position of leadership in tilt-rotor technology. Bell engineers proposed building a development aircraft with company money, but management was concerned about the lack of a future market to justify such an expenditure.

"Finally, Jim Atkins, who strongly backed the program, convinced Ed Ducayet, who was president of Bell then, to fund a 10,000-lb. demonstrator aircraft over an extended period," Wernicke said. "We got money in 1968 for rotor development, then in 1969 and 1970 we received funding for transmission development and a test stand. We ran the transmission in 1971 and 1972, with much of the work being directed by Bob Lynn.

"While we were running the transmission in 1971, NASA and the Army Air Mobility people announced that they would jointly sponsor a competition for a demonstration craft to prove the concept of tilt-rotor technology," Wernicke added. "In 1972, Bell was selected and we were told that we had to use the T53 engine, which meant that we had to modify the transmission that we already were running."

A speed-up gear box and a coupling gear box were added to mate the transmission to the new Lycoming T53, Wernicke said. The aircraft, which had been given the company designation of Model 301, grew from the originally planned 10,000 lb. to 13,000 lb. to take advantage of the added power and thrust available.

Up to this time, all of the development work on the Model 301 had been funded entirely by Bell, except for some whirl tests conducted at Wright-Patterson, which were co-funded by Bell and the government.

"In 1972, we got a contract to build two full-scale aircraft," Wernicke said. "The demonstration aircraft were to have two 25-ft. prop-rotors made out of stainless steel because we couldn't bond titanium, and composite technology was not sufficiently advanced at that time to allow us to use composites. Initial whirl tests showed that the rotors produced about 29% more static thrust than had been predicted, and this allowed us to safely increase the gross weight."

The Model 301 was designated the XV-15 by NASA. It was basically similar to the XV-3, although it had a twin tail and an overall more streamlined appearance. Also, it had two swiveling engines, each mounted in a wingtip pod. The two engines and their associated transmissions were linked by cross-shafts in the wings, so that the XV-15 could fly on one engine.

"We rolled out the first XV-15 in 1976 and it flew in 1977, but NASA was very cautious and would only let us fly it in the helicopter mode for a long time," Wernicke remembered.

Ron Erhart, now chief pilot at Bell, began working on the XV-15 program when

The original XV-3, shown here before the formal unveiling, had three-bladed rotors and an unmodified vertical tail.

First fuselage of the V-22, manufactured by Boeing, arrives at Dallas Naval Air Station.

This mockup was a fore-runner of the XV-15. It was designated the Model 300 and had a conventional tail. It was never built as a flying air-craft.

the first simulation work was being done, before the two test vehicles were built. He then left to attend the Navy's test pilot school at Patuxent River, Maryland, for almost a year. When he returned, he went back to testing the XV-15.

"Dorman Cannon and I were the entire flight crew. We had a certain budget of flying time, and within that budget there was no time to check anybody else out on the XV-15," Erhart said. "We just swapped seats for different flights. It was very easy to fly right from the first, and it flew almost exactly like the simulation in our pre-flight testing had predicted it would. We ended up tailoring the stability augmentation system to make it a little less sensitive in the airplane mode. That's really all we did to it.

"The XV-15 program was frustrating at first," Erhart recalled. "It was controlled by NASA and the Army, and they were just so ultra-ultra conservative that they wouldn't let

us do anything. We couldn't go five knots faster without having all these meetings and analysis and so forth. We could only hover and air taxi and move the nacelles a few degrees. And then we had to go to NASA Ames [Research Center] for a very long wind tunnel entry there.

"Before we went out there, we had a big ceremony here — kind of a show-it-to-Congress affair — and all of Bell's executives were there," Erhart said. "Jim Atkins was president then, and he came over to me and asked, 'When are you guys ever going to convert this to an airplane?.' I said that if we followed NASA's schedule, it was a year and a half away. Then I said if he wanted it converted sooner, he would have to get an old pickup truck, put a million dollars in the back and park it at the Waco airport.

"I told him if he did that, then Dorman and I would take off, convert to airplane mode, fly around so they could get a lot of pictures and then go land at Waco, hop in the truck and take off," Erhart said. "Because if we do that, you're going to have to fire us because we will have broken all these NASA rules and regulations. But we had that much confidence in the XV-15 even at that time. We were ready to convert right then, if NASA had let us."

In fact, the XV-15 was not allowed to make a full, free-flight transition until July 24, 1979, a few months after XV-15 No. 2 joined

the flight test program. By the end of summer, 1980, the XV-15 had flown at speeds of more than 300 mph. in the airplane mode. Engineering development flying continued into 1981, and the XV-15's capability to transition from helicopter to airplane modes while flying through a wide range of speeds was demonstrated.

"Later, when the V-22 came along, we had to divide the test pilots into two distinct groups — one to fly the XV-15 and the other to fly the V-22. This was caused by the Marine Corps insistence on an aircraft-type throttle in the V-22, rather than the helicopter-like collective control that was in the XV-15," Erhart said. "Gen. Harry Blot, who was the Marine Corps program director, thought he was going to have to convert a lot of pilots out of the Harrier VTOL aircraft to the V-22. So he felt that a collective would add unnecessary complexity to the conversion process. There was a lot of opposition to the idea, but, in the end, Gen. Blot got his way. We call the control a 'Blottle.'"

About the time the XV-15 was demonstrating its speed and conversion capabilities, the military began the Joint Services Advanced Vertical Lift Aircraft Program — JVX for short — and the XV-15 became a demonstrator aircraft for this developmental

V-22 wind tunnel model during NASA testing at the Ames Research Center in California.

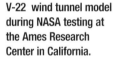

The XV-15, in camouflage paint, performs tactical tests for the U.S. Army at Yuma, Arizona.

The XV-15 in wing-borne flight with the rotors fully forward. This is the configuration in which the aircraft appeared at the 1981 Paris Air Show.

Two generations of tilt-rotor aircraft are on the ramp at Arlington Airport. The XV-15, in the foreground, preceded the V-22, seen in the rear.

Comparative view of the XV-15 (foreground) and the V-22 shows the relative size of the two tilt-rotor aircraft.

program. The XV-15 demonstrated the tilt-rotors' capability to accomplish special electronics missions, had its radar signature measured, and conducted an evaluation of its ability to operate from smaller aircraft carriers.

"We flew all the high-ranking military people and a lot of Congressmen [in order] to start selling the JVX program, which was to have been a replacement for the Marines' H-46 assault helicopter," Erhart said.

Still, the aircraft had not really created the splash of public interest that Bell had anticipated. Much of its development flying had been out of sight to the general public, and most of the military work with the XV-15, while not officially classified, was not publicized, either.

In early 1981, Jim Atkins decided to seek U.S. government permission and assistance to take the XV-15 to the Paris Air Show, then as now, the world's preeminent aerospace showcase. At the time this was a hotly

debated decision within the Bell management. "The XV-15 was an experimental aircraft with limited-life components," Webb Joiner, now president of Bell and then financial vice president of the company, recalled. "People were pointing out that there was no demonstrated reliability in the aircraft and asking what sort of impression it would make if the XV-15 crashed? What if nobody showed any interest in it? What kind of impact will it make even if it operates perfectly? And a lot of questions like that. But when crunch time came, Atkins said we were going."

Dorman Cannon, who later became V-22 project pilot, recalled that he got a phone call from Atkins one day asking what he thought about taking the XV-15 to Paris. "I told him that the ship had not yet made a full conversion and that our flight test work was still immature. I said I thought we shouldn't go," Cannon said. "A few minutes later, the phone in Ron Erhart's office rang and Atkins asked him the same question and got the same answer.

"A few weeks later, a memo came out listing the aircraft we would take to Paris, and the XV-15 was conspicuous because it topped the list," Cannon said. "Obviously, Mr. Atkins had more confidence in us than we had in ourselves."

But even Bell's best efforts could not get the XV-15 to Paris without help.

"We asked the Air Force to transport the aircraft to Paris," Atkins said. "It was

impossible for us to take it there unless the government would let us use a [Lockheed] C-5. Hans Mark was Secretary of the Air Force then, and he was a big supporter of the tilt-rotor concept. He helped us to get the transport we needed to take the XV-15 to Paris.

"Hans Mark was very important to the development of tilt-rotor in general and the XV-15 in particular," Atkins recalled. "He was at NASA Ames Research Center and we went to him and submitted proposals. With the rotor instability problem in hand and work on a transmission underway, we were able to sell the program to the people at Ames. We had some differences in cost and contract prices, but one day Hans Mark came into my office with a group from NASA and we talked. And that afternoon we had a contract for the XV-15. We did that program for a very small amount of money — less than $15 million."

"After Hans Mark left NASA, he ended up as Secretary of the Air Force," Atkins said. "He was an engineer and he had a lot of experience in talking to congressional committees. He had a big influence, based on his reputation as an engineer, in advising the committees that tilt-rotor technology was real and was promising."

The NASA contract was in effect for about seven years, Atkins said, and the work was closely supervised by NASA officials.

"They didn't have a lot of money to spend, so we had a low-budget program," he recalled. "We put a lot of concentration on it and we did some R&D work with our own money to supplement the contract."

Even after the XV-15 was transported to the Paris Air Show, it cost Bell a considerable sum to operate it there, Atkins said. It was a research and development aircraft and therefore had high operating costs and needed a lot of people to support it. Actually, the Air Force didn't fly the XV-15 to Paris. The aircraft was taken to Farnborough, England, and there assembled. It flew several demonstrations there and then flew on to Paris

The V-22 hovers with the landing gear extended during its first public flight at Arlington Municipal Airport.

The XV-15 prepares for takeoff from the a carrier during shipboard operations tests.

V-22 approaches and Air Force KC-135 during aerial refueling tests.

V-22 is shown during conversion with the rotors tilted forward about 45 degrees.

under its own power.

"The XV-15 turned out to be a huge success in Paris," Atkins remembered. "And every time it was supposed to fly in the air show flight program, it was on the line and ready to go. Dorman Cannon was the pilot, and he developed the flying display which had a particularly audience-pleasing maneuver when he came in to land. It really attracted attention and was the big hit of the show. We had major visitors from all the services come over to see it. I believe that the Paris Air Show flight demonstration was a very significant part in the government's decision to go forward with the Osprey."

The maneuver that impressed Atkins was called "the Whifferdill" by Bell pilots and consisted of making a series of flat turns while air taxiing down the runway after landing. "I never thought it was anything very spectacular," Cannon recalled, "but it seems to have impressed a lot of people."

After the XV-15's Paris demonstration, the Defense Department began a program formulation study, in which the concept of a tri-service development program evolved.

The JVX program, under which the V-22 first evolved, was originally managed by the Army, but management was transferred to the Navy in January, 1983, about a month before Bell and Boeing submitted their joint proposal for a tilt-rotor transport.

"The Navy and Marines appeared to have better use for the V-22 than the Army or Air Force from the standpoint of the aircraft's shipboard capability," Atkins recalled. "After taking over management, the Navy told us that we would have to have an industrial partner in the V-22 program, and we selected Boeing.

"Boeing was chosen as our partner for a number of reasons. In the first place, the name Boeing meant more to the industry than any other manufacturer, and especially in the connotation of a commercial program, which we were pushing.

"Boeing also had a lot of technology — not in the tilt-rotor field, but in avionics and fuselage manufacture with new materials — which they could bring to the program.

"Finally, it was thought that the relationship between Bell and Boeing could be better than it might be with other airframers. There was no competition. Bell selected Boeing as its partner," Atkins said. "I worked out the details of the agreement with Joe Mallon, who was then president of Boeing Vertol. The first contract between the two companies was for a design study."

Events moved rapidly from then on, with the Navy awarding the Bell-Boeing

consortium a two-year preliminary design contract in April, 1983. A follow-on preliminary design contract was signed in May, 1984. In January, 1985, the tilt-rotor craft was designated the V-22 and named the Osprey.

In February, 1985, the Bell-Boeing Team presented its full-scale development proposal to the Navy, and work on full-scale development began in June, 1985. By the end of the year, the program had received full approval by the Navy, and the Allison T406 engine had been selected as the power plant. In May, 1986, six flight and three static test aircraft were authorized.

"We built an erector set-type assembly to test on the tie-down stand in Arlington," Dorman Cannon, who had become V-22 project pilot, said. "It was a framework that supported the wing, rotors and fuel system components, and it was controlled by a partial cockpit located inside a nearby blockhouse. The cockpit had multi-function displays, but all they were programmed to show was the fuel system — there were no flight instruments.

"The blockhouse operation was run by Dave Lackey, who had formerly worked at Cape Canaveral, and he ran it just like he was still doing space shots — we called it Cape Lackey. The simulated aircraft was linked directly to the fuel farm at Arlington Airport, which meant we could refuel constantly. Since the V-22 could burn 2,000 lb. per hour in certain configurations, this was a real benefit."

Before the first flight, the test rig erector set assembly and the first V-22 itself had together made several hundred simulated flights on the test stand, during which conversions had been made, high-speed runs had been completed and the capabilities of the V-22 generally defined.

First flight of the V-22 occurred on March 19, 1989, a Sunday. It stayed aloft 12 minutes, and the rotors were tilted only five degrees.

"We flew on Sunday, even though it was a cloudy, gray day, because that's the day the V-22 was ready," Cannon recalled. "The program was behind schedule and we couldn't afford to wait. The V-22 flew very similarly to the XV-15, which we had expected. Even during the first hour of flight, I felt like I had flown it before. I think the most accurate analogy I could think of was that the XV-15 felt like a Ford pickup and the V-22, which was three times larger, was like a Peterbilt truck."

Six V-22 test vehicles were authorized, but only five were completed because of funding shortages. The sixth was never assembled and was used to provide spare parts for the first five. The first, third and sixth V-22s were assigned to Bell, while the second, fourth and fifth aircraft were to go to Boeing. During the course of flight test aircraft four and five were lost, which left Bell with two aircraft and Boeing with one.

"Our job at Bell was essentially to open the flight envelope, and then Boeing was to come along behind us and do specific

The XV-15 lands on the parking lot in front of the Capitol Building in Washington D.C. The demonstration made a major impact on Congressional support for the program.

Air flow tufts are visible on the wings, nacelles, fuselage, tail surfaces and flaps of the V-22 during an early test flight.

tests. We cleared the way for them," Cannon said.

In an aircraft with a fly-by-wire control system and electronic engine controls, test work was not without its unexpected incidents.

"Roy Hopkins and I were flying the No. 1 V-22 on the test stand once in the airplane mode and at a simulated speed of more than 200 kt.," Cannon related. "All of a sudden both engines quit simultaneously. Fortunately, the aircraft was telemetering in real time more than 1,000 parameters of data to the test center. This enabled us to find out pretty quickly that both engines had died of

fuel starvation. Each engine had a separate feeder tank from which they drew fuel. These tanks were constantly topped up from the main fuel tanks, so theoretically, it should have been impossible for both engines to fail simultaneously. But we found that the valves in each tank were reacting to a natural harmonic which caused both of them to float to the closed position and stay there. The valves were quickly modified to prevent that happening again.

"Another time, we were simulating engine-out situations in flight, and when we pulled one engine back to flight idle, it kept right on spooling down until it stopped," Cannon said. "We made a single-engine landing and began to look for what had happened to our engine. Eventually, we found that we had been at about 7,000 ft. density altitude and that the electronic fuel control for the engine had never been tested at that exact density altitude. And at that exact altitude, and no other, the fuel controller's fuel-flow schedule was insufficient to keep the engine running. We had to send the engine con-

Three of the six V-22 test vehicles are visible inside Bell Plant 6 at Arlington Airport.

Reminiscences:
Ron Erhart, test pilot

Back in early 1984, a group of us were up in northern Minnesota doing cold weather tests on the Model 222 and the temperature was about 30 deg. below zero [Fahrenheit]. This was the year that the famous Siberian Express cold front came through and dropped temperatures below freezing in all 48 contiguous states. Everybody was griping about the cold, and so were we. We needed temperatures of 40 deg. below to get our tests run properly and we were just sitting around hoping for colder weather.

That was the year that the Washington Redskins played the LA Raiders in the Super Bowl and somebody had the idea of getting Bronco Nagurski to go out to California and flip the coin before the kickoff.

A network television news team came up to his hometown and did a film interview on him. They came back to catch a plane to LA or wherever they were from when they saw us standing around our helicopter. One of them walked over and asked what we were doing there and we told him we were waiting for colder weather. That night, we all were on the national news as the Texans who didn't think it was cold enough.

Another time, we were doing snow ingestion tests on the OH-58 at Sault Ste. Marie, Mich., where the heaviest snow fall in the U.S. had been predicted. That was the year that had the latest recorded snowfall in the area. It finally snowed, but not heavily enough for us to complete our tests. I was sitting at the counter in the airport dining area when an airline pilot came in and sat down beside me. 'Weather giving you problems,' he asked. I told him it was. 'Us to,' he said. 'We're waiting until it's snowing a little less so we can fly.'

We're waiting until it's snowing a little more so we can fly, I told him.

Ron Erhart joined Bell in 1964 as a test pilot. In 1987, he became only the third chief test pilot and director of flight operations, succeeding Lou Hartwig and Floyd Carlson.

Overhead view of the No. 1 V-22 shows the unusual forward sweep of the wings. The rotors were turning when this photo was taken in January 1989, while the aircraft was on the outdoor tie-down rig at Arlington Airport.

troller back to the factory to have the electronics card modified.

"That's why you have test pilots." he added.

Development of the V-22 continued, and while it did, a continuing war was waged in Washington between the Congress, which supported further development and volume production of the V-22, and those in the Pentagon and other agencies of the executive branch, which tried to reduce the scope of the program, or kill it outright.

After several ups and downs in the funding fight, the Defense Dept. announced in late 1994 that it was committed to full-scale production of the V-22.

Tilting at rotors has been a significant part of Bell Helicopter's history and promises to be an even greater part of its future.

Reminiscences:
George Hall — development engineer

George Hall worked at Bell Helicopter until he retired in 1990. He resides with his wife, Joanne, near Possum Kingdom Lake, west of Fort Worth.

Most people who worked at Bell in the very early days had no idea what Arthur Young's objectives were. They thought he wanted to invent a helicopter. But what he really wanted to do was to document the mental processes of problem solving. To him, the helicopter was a means to this end.

I was the airport manager at Paoli, Penn., in the early 1950s and Art Young was my neighbor. This was after he had left Bell. He used to come by the airport and sometimes talk to my kids, but I had no idea who he was. I had been a test pilot and flight test engineer with Piasecki and one day someone mentioned helicopters and we both learned of each other's previous involvement with rotary-wing aircraft.

Arthur remained an inventor at heart — at least he needed to invent to document the process and he always needed more ideas. He told me about this idea he had for a variable diameter rotor. He said he had tried to forget about it, but it kept coming back to him. It sounded interesting to me, so I went to work with him on the concept. He funded the project in the first few years out of his own pocket. Then he approached Bell through Bart Kelley and they agreed to further the work, so I went to Bell. Art had given me a share of the patent rights in the variable diameter rotor, so it tied Arthur and me and the variable diameter rotor and Bell Helicopter all together.

I never had a better friend, associate and teacher than Arthur Young. I learned more from him in a week than I did in my entire previous career. He worked by what I call the Buddhist experience: put the subject you are studying on like a robe and learn to live inside it.

If you followed him in doing this, you would discover answers to problems. He would never tell you, but pretty soon you'd find yourself saying 'I'll be darned, I never knew that.'" I consider it an unbelievable stroke of good luck that I became associated with Art, then with Bart Kelley and Bell Helicopter.

I came to Bell in the mid-50s, and worked on the rotor concept until Bell selected the tilt rotor as the way to go in developing future vertical flight aircraft. We had a full-sized rotor working that would go from 25-ft. diameter to a 15-ft. diameter. We installed in on N-167, the same helicopter that [Elton] Smith flew from Fort Worth to Buffalo non-stop. We did nearly 5,000 full cycle conversions, but never flew the rotor. We pulled enough power to fly in some of the ground tests, though.

A V-22 approaches the deck of the USS Wasp during shipboard compatibility testing. Ability of the aircraft's wing to swivel and rotors to fold allow the V-22 to operate from smaller carriers using a minimum of space.

3913

CHAPTER EIGHT
The Big Business Rotary Club

A Model 206, a Model 206L and a Model 412 (right) operated by PHI approach an oil rig in the Gulf of Mexico; (left, top to bottom) Model 205A sprays foam on a fire; Model 47D, flown by Elton Smith from Fort Worth to Buffalo; Model 206 JetRangers move down the production line at the Globe plant about 1964.

Back in 1946, when Larry Bell first had a certificated helicopter to sell, he first and foremost looked to the civil market for his bread and butter.

The military would, of course, want a few helicopters here and there. But to most people, the war had been fought and won, and there would be little or no need for a big expensive army, navy or air force in the immediate future. And anyway, they could use the same weapons that won the last war, if it became necessary.

With World War 2 over, millions of GIs were flooding back home, ready for school, jobs, families and what many people fore-

The New York Police Department was an early operator pf Bell helicopters, This is a float-equipped Model 47J.

Bell brochure from 1948 emphasized that the helicopter could not only hover and fly backward or sideways, but "fly at any speed up to its maximum.," which was 95 mph. at sea level.

saw as a new world, transformed by civilian use of all the wonderful things developed during the war — such as helicopters.

Larry Bell was not alone in his assessment of the situation. Most aircraft manufacturers thought the same way. In the coming future, everyone would use a private aircraft for nearly all their travel. For shorter distances, this could well be a helicopter, which could be parked in the family's driveway at night and landed on a rooftop near Dad's workplace during the day.

Helicopters were seen as being the answer to many pre-war problems. One of

these was rapid delivery of individual packages from department stores downtown (which is where they all were located then) to homes in the suburbs or even farther out. Another was extended commuter bus service. People could live as far out as 100 or 125 miles from their workplace and commute to the city center (which is where everybody worked then); the heli-bus would stop at a local bus stop, just like the old earth-bound buses used to do. And local mail service would be greatly improved because letters could be transferred from the main office downtown to outlying offices much more rapidly.

A hundred other fanciful uses were envisioned for the new helicopters in the helicopter-centered world of imagination. Unfortunately, reality quickly intruded and the bubble burst.

The first question that arose concerned learning to fly one of these strange machines. Just who would teach Mr. Average Suburbanite to operate a helicopter? The military had trained only a handful of helicopter pilots during the war, although it had trained hundreds of thousands to fly fixed-wing aircraft. Could some of these pilots be trained to fly helicopters and then be used to train others, until the dream of a helicopter in every garage became a reality?

The second question was what could helicopters do *NOW* to justify Bell or any other company putting them into volume production? Despite all the Wizard of Oz predictions, nobody could immediately point to a specific market and say that helicopters were the only way to go.

A third question concerned maintenance. If everybody — or even a sizeable portion of the public — had a helicopter, who would keep it going according to the rules laid down by the then Civil Aeronautics Administration? It didn't look like the mechanic at the corner garage could do it without a lot of training and the purchase of a lot of expensive tools.

Larry Bell attacked these problems in three ways. First, he established schools at

Niagara Falls to train helicopter pilots and mechanics. At this time, Bell had only five or six helicopter pilots, so it was cutting the force pretty thin to have them train pilots, fly test and acceptance flights, and demonstrate the usefulness of helicopters not only in the U.S., but around the world.

Secondly, he began to seek areas where helicopters could be used immediately, such as agriculture and pest control and oil exploration and drilling. While there were customers to be found in these areas, they did not immediately generate anywhere near the number of sales Larry Bell and others had anticipated. Other areas also were slow to develop as markets, and the concept of a helicopter in every garage died rapidly.

Larry Bell's third approach was to demonstrate his helicopter anywhere and everywhere. It didn't matter who saw it or whether they were ever likely to purchase one. Bell's idea was that the more people who saw a helicopter fly, the less opposition to helicopter use would be generated by people who were ignorant, scared or both.

This approach eventually paid off, but not as rapidly as Larry Bell had hoped. When production was transferred from Buffalo to Fort Worth in 1951, only 388 Bell helicopters had been manufactured. This total included more than 110 helicopters sold to the military.

Once Bell had relocated to Fort Worth, the development of the Model 47G was begun. This helicopter was a much better aircraft for civil use and was accepted more readily by the commercial market than any previous Bell design. Production of the Model 47G and its variants continued until 1974, and new versions of the basic design were being introduced as late as 1968. For several years, the Model 47G was Bell's only commercial product, and it sustained the company until newer models could be designed and developed. But, still, from 1950 onward, it was mainly military orders that kept Bell running.

Bell Aircraft Corp. was controlled by a parent organization, The Equity Corp. This was a holding company funded largely by money from the Rockefellers. Bell Aircraft changed the structure of Bell Helicopter in 1958, dropping it as a division within Bell Aircraft and incorporating it as a wholly-owned subsidiary, Bell Helicopter Corp. The Texas division had been operating more or less independently in any event, and giving it subsidiary status paved the way for Equity Corp. to take an even more drastic step — selling Bell Helicopter outright.

Negotiations lasted several months,

Sabena Belgian Airlines used this Model 47D in an early experiment in carrying the mail. The photo was taken at Niagara Falls, probably in 1950. Skid landing gear indicates that the helicopter had been modified from its original configuration.

Larry Bell congratulates Elton Smith after his 1,217.137 mi. non-stop flight from Fort Worth to Niagara Falls. The helicopter, N167B, later was used for experimental work in Fort Worth.

Model 47D-1 supports a logging operation in mountainous terrain. Site is not known for certain, but may be in the Canadian Rockies

Model 47D-1 with float landing gear was used by the Bell Helicopter Training School in Niagara Falls, around 1949.

Cabin mockup of the Model 47H had the pilot on the left, with two passengers seated to his right.

Among the corporate users of the Model 47G was Mobil Oil, which attached its Flying Red Horse trademark to the tail boom of this helicopter.

but in mid-1960, Bell Helicopter Corp. was sold to Textron, a company which had begun as a textile manufacturer. The firm was in the process of diversifying and becoming what was then referred to as a conglomerate. It had little or no previous experience in the aviation field, and there were many who thought that the Textron management had been hornswoggled, if not downright cheated, by letting itself be talked into buying an unpromising company at an unreasonably high price in an industry with such an uncertain future.

"John E. Bierwirth was on the board of Equity Corp. and was also CEO of National Distillers," Jim Fuller recalled. "He contacted Royal Little, chairman of Textron, who was just beginning his effort to turn Textron into a conglomerate, and began negotiations. Eventually, there was a meeting in Mr. Bierwirth's offices on Park Ave. in New York. Harvey Gaylord went to it, and I went along to carry the bags and cases and such.

"I was there in the board room setting up everything for the meeting and this little old man came in, wearing khaki pants, white suspenders and a kind of nondescript shirt and tie. I thought it was the janitor getting the place ready for the meeting. Then everybody else came in and the little old man took his seat at the head of the table and I realized that he was in fact Royal Little," Fuller related.

"The final deal was hammered out at that meeting," Fuller said. "Textron bought all of Bell's aviation and defense facilities

Prototype of the OH-4 hovers at the Fort Worth factory in the early 1960s.

which would go to make up their new subsidiary, Bell Aerospace. They were not interested in the other Bell Aircraft units, such as Wheelabrator and a number of other companies. All they wanted was Buffalo, Texas and any other defense or aviation facilities.

Larry Bell, center, is shown the interior of the Model 47H, probably in 1955.

"There have been a lot of numbers tossed around about how much money Textron paid Equity Corp. for Bell Helicopter and the other units it got. The price, according to my recollection, was $18 million," Fuller said. "There was a widely read national financial publication which had a story saying that the 'sly old fox,' meaning Royal Little, had been outfoxed by the Equity Corp., if he had paid that much money for Bell Helicopter.

"I can't confirm this, but my understanding is that within a year and a half — certainly less than two years — Bell Helicopter alone returned to Textron as profit all the money Textron had put in," Fuller said. "That doesn't count the other divisions they bought. From that point on, Mr. Little

and the other officers at Textron were very supportive of the helicopter operation, which they should have been, because it turned out that they had bought a jewel."

The sale was not only a total surprise to a lot of Bell employees, but the buyer was almost completely unknown. Webb Joiner, now president of Bell Helicopter Textron, recalled that on his first day on the job, Jim Atkins, then treasurer of Bell and later president, called him in and said, "We're selling the company!" "Who to?" Joiner asked. "Textron," replied Atkins. "What is Textron?" Joiner asked. He had never heard of the company before.

"My first job at Bell was researching data for the sale of Bell Helicopter," Joiner recalled. "We were just gearing up to go to 10 Hueys per month. Our total sales in 1960 were on the order of $35-$37 million. Within five or six years we were up to $600-$700 million in annual sales. Virtually all of this growth came because of the Huey."

[A personal aside. The author of this book was, at the time Textron bought Bell Helicopter, the aviation writer for the *Fort Worth Star-Telegram*. Shortly after the sale was announced, I attended an aviation convention in Los Angeles. At one of the sessions, an Army officer gave a briefing on the Army's future plans during which he said the service planned to buy 10,000 new helicopters. When quizzed after the briefing ended, he said that most of these would be "that new transport helicopter Bell is building in Texas" (the Huey). The next day, there were banner headlines in the *Star-Telegram* reporting this great economic boon that Bell had brought to the city. Copies of the paper were shipped to Textron headquarters and several days later, a Textron official called to talk to me. "Thanks for that great story," he said. "We have been getting a lot of criticism for buying Bell, but now we just show our critics the *Star-Telegram* piece and it shuts them right up."]

One result of Textron's takeover was the move from Bell Helicopter of Harvey Gaylord. He soon was elevated to president of Bell Aerospace, with headquarters in Washington, D.C. Edwin J. Ducayet, his assistant since before Bell Helicopter moved to Texas, was named as his successor.

Whereas Gaylord was outgoing and personable — "a PR man's dream," one Bell official called him — Ducayet was more reticent. Some even called him shy. But virtually everyone of his contemporaries held him in the highest esteem.

"Duke was a tremendous individual," Cliff Kalista, international marketing vice president, said. "He never put anyone down. He was always quiet and uplifting. Maybe it was shyness, but it got results. Also, Duke was an engineer and understood production.

"Gaylord, by contrast was very outgoing and believed in public relations," Kalista added. "He did not have a technical education, so he had to depend on his staff

Model 47G sprays a cotton field. This helicopter is equipped with both a spray bar and hoppers for dust distribution.

"Later I learned that Harvey Gaylord wanted to ensure that Ed Ducayet succeeded him and at the time, Ducayet's title was special assistant to the vice president in charge of the Texas division. So by promoting all of us to vice president, Gaylord was able to elevate Ducayet to a position where others in the company who had been there longer

Model 205, civil version of the military UH-1D, was introduced to the civil market in 1965. This is an early production model.

and he knew how to use them and get the most out of them."

Gaylord's departure was preceded by a puzzling event. "All of the department heads were elevated to vice president status near the end of Mr. Gaylord's presidency, and I always wondered why," Fuller said.

couldn't jump in and try to grab the job."

Also concurrent with the Textron takeover was an increased effort to market helicopters for civilian use. The Model 47 was still selling, as it would for another decade or more, but there were newer and

PIKES PEAK
ALTITUDE 14.110 FT.
TEMPERATURE 6°Cent
DENSITY ALTITUDE 15400

Model 47G-3, modified with a turbosuper-charged Lycoming TVO-435 engine, hovers atop Pikes Peak, Colorado, in the early 1960s. The helicopter, with a few other modifications, was subsequently marketed as the Model 47G-3B-1.

better helicopters flying that had commercial potential.

"When I came to Bell in 1960, our commercial sales were about $8 million per year," Dwayne Jose recalled. Jose had been in the sales department at Cessna for several years, and the job at Bell had been vacant for nearly a year and a half. The salesmen in various regional offices in North America sold Bell helicopters in their given areas, but there was little coordination of their efforts. Cessna, now also owned by Textron, at that time had annual sales of more than $25 million, and Jose was so unimpressed with Bell that he turned the job down the first time it was offered. He accepted later when he was offered control of both domestic and interna-

tional marketing.

"In the commercial line then we had the Model 47G and Model 47J and that was all. The Huey was there, but it wasn't certificated for civil use, and we couldn't afford to certificate it," Jose said. "But there was the prospect of selling the Huey abroad sooner or later and it came sooner rather than later. On a trip to Australia, I stopped off in Japan and talked to Mitsui, our agent there. They were interested in a license to build the Huey in Japan, and we negotiated one which went into effect in late 1961 or early 1962."

Mitsui also had held the license for the production of the Model 47 in Japan and had sub-licensed Kawasaki to manufacture that helicopter. But Kawasaki had, by this

costs came to around $3.5 or $4 million. And that's how we got the commercial Huey."

The Model 204B was certificated in the U.S. in the spring of 1963. Fuji built more than 125 for Japanese military and civil users. Agusta, which held a license for the 204B in Italy, began production in 1967 and eventually sold well over 200 machines to both civil and military customers. Bell built about 75 Model 204Bs for the U.S. civil market and export. Bell's production of the Model 204B was hampered partly because of the huge demand for the military Huey and because of U.S. civil requirements which made it difficult to build both machines on a common production line.

"We were able to handle the orders for civil Hueys," Roy Coleman, head of production, said, "but it was complicated because the military ships were not type certificated. For example, the military Hueys had doors with quick-release mechanisms so that they could be rapidly jettisoned. The CAA wouldn't allow that for civil versions. Finally, we had to earmark certain airframes as civil production and sort of keep them separate from the military helicopters, which made up most of the production."

Jose commissioned several studies when he first joined Bell, which helped to revive and

time, negotiated a license arrangement with Vertol and so were ruled out for the Huey. Mitsui suggested Fuji as a possible manufacturer, although they had no helicopter experience at that time.

Bell agreed to Mitsui's suggestion. Mitsui, as the license holder, was then faced with the task of qualifying the Huey for the Japanese military and getting Japanese civil certification.

"We worked a deal out on the back of an old envelope," Jose recalled. "Mitsui paid $50,000 cash for the license and agreed to pay half of the civil certification costs in the U.S. This certification could then be transferred to Japan, which used the American certification requirements. The certification

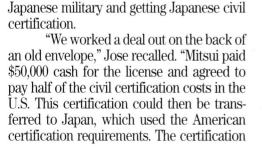

Second production version of the Model 206 JetRanger was pressed into service as an aerial ambulance at this accident near the Bell factory in Fort Worth.

An early user of the Model 204 was the National Aeronautics and Space Administration, which operated this helicopter.

155

First CUH-1D for the Canadian Defence Forces was a standard UH-1D. Later, Canada ordered large numbers of UH-1Ns, powered by Canadian-built Pratt & Whitney PT6 engines.

expand civil helicopter sales.

"First, we had the Arthur D. Little Co. do a study on the state of the industry," Jose recalled. "We located all of the civil helicopters in the U.S. and Canada and tried to find out who owned them, what model helicopter they had and how they used it."

The study showed that from 1946 to 1960, only about 1,000 civil helicopters had been built for use in the U.S. and Canada. Of these, about 67% were Bell designs. About half of the 1,000 helicopters operating were used in the extractive industries, primarily oil exploration and production, mining and pipeline patrol. The other half were divided between agriculture, personnel transport, traffic control and police and fire use.

"Our job was to increase the size of the market, while holding on to our share of that market. The first thing we did was

increase our sales offices from eight to 36 in the U.S. and Canada and made sure the salesmen were all singing the same song," Jose recalled. "Before, you couldn't find any two salesmen who had the same ideas about what was needed. And we didn't try to assess the market just from the factory, anymore. We got out and began to establish a rapport with people who operated the helicopters.

"As a means of boosting piston-engine helicopter sales, we saw the agriculture market as a great missed opportunity," Jose added. "We cooperated with the University of California at Davis, the University of Mississippi and Cornell on a study of the agricultural uses of the helicopter. The University of Mississippi performed a low-speed lab study and wrote a manual on the uses of helicopters in agriculture. We also sent a fixed-wing agricultural expert around the world — Greece, India, Australia — to report back on the needs there."

These studies resulted in the development of the Model 47G-5 and an agricultural variant, the Ag-5, which were basically simplified versions of the existing 47G-2. This and other efforts paid off to the extent that within less than three years, civil sales had increased by almost 37% to $11 million.

In 1963, the first production run of civil Hueys — 10 helicopters — came off the Fort Worth production line.

"It was tough to find a home for those first Model 204Bs," Jose recalled. "Partly it was because a lot of used Sikorsky S-58s were available at lower prices, but mostly people were just not sure about turbine engines in helicopters. They were not sure about what they could do and how reliable they would be."

One of the first attempts to develop a three-bladed rotor at Bell used this Model 204B as the testbed helicopter.

One of the first major sales of the civil Huey was in South America, Jose said. In 1963, Texaco had a large lease in Colombia and needed a helicopter subcontractor to support their exploration and drilling efforts.

"The terrain wasn't very high, but it was terribly hot," Jose related. "And the rainfall totaled about 200 in. per year, so they couldn't build any roads and expect them to stay. All their expendables and equipment had to be moved by helicopter. One helicopter operator had done some work on the project earlier using S-58s, which really had to strain to lift the two-ton loads that were needed. The engines were taking a beating, and they had to change spark plugs about every 50 hr. Then Texaco rebid the helicopter contract and Heli-Col, a subsidiary of American Airlines, won. Heli-Col debated which helicopter to use: the older, cheaper S-58, or the new, untried, turbine-powered Huey.

"Finally, Heli-Col decided to hold a competition to see which helicopter was best, and our agent in Bogota arranged for a Huey demonstration in New York," Jose recalled. "After our portion of that was done, the Texaco project engineer said it wasn't good enough. He wanted to see it done again in Fort Worth, where the heat would approximate that encountered in Colombia. So we all came back to Texas and did the demo over again. Finally, they were convinced, and we

Bell helicopters are used around the world in a variety of missions. This Model 412 is used in Sweden as an aerial ambulance.

The Japanese national police used this Kawasaki-built Model 204, shown here over central Tokyo.

Model 206 on rough-sea floats was used by Petroleum Helicopters, Inc. to service off-shore oil rigs in the Gulf of Mexico and elsewhere.

sold them two Hueys and leased them a third. Later on, they bought a lot more.

"After the first project, they built a pipeline over the Andes Mountains using the Huey, which received a lot of publicity. That led to power transmission line work in Eastern Canada and finally to the James Bay project," Jose said. "And the civil Huey was off and running."

Subsequently, the Model 205 — the basis for the UH-1D/H — received civil certification. It was produced by Bell and by Agusta in Italy, and Fuji in Japan.

The piston-engined Model 47 helicopters remained in production at Bell, but they were getting expensive to build and expensive to operate.

"In 1963, before the Army had picked a winner in the Light Observation Helicopter competition, Jim Atkins asked for three stud-

ies," Jose said. "He wanted to know what we could do commercially if the Bell entry, the OH-4, won the competition; what we could do if two companies were winners, and what we could do if we lost. We did a market study and told him that if we won or were co-winners, we should immediately develop a commercial spin-off. And even if we lost, we thought we could sell over 500 units of a commercial spin-off in five years, plus negotiate production licenses in both Italy and Japan."

Bell was eliminated from the LOH competition in March, 1965, and work was immediately started on devising a commercial spin-off of the OH-4. Jim Atkins, who was executive vice president by this time, told Jose to "go see Charlie Seibel and get a small team to work on getting the space needed for civil use inside the existing OH-4 fuselage."

Funds were short at this time, because everything was being directed to the production of the Huey and the development of the Cobra. The money for this effort was spread among several different company accounts.

"We tried several ideas and none worked," Jose recalled. "We even tried to put blisters on the doors to give us extra passenger space and that didn't work. We were about to come to the conclusion that there was no way we could do this, but we decided to try an outside design consultant. We called in Charles Butler of New York, who had done the interior of the Concorde supersonic transport. Also, Charlie Seibel had a designer he had known at Cessna come in. They both told us the same thing

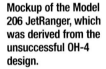

Mockup of the Model 206 JetRanger, which was derived from the unsuccessful OH-4 design.

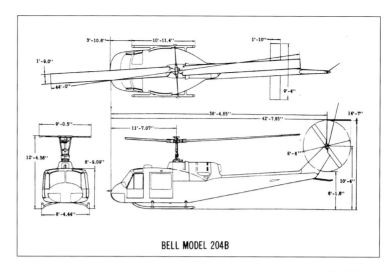

BELL MODEL 204B

— throw away the existing OH-4 fuselage and start over again. One of them said the OH-4 was so ugly 'it probably lost the Army competition on looks alone.'"

A new fuselage design was built in mockup form in the wood shop at Bell, but it still had one major drawback.

"It had no baggage space," Jose said. "So I went over to the drawing and took a Marks-A-Lot pen and just drew in an addition to the rear of the new fuselage and asked if they couldn't do something like that. They did and we had a baggage area of 16 cu. ft., more than the average car. It cost us a couple of knots in speed, but we could carry something."

At about this time, before the new commercial turbine helicopter — it had no name as yet — went any further, Charlie Seibel moved over to the HueyCobra project. Paul Kessling came in as the new project manager.

"Jim Atkins called us both in and he was mad as hell," Jose said. "He had seen the partial mockup and he said 'that's not what I told you I wanted!' We told him we couldn't be successful with the original design. He thought about it for a while and then, in May of 1965, told Kessling that he wanted a complete full-scale mockup by August. I did the market planning and we had hardware ready to fly by the end of the year. By this time, Hiller was already making deliveries of their competitor, the FH-1100."

Bell displayed a mockup of the new helicopter — Ed Ducayet had named it the Model 206A JetRanger — at the National Business Aircraft Assn. show in October, 1965, announced the program and began taking orders. "We laid on a big advertising campaign and by the time of the Helicopter Assn. of America show in January, 1966, we had about 60 orders," Jose recalled. "It wasn't long before we had 100. We began making deliveries in January, 1967, and after five years, we were within one percent of our prediction of 500 helicopters, even though we were selling into a soft market and had some early engine problems.

"We had asked our ad agency to give us a list of possible names for the new helicopter, but Ducayet decided on the

JetRanger — which wasn't on the agency's list — because it followed the Model 47J Ranger," Jose recalled. "He probably had decided on that name before we ever asked the agency for suggestions, but I was so glad not to be out of the small helicopter business I didn't care what he called it. The Bell management made a calculated decision to stay

in the small helicopter business. They could have written off the losses on the OH-4 and gotten out and I doubt anyone would ever have faulted them for doing so."

Eventually, the Model 47 was completely phased out as it was replaced by the turbine-powered JetRanger. "After we got down the learning curve a little, it was actually cheaper to build a JetRanger transmission than to

The U.S. Navy looked at the Model 206 as a potential anti-submarine warfare helicopter. This prototype has folding rotor blades and carries an anti-submarine torpedo under its fuselage.

A Model 222 flies over Lake Arlington near the Fort Worth factory. The 25,000th helicopter built by Bell was a Model 222.

build a Model 47 transmission," Jose said.

The Japanese license never materialized, but Agusta in Italy eventually built a large number of JetRangers. The design evolved from the original JetRanger to the JetRanger II and, eventually, the JetRanger III. Major changes in both were more powerful engines.

As it turned out, the Army re-opened its LOH competition in 1967 because of rapidly climbing costs of the original winner, the Hughes OH-6. The second time around, the Bell 206A was selected, and an initial order for 2,200 was placed by the military. The Army called it the OH-58.

However, the story of the civil JetRanger does not stop there. Oil rig operators, primarily those in the Gulf of Mexico, wanted a helicopter with bigger internal capacity to support their off-shore drilling rigs. The five-seat JetRanger did not have the needed capacity, but they did not want to invest in a more expensive Model 205, which could carry 15 or more. A number of suggestions were proposed at Bell, but the best one came from Bob

Moore, an applications engineer.

"Bob proposed that we put a 30-in. splice in the JetRanger fuselage," Jose said. "He had done a very thorough analysis and showed that it was at least doable. The engineers began calling it the LongRanger, and the name stuck. It turned out to be something we had just backed into, but it gave us a new model — the 206L — for our product line."

The LongRanger seated seven people and had a greater range than the earlier JetRanger. Bell announced the program in September, 1973; the LongRanger was certificated by the FAA in time for deliveries to begin in October, 1975. Like the JetRanger, the LongRanger evolved into the LongRanger II and the LongRanger III. In both instances, engine power was markedly increased over the previous version. A LongRanger II, in the fall of 1982, flew around the world in less than 30 days. It was piloted by Ross Perot Jr. and Jay Coburn. A LongRanger II also made the first transatlantic crossing by a light helicopter.

Production of the LongRanger exceeded 1,000 units, including several hundred built at Bell's factory in Canada, where it remains in production in 1995.

Another Bell helicopter to carry the name Ranger was the Model 400 Twin Ranger. Although the Twin Ranger was basically a new design and not a derivative of the earlier JetRanger, a LongRanger was used as the development test bed. The Twin Ranger had a four-bladed rotor that was developed originally for the OH-58D military helicopter. Power was provided by two Allison 250 turboshaft engines. The Model 400 was never built, but the twin-engine Model 206LT is being produced as the TwinRanger.

Another model derived by Bell engineers from an earlier helicopter was the twin-engined Huey, which evolved into a model which also sold well over 1,000 units. That effort began back in the early 1960s, when it was obvious that the Huey needed more power and the best way to achieve this goal seemed to be to make a twin-engine version of the helicopter.

Bell funded the conversion of a UH-

A Model 222 with a fenestron-type enclosed tail rotor was tested at Fort Worth, but no production was ever ordered.

1D into a twin-engine helicopter designated the Model 208. It was powered by two Continental T72 turbine engines which drove the rotor through a combining gear box. The Model 208 first flew in mid-1965. Hans Weichsel guided the development of the new Huey version with an eye both on military sales and off-shore work, for which a twin-engine helicopter had some obvious advantages.

At about the same time, the Canadian Defence Forces completed an air mobility study. The U.S. Army and the U.S. Marine Corps were using the UH-1D/H Huey, and Bell was producing the Model 205, the civil version of the UH-1D. Bell also was developing the Model 208, and the Canadian military was interested in acquiring one of these helicopter types as means of implementing the results of their recent air mobility study.

"The problem for them was the Canadian Dept. of Industry, Trade and Commerce, which refused to agree to the acquisition of a new helicopter for the military unless there was substantial offset work for the Canadian aircraft industry or a significant amount of Canadian-built equipment in the machine," Dwayne Jose recalled. "Pratt & Whitney of Canada came and talked to us about a twin-engine Huey

using two PT6 engines which were built in Canada. They proposed that Bell design and build the combining gear box and other needed components for such a helicopter while they would provide enough Canadian content with the engines that the Canadian DOITC would agree to the purchase."

Bell officials studied this proposal, but balked at the idea of having to design the gear boxes and other equipment associated with the PT6 installation.

At the same time, Hans Weichsel and the military marketing group were talking to the U.S. military about the Model 208. But the cost was too much for the U.S. military, which apparently backed away from any twin Huey concept.

A disagreement ensued inside Bell, with the military marketing office preferring to continue to work toward U.S. military acceptance of the Continental-powered

The first Model 222 is shown here in Pan Am Airways markings at Dallas-Fort Worth Airport. The helicopter has outlasted the airline.

Agriculture remains one of the largest markets for Bell helicopters. Here, a Model 206L sprays a field.

Reminiscences: L.M. (Jack) Horner – former president of Bell Helicopter, 1984-1992

I came to Bell in May, 1974, to replace Matt Barcelona when he retired. I had been vice president of manufacturing at Sikorsky and I became vice president of operations at Bell. The job I came to at Bell was basically the same job I left at Sikorsky. At both places, I tried to build the most inexpensive helicopter possible that would do the job and sell. I've always believed in meeting schedules, particularly with new products, so I tried to do a lot of little things that were different to help people meet the required schedules.

Also I tried to get a closer tie between manufacturing and engineering and to put the computer to work at Bell. It was something that was coming and I tried to facilitate it and keep our operation up to date.

The war in Vietnam was over by the time I came to Bell and the last few Hueys were being delivered. The Cobras were still in production, but it was obvious that we needed to develop and build some new and different types of helicopters. Bell's strong point, to my thinking, is in evolution, rather than revolution, and we developed helicopters such as the LongRanger based on existing designs.

Things got pretty wild in the early 1980s. We were building 600 or 700 helicopters per year. We got a lot of business from the resource industry, primarily oil, but also timber, coal mining, gas production and electric power generation and transmission. The banking business and emergency medical service markets were just starting to develop. McDonalds' even used a helicopter to select sights for their hamburger franchises.

Then, when we got where we were producing a lot of helicopters for a very large market, the market just disappeared. Not only did the military market decline, but the oil boom burst and we went way down. Production dropped from about 700 per year to 200-250 per year. That's not terribly unusual. The helicopter market is a cyclical business and you have to recognize the cycles. History is a great teacher, in this respect.

We set out to sell into the international market and we had to develop and build helicopters which were attractive in that market. A lot of effort went into selling to non-U.S. government and international buyers. We built a tremendous reputation in the international market. Dwayne Jose was a great innovator in this effort.

After Jim Atkins negotiated the Canadian deal, we planned to put Twin Ranger production there, but the market just disappeared for the light twin -- not only the Twin Ranger, but all of its competitors as well. We had a plant in Canada and a very good relationship with the Canadian government and they had good capabilities in helping us with financing. We decided we could build our light helicopter line more economically outside Fort Worth, because Fort Worth was being driven by government business, which requires a full set of rules which are expensive.

So we made the decision to move the whole light helicopter line to Canada. We can build the helicopters less expensively and we got tremendous help from the Canadian government in financing our international commercial marketing effort. All of the flight-critical items are still manufactured in Fort Worth and assembled in Canada. At the time we moved, we were making about 20 commercial helicopters a month.

This was a time of major transition. We moved the medium helicopter fuselage manufacturing to Korea under an offset deal. We closed the refurbishment factory at Amarillo, and the Globe plant and several other local facilities, then built a new facility in Fort Worth at the same time we were building a factory in

Canada. We just about doubled the size of the machining center in Fort Worth. All of this was done to help control our costs.

We still had Cobra and OH-58 production at Fort Worth and put a lot of energy in the V-22 development. This also was a period of high intensity in technology development, particularly in what was needed for the V-22 and in composite technologies. As far as technology development goes, the XV-15 was a good program.

We had then and still have only about five major market groups: the U.S. military, the foreign military, the oil and gas industry, the executive management field and everything else. To succeed in these markets we have to make sure there are no surprises to the customer -- we tell him exactly what we are going to do and then we do it -- and we had to have the best market support in the world.

We built a $500-$600 million international market this way. And we continued to look for things that a helicopter could do -- things that nothing else could do. That's the whole secret.

In 1974, when I became president, Bell was about 60% of Textron. For a time, Bell was Textron. Now, Bell is about 10-12% of the parent company.

Reminiscences: Bob Wheelock, flight test engineer

We were testing the Model 205 with the 540 rotor system on it out in California. Turp Gerard was the pilot and I was flight test engineer. To get a lot of performance data we'd fly down to Bakersfield, which was nearly at sea level.

But every time we'd fly over Bakersfield, the helicopter would begin to bounce. Once Turp moved the stick, the bouncing would go away, but it would return the next time we flew over Bakersfield. We called it the Bakersfield Bounce.

We tried everything to find out what was causing it. We measured the flapping angle of the blades and we tried to induce the bouncing at zero flapping angle.

Finally, we traced the problem to the rotor bearing, which was just a teflon coated metal face. There were no roller bearings. We found that since only one of the metal faces had a teflon coating, the teflon would wear off and cause the bearing to not run smoothly. Instead, it had a jerk in it, which caused the bouncing. We solved the problem by putting a teflon coating on both metal faces and that stopped the bouncing.

We never did figure out why it happened only over Bakersfield.

Robert "Bob" Wheelock rose to be chief flight test engineer. He resides in Fort Worth.

First Model 222 is assembled at the Fort Worth factory. Unlike some other successful Bell helicopters, the 222 was not derived from a military design.

Japanese national police used this Model 222 in their work. It is one of a number of Bell designs they have operated.

Model 208. Weichsel opposed giving Canadian Pratt & Whitney the technical data on the Huey needed to enable them to engineer a version of the PT6 to power it.

"Bob Lichten was the only engineer to favor the PT6," Jose said. "The commercial marketing people saw a link between a Canadian military order and possible commercial orders for the twin Huey, but we weren't going to get either if we didn't use the PT6."

The dispute finally was settled by Ed Ducayet, who decided to release the technical data to Pratt & Whitney, but apparently told them that Bell was not interested in developing or building the needed gear boxes. The Canadian engine builder then devised the PT6 Twin Pac design, which had two engines and all the associated gears in one package that could be dropped into the Huey intact.

"This went to the Canadian military as an unsolicited proposal in the fall of 1966, but nothing moved until the following June at the Paris Air Show," Jose said. "A group of us from Bell then had a three-martini lunch with Thor Stephenson, Dick McLaren and Tony Clark, who were the top officers at Pratt & Whitney, and with senior officials of the Canadian DOITC. We found out that what we needed was a letter from the Canadian military requesting an unsolicited proposal. About 30 days after the air show, we got it, and we had a proposal to them by October."

The deal was struck, and in January, 1968, Bell ordered 100 sets of PT6 Twin Pacs from Canadian Pratt & Whitney. The Canadian government agreed to help fund the engineering costs of developing the Twin Pac itself and also the costs of installing it in the Huey airframe. The re-engined helicopter was designated the Model 212. The Canadian government announced in May that they were participating in the program, and soon afterward the Canadian Defence Forces ordered 50 Model 212s, with the Canadian military designation of CUH-1N.

"The U.S. Air Force, Navy and Marine Corps quickly placed orders because of the low price we could offer," Jose said. The U.S. Air Force ordered 79 of the helicopters, which were designated the UH-1N, some of which saw action in Vietnam. Others were used as rescue helicopters and for liaison work. The Navy and Marines ordered more than 200, of which about 60 saw action in the 1991 Desert Storm operation. All told, the U.S. services ordered more than 300 UH-1Ns. More than 30 foreign military organizations also ordered the helicopter.

The Model 212 received civil certification from the FAA in 1970, and in 1977 received FAA approval for single-pilot IFR operations while equipped with floats.

In 1988, the Model 212 returned home, after a fashion, when production was transferred to Bell's new Canadian plant in Mirabel, Quebec. More than 1,000 military and civil versions have been produced. The Model 212 also was built in Italy by Agusta, which developed several new military ver-

Prototype Model 400 twin-engine design flies over Lake Arlington, near the Fort Worth factory, in 1986 (above).

NASA used the Model 205 for a number of research missions, including advanced rotor studies shown here (upper left).

Polish police acquired a Model 412 for use in the European country. The helicopter is pictured here over downtown Fort Worth.

The fourth Model 222 performs a roll while being tested with the four-bladed Model 680 rotor system. The 680 rotor also has been flown with the AH-1W gunship.

First prototype Model 430 flies over a frozen lake in Canada, where the 10-place helicopter was being certificated.

The first two production Model 222 helicopters are shown on the assembly line at the Fort Worth factory.

Model 222 configured as an air ambulance saw service with the Uniwest Foundation and three cooperating hospitals.

sions of the helicopter.

Bell developed an advanced version of the Model 212 in the late 1970s, designating it the Model 412. The major differences were a four-bladed rotor — the first four-bladed design produced by Bell on other than a research helicopter — and improved vibration suppression. Certification was received early in 1981, and the first commercial deliveries began at that time.

Production of the Model 412 also was transferred to Canada in early 1989, and the helicopter also is being produced under license by IPTN in Indonesia and Agusta in Italy. Over a period of several years, the production work on all of Bell's civil helicopter line was moved to Canada to clear the Fort Worth plant for construction of the V-22 Osprey. Many of the machined components and other high-technology items still are manufactured in Fort Worth and sent to Quebec for assembly.

Other civil helicopters developed by Bell over the last decade or so include the twin-engine Model 222 and an improved derivative, the Model 230. The 222 began as a completely new design — that is, not derived from an earlier military or civil helicopter — and made its first flight in 1976. The first version of the 222 was powered by two turboshaft engines, with several engine

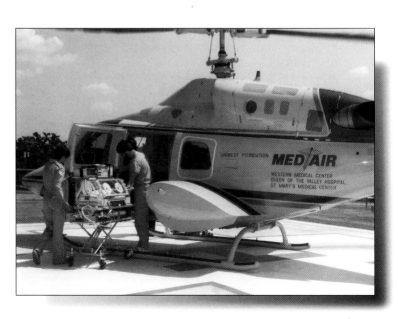

Reminiscences:
Dr. Dora Dougherty
Strother

Shortly after I came to Bell in 1958, I was at a reception and wound up in a group that included Ed Ducayet, then president of Bell, and an Army general whose name I can't recall. They were recalling the worst aircraft they had ever been associated with — the real dogs — and when it came around to me I mentioned the Curtiss SB2C Helldiver of World War 2. I had been a WASP pilot and had flown the Helldiver on target tow missions and didn't think much of it.

Mr. Ducayet looked at me for a moment and then said "I don't suppose you happen to know who the project engineer was on the Helldiver, would you?"

I said that I didn't but that I had just got a real good clue. I knew Mr. Ducayet came to Bell from Curtiss, but I had just never associated him with that particular aircraft. The Helldiver was one of a number of aircraft I flew during the war. Another was the Boeing B-29, and I was checked out on that aircraft by Col. Paul Tibbets, who later flew the atomic bomb mission to Hiroshima. I was one of only two women pilots to qualify on the B-29.

I got my doctorate at New York University and worked at the University of Illinois aviation psychology laboratory and at the Martin Co. in Baltimore before I came to Bell. I had learned to fly fixed-wing aircraft before the war, but had no helicopter experience.

My first work at Bell was in the Army/Navy Instrumentation Program (ANIP), and we did work on developing a contact analog picture of the real world in an attempt to allow pilots without instrument training to fly helicopters under instrument conditions. During this program, we built the first six-degree-of-freedom flight simulator in the world. We had a staff of 15 or so in the aviation psychology department and I felt that we needed piloting experience as well as academic training to do the job properly. So my boss arranged for me to take helicopter training

at Bell when an instructor pilot and a helicopter happened to be free. I got my rating in 1960.

In early 1961, Bell went all out to set a lot of world helicopter records. Al Averill and Lou Hartwig set a number of altitude, speed and distance marks. Then someone suggested that I be allowed to try for some of the women's records. I had very little time in helicopters then, but they sort of twisted my arm.

The first record I set was an altitude record of 19,000 ft. in a Model 47G-3. I wore a borrowed jacket and had an oxygen mask that didn't feel just right, but I got up to the desired altitude. I was supposed to stay over the Bell factory, but a strong west wind came up and by the time I got to the altitude I was aiming for, I was about over Love Field in Dallas. I came down into the wind, and was making only about 15 mph. over the ground. I just barely got back to Bell without running out of fuel. Mr. Ducayet came up and I had just taken my oxygen mask off and had rubbery goo all over my face, when he decided the proper thing to do was kiss me on the cheek. Bart Kelley and all the engineering staff were there, also, and they, I guess, felt they had to kiss me on the cheek, also. Anyway, they all did.

Sometime later, I set a distance mark of 340.346 miles, flying the Model 47G-3 from Fort Worth to Jackson, Miss. They had to put auxiliary tanks on the helicopter to get enough fuel to go that far. I only had 39 hrs. in a helicopter then and was a little concerned, but Dick Byers told me that as the fuel burned off, I would notice a little vibration now and then. That was exactly the right thing to say, because the helicopter rattled all the way to Jackson and I didn't worry a bit about it.

Much later, I was invited to the White House. Most of the other ladies invited were garden club women and we didn't have a lot in common to talk about. We were all standing on the Truman balcony when the President's helicopter arrived. One of the women turned to me and said, "I just hate those helicopters. All they do is come in here and blow the blossoms off of the Andrew Jackson magnolia trees."

Dr. Strother was manager of human factors and cockpit design when she retired from Bell Helicopter in 1986. She now lives in Fort Worth. Her husband, Lester Strother, is a Fort Worth journalist and author.

types considered. The Lycoming LTS-101 was selected and an uprated version of the engine also powered the improved Model 222B. A utility version, the 222UT, also was developed. In 1981, one 222 had the distinction of being the 25,000th helicopter sold by Bell. Production of this model was terminated in 1988.

The Model 222 was superseded by the Model 230, powered by two Allison 250 turboshaft engines. Other changes from the Model 222 include greater fuel capacity for extended range and skid landing gear as well as a three-wheel landing gear arrangement.

The next Bell commercial helicopter, currently under development at the Canadian plant, will be the Model 430. This new 10-place twin-engine model is expected to be certificated in 1995, with first deliveries anticipated by early 1996. The Model 430 is powered by the Allison 250-C40 engine and has a four-bladed Model 680-type rotor

The Model 206L gave the JetRanger design the capacity it needed to adequately support off shore oil-rigs and perform other heavy-lift missions.

blade. Bell is aiming it at the corporate, off-shore support and emergency medical services markets.

The latest Bell commercial helicopter has been designated the Bell 407 and Bell 407T. It was announced in early 1995 and will carry up to seven persons. The Bell 407 will be a single-engine helicopter, and the companion Bell 407T will have twin engines for added safety. It will have a four-bladed rotor system of advanced design. Two development test aircraft are currently flying in Canada.

Bell's latest civil helicopter is the Bell 407, which is being developed in both single-engine (shown here) and twin-engine versions.

Two Model 214STs fly formation over the ocean (right); left, top to bottom, tilt-rotor Eagle Eye drone under construction; various models in the Bell training hangar; British Caledonian Model 214ST on a North Sea oil rig.

CHAPTER NINE
Over There

Larry Bell and the Model 47D were pictured on a proposed postage stamp.

The first Bell design to have been built under license abroad was the Model 48, a limited number of which were built in Italy by Agusta as the AB 102. In it, Pope Pius XII received his first helicopter ride. This photo was taken in Italy, probably in 1948 or 1949.

Aircraft are the most international of all means of travel. There are no shore lines to stop them and no man-made boundaries in the air.

It was, therefore, quite natural that the helicopter in general and Bell helicopters in particular, were found in other nations soon after they were on the market. Their numbers were at first small, but quickly operators found many uses for them, and the commercial potential, both in Europe and the Orient, seemed great.

In the late 1940s and early 1950s, Bell Model 47s were acquired by several European armies and navies for testing, and the British army eventually bought more than 250 of the type, most of which were built under license in Britain.

Model 47s also demonstrated their capability to fly above the Alps, participated in a number of dramatic rescues and began to carry the mail experimentally in Belgium.

Other manufacturers saw this potential and quickly realized its importance to them. In Europe, Agusta of Italy built a few versions of the Model 48 and later secured a license to build the Model 47. It began production of the Model 47G in 1954 and, later, other versions of the Model 47. Agusta thus began a long-term relationship with Bell which continues to this day.

In the mid-1950s, Kawasaki of Japan licensed the manufacture of several versions of the Model 47G, through Mitsui, Bell's agent there. The company built more than 300 Model 47s, with just over 100 going to the reconstituted Japanese military. Kawasaki also later manufactured the Model 47J. Several hundred Model 47s were manufactured by Westland Helicopters in Great Britain in the early 1960s. Nearly all were for the British army, although a number of them were later sold to the civilian market.

In April, 1953, the 1,000th Model 47 was flown by Bell, just a few weeks shy of a decade since the Model 30 had made its first tentative free hovering flight at the development center in Gardenville, N.Y. The 2,000th helicopter flew in 1957, just four years later. Clearly, things were accelerating, and Bell had to grow to stay ahead in the rapidly expanding market.

A major breakthrough came in the early 1960s, when both Agusta of Italy and Fuji of Japan were licensed to build the Model 204 Huey and its follow-on, the Model 205.

However, just licensing other firms to build Bell designs abroad, while necessary to penetrate some markets, was not the answer to Bell's needs for major advantages which could be gained by international production. That required Bell to establish itself in other nations. If it could do so, then it would truly become a worldwide power among those companies in the helicopter field.

But it was an innocuous article in a Canadian magazine which ultimately triggered Bell's most successful international program, which now has advanced to where production of virtually all of its commercial helicopters are assembled at Bell Canada's factory in Mirabel, Quebec.

The article in the early 1980s reported that the Canadian government wanted to establish a helicopter industry and briefly outlined what the government expected to be able to do for the selected company when that company established a presence in the country. The article caught Jim Atkins's eye, and he passed it on to Dwayne Jose in the civil marketing department, asking him to find out more details.

Bell already had a relationship with Canada, in that it had provided 50 UH-1N twin-engine Hueys to the Canadian military on the basis of a commercial sale. Furthermore, large numbers of Bell helicopters had been operated commercially in Canada since the late 1940s, shortly after Bell received certification for the Model 47 and began to market it.

"Canada is a country that makes considerable use of the helicopter because of the nation's various physical characteristics," Jim Atkins said. "There was a very large operator in the Vancouver area and another in Toronto, both of which often operated in the wilds of Canada. All of these contacts, both civilian and military, helped form a sort of band of friendship between Bell and Canada."

Atkins traveled to Canada a number of times during the negotiations for the UH-1N sale and found the government officials there "very friendly." They expressed an interest in working out some sort of co-production arrangement, but were vague about what they could or would do and what they wanted. Nothing came of the talks until 1982.

"In 1982, our sales department determined that the Canadian government was leaning toward creating some sort of a helicopter industry in the country, and that they were probably going to do this by holding a competition between the various manufacturers," Atkins said. "That included Aerospatiale and Messerschmitt-Boelkow-Blohm from Europe and Hughes and ourselves from the U.S."

Knowledge of the forthcoming competition generated a lively discussion and debate within Bell. Some questioned whether Bell should move some of its production to Canada or even get involved in the competition. Others opposed taking work out of the Fort Worth plant.

At the same time, the V-22 Osprey program was beginning to take shape, and the argument was advanced that Osprey production was going to entirely fill up the Fort Worth plant and that Bell probably was going to need a second plant somewhere in the relatively near future. If Bell were to do the assembly of the Osprey, in addition to the rotor systems and the transmissions and other components of the power train, the present plant was definitely too small.

"The rate of production also would affect this," Atkins said. "Back then, we were thinking of eight or 10 Ospreys per month. Now I understand that number is more likely to be four per month, which would make a difference. We took the course of action of going forward with the government of Canada and investigating their plans and trying to help formulate their plans, without making an immediate decision [on whether or not] we were going to compete.

"It was a hard decision to take anything away from the Fort Worth plant," Atkins recalled. "The Canadians were not interested in just an assembly plant; they wanted engineering and all the good things that go with high technology. And they wanted the program to be broader than just production for Canada. They wanted to build helicopters for export."

In Canada, the program was being developed by the Industry Dept. under Ed Lumley, the industry minister. He assembled several key people to formulate the plan and put as much emphasis behind the program as possible. In early 1983, after consulting with Robert Ames, the group vice president at Textron who had responsibility for Bell, and Jack Horner, who had been tapped to become president of Bell Helicopter when Atkins retired, Atkins made the decision to fully explore the Canadian possibilities and negotiate an agreement, if possible.

"Then, it was a program that changed

Bell Advanced Tilt Rotor (BAT), shown here in mockup form, was proposed for the Army's LHX light helicopter program in 1984, but was dropped when it could not meet the Army's stringent weight requirements.

Venezuelan Air Force operated four Model 214STs as combat transport and liaison helicopters.

Model 214ST protype demonstrates its heavy lift capability during promotional work in the early stages of the program.

every day, depending on who in the government you talked to," Atkins recalled. "I made quite a number of trips to Canada to talk to Robert Brown, who had been named the chief formulator of this program in Canada, directly under Ed Lumley. The competition was something that was hard for [us at] Bell to get our hands on.

"Aerospatiale was preparing for it and was actively working with the government of Quebec province," Atkins recalled. "Boelkow was never a real competitor, nor was Hughes, so it appeared to be a contest between Bell and Aerospatiale."

The Canadian government asked for proposals for a helicopter facility in Canada and gave each competitor the privilege of selecting the site where their plant would be located. Each company had to name that site in its proposal. Bell studied several sites, most of them in Ontario or Quebec, but also some locations in other provinces. The plan called for the Canadian government to pay part of the cost and for the government of the province in which the plant was to be located to pay a share.

"We noticed that all the automobile manufacturers were located in Ontario, while Canadair [a major aircraft manufacturer] was in Quebec," Atkins recalled. "We visited various government agencies to discuss the location, and nobody ever said it's got to be here or there, but it became very clear that if you wanted to win this competition, you better put your plant in Quebec.

"That raised a lot of fears about problems we'd encounter by attempting to operate in the French language and under the work rules in force in the Province of Quebec," Atkins said. "These rules were pretty worrisome, the way they were first expressed to us. We also were worried about people and how the location of the plant would affect the people we would employ."

The Canadian government suggested

a site near Montreal's new international airport, which was fairly far off the main highway. Bell rejected the site. The company decided that it needed a site near the existing factory of a major U.S. company, and on a main highway near Montreal.

"A little way out from Montreal we found a General Motors plant and we worked our way down the highway until we found a location that looked great to us," Atkins said. "We found this big open area where we could build a new plant, and our French legal firm tried to make sure we could acquire it. There were a lot of problems, but eventually, we got enough assurances that we could get the land that we determined that Mirabel, Quebec, should be our spot."

There were four major reasons that prompted Bell to move to Canada. First, there was the belief that the Texas facility could not handle the anticipated large production volume of the Osprey and maintain full production of the rest of the Bell line. Company officials recognized the fact that there might be some delay between development of the Osprey and actual production, which could mean a temporary reduction in the number of workers at Fort Worth. On the other hand, the Osprey program would require Bell to keep its engineering team together, use its talented machining work force to full advantage, and make use of all the transmission know-how and the advanced production machinery then in the Fort Worth factory. There would be little or no excess capacity in the Fort Worth factory when the Osprey program reached full production.

Secondly, Bell wanted to keep Aerospatiale out of North America as much as possible. Bell respected the products that the French company built and the quality that was engineered and built into them. They also knew that Aerospatiale could get major financial assistance from the French government and that Aerospatiale had strong political connections in Quebec and elsewhere.

"Aerospatiale was a strong competitor, and to have them sitting in an adjoining country just didn't make any sense to me," Atkins stated.

Another reason came from the Canadian government. Bell was led to understand that the government would provide major support, including partial funding for the construction of the new plant, funding for a portion of the research and development required, and would pay for the training of workers hired locally. This support was seen as allowing Bell to put new civil helicopter models into production that otherwise could not be developed because of Bell's limited research and development budget.

The Canadian government also was thought to be capable of acting as one of Bell's salesmen in international efforts. The country could help with export financing in a way that the U.S. government could not. U.S. law requires that the government remain neutral when two or more American manufacturers are selling similar products to the same customer.

Canada, in effect, stood ready to make the winning competitor a part of the Canadian team, assisting the company to sell its products internationally as a vehicle to providing both employment and technological development in Canada.

The final agreement was based on the total estimated cost of moving, training, plant development and construction, tooling and development of the projected Models 400 and 440. The total cost came to approximately $400 million, and the two parties had a specific agreement on who paid what. The Canadian government eventually paid slightly over half of the total cost.

The agreement initially allowed for development of a fuselage for the Model 440 made of composite materials. When the Model 440 was canceled, the contract was renegotiated to reflect this.

A major problem existed concerning Quebec Province and its requirements for business operations within its borders. Questions that needed answers ranged from the critical to the ridiculous. One such question concerned the name on the factory — could it read Bell Helicopter Textron or would it have to be displayed solely in French. Other questions concerned whether the factory could operate in English, or would all the documentation have to be translated into French.

More serious were the work rules Quebec imposed. The Quebec minister in charge was a strong separatist, seeking independence for Quebec from Canada. He

agreed to negotiate the rules, however. Bell and Quebec officials eventually reached an all-encompassing agreement which spelled out in detail how the regulations could be applied by Bell.

The agreement with Quebec was signed near midnight on Jan. 4, 1984, in Quebec City. As the Bell representatives arrived back at the hotel where they were staying, a message arrived telling them that Bell had been selected by the Canadian government as the winner of the competition and urging them to come immediately to Ottawa to sign it. The French government had been unofficially involved in the program from early on until the night the contract with Bell was to be signed. One Bell official said "they were always around."

On the night the agreement was to be signed, a high French government official called top-level officials in the Canadian government and pressured them not to select Bell. This accounted for the urgency in signing the final contract, since the severe pressure might eventually force the Canadians to change their decision.

Bell had a business jet standing by at the Quebec airport, and the negotiating team flew immediately to Ottawa, where the contract was signed at 3 a.m., Jan. 5, 1984. It was the end of what one participant termed "quite a war." A formal contract signing ceremony later was observed in Ottawa with senior officials of Bell, Textron and the Canadian government present.

Opposition to the agreement existed within Bell and within the Textron headquar-

Interior of the Model 214ST could be configured to carry 18 passengers in this high-density seating arrangement.

Alternate landing gear of the 214ST included a three-wheel arrangement for easier ground handling. This version was certificated in 1983.

Bell Helicopter Canada's factory at Mirabel, Quebec, provides the company with a major international production facility.

Model 214ST operated by Helicopter Service of Norway lifts a man from the North Sea. U.S. registration indicates this was a leased helicopter.

ters right up until the contract was signed. Opponents in both camps now have apparently changed their minds. One senior official later called the agreement a "jewel of a deal for the company."

One overriding goal in the negotiations for Bell was to craft an agreement that both future Bell managements and Textron Inc. could live with.

The Canadian government also achieved success in that it got what it wanted in the way of a helicopter industry. All Bell helicopters other than the OH-58, the AH-1, and the V-22, are or soon will be, assembled in Canada. While the Canadian factory does not include a machining or rotor manufacturing capacity, it does have both aeronautic and avionics engineering capability. The Model 230 currently is being built there. An advanced version of this helicopter, with a four-bladed rotor system, is under development there and will be initially certificated in Canada. A significant number of Canadian suppliers also have received subcontract work from Bell Canada.

Lloyd Shoppa, now senior executive vice president of Bell, was the President of Bell Helicopter Textron, Canada for a time and is generally credited with making the facility perform as it has, with high employee morale and a strong competitive spirit among the work force. "The Bell team made the program happen, but it was Shoppa who made it work," one senior official of Bell said. "He handled the language problem well and cultivated good relations with the Canadian government."

Canada's recent purchase of 100 Model 412s at an estimated cost of $800 million was, in part, the result of Bell's efforts to develop and sustain good relations with all groups in Canada. It also underlined Canada's determination to support Canadian companies in filling their military requirements.

"We found that if you were honest with the Canadian government and if you had the capability to do what you say you can do, they will support you to the fullest extent they can," Jim Atkins said. "But they still reserve their independent position when they are buying equipment."

The original agreement provides for continuing joint funding of several types of operations. New facilities under construction in early 1995 were jointly funded by Bell, Canada and Quebec Province.

The Canadian government continues to support Bell sales internationally. At the 1994 Farnborough Air Show in Britain, the government displayed the first of the 100 Model 412s it had ordered, with all of the additional equipment on board. Later, the helicopter was taken on a tour of several European nations in which Bell representatives were allowed to participate and discuss sales possibilities.

The Canadian program was not the only attempt by Bell to expand internationally, although it was the most successful. By far the largest of Bell's overseas efforts, however, was the Iranian program, which at its peak employed more than 5,000 people in Iran.

"The Iranian government came to us sometime in the late 1960s and wanted to buy a number of helicopters," Jim Atkins recalled. "I can't remember the exact number, but it was on the order of 25 machines. At that time, we were building 150 Hueys and 15 OH-58s for the U.S. government each month [plus a few commercial machines], so we were pro-

ducing over 200 ships each month.

"Based on the big commitment we had to the Army for Vietnam, I suggested to Ed Ducayet that we not accept the Iranian business, but rather refer them to our licensee in Italy, Agusta." Atkins said. "The Iranian government did go to Agusta and did buy some machines from them at that time. Later on — I believe in 1971 — Iranian officials visited Bell at the Paris Air Show and indicated that the government needed assistance from Bell. They had the vision that they would have a much larger aviation program, and they felt that the assistance of a major U.S. helicopter manufacturer and government contractor would be needed. Later in 1971, they extended an invitation to Bell to visit Iran. Frank Sylvester, who was Bell vice president of international marketing, and I went to Iran and made the initial contacts.

"We met with the minister of defense and his assistant," Atkins said. "They were interested in an overview of Bell, the company and its product line. They had been well-briefed by the U.S. government. I believe that some Iranian representatives had participated in some of the test work at military bases where Bell helicopters were located. They pointed out to us that conditions in Iran could be extreme. Performance in the U.S. might be one thing, but performance in their country might be an entirely different thing.

"As this same visit proceeded, Frank and I began to talk about improvements to our product we had been working on back in Fort Worth," Atkins added, "and it was obvious that this was very intriguing to the Iranians. The results of the visit were transmitted to the Shah by his minister and we promised to get together for further discussions."

The Bell team came back to Fort Worth and analyzed the situation. Bell at that time was in a period of declining production rates and viewed Iran as a possible major customer. While no specific numbers had been mentioned, the Iranians were talking about a large program, and the nation was then producing five or six million barrels of oil per day. They had the capability of financing a major effort.

Atkins ordered some design studies to improve the UH-1H Huey and the AH-1G, both of which were being mass produced at that time for the U.S. Army.

"We laid out for the engineers the in-country problems in Iran — weather, heat, humidity and high altitude — and the desire of the Iranians for twin-engine capability," Atkins explained. "The design studies produced a Model 214 which was to be a commercial helicopter. I think we were pretty far along on the Model 214A before the Iranian thing came up and we moved to a Model 214ST. We went to the Lycoming T55 engine in order to provide the power the engineers thought would be necessary. The 214ST was still a single-engined helicopter at that time. We had already put the Pratt & Whitney Canada PT6 Twin Pac in the AH-1J for the Marines, and we piggy backed off

Bell Advanced Composite Aircraft Program (ACAP).

Prototype Model 214ST shows its ability to operate from a standard offshore oil rig heliport during sales demonstrations.

Two unmanned tilt-rotor designs proposed by Bell for military use include the Pointer (top) and the Eagle Eye. Both were conceived as reconnaissance or data relay aircraft.

that and did other improvements to the Cobra for Iran."

Bell submitted an engineering proposal to Iran, defining the configurations of the 214ST and the AH-1J+ and giving a rough estimate of the costs involved. After studying the proposals, the Iranians requested Bell to build prototypes of helicopters and bring them to Iran for demonstrations in the summer of 1972 during the hottest part of the year. The prototypes were to be built at Bell's expense. In return, Bell and the Iranian government concluded what Atkins termed a "handshake agreement" that Iran would purchase both models if they met the performance criteria which Iran specified.

"We had no guarantees that they would buy anything, other than a general feeling that they were very supportive of the program," Atkins recalled. "We might have invested a couple of million dollars in the program. We could do things cheaply in those days." The schedule gave Bell less than eight months to build the two prototypes and prepare them for shipment to Iran. Bell pilots and engineers worked out a test program to be conducted in Iran during one month at about six locations where extreme conditions could be expected. The Iranians provided air transport for the two prototypes in Lockheed C-130s in late July, 1972. A 40-member team, which included engine and armament company representatives, accompanied the helicopters. After the demonstration program was complete, the two prototypes were returned to the U.S. and later used for development of the production helicopters.

Within two days after the completion of the demonstration work, Iran ordered 500 helicopters from Bell. The original order was for 287 of the 214STs and 212 AH-1J+ Cobras. However, because of Iran's desire for early delivery, the first group of helicopters delivered were 214As. "This production helped ease the problem caused by the reduction in orders from the U.S. Army, which was phasing down from Vietnam," Atkins said. "It didn't take up all the slack, but it helped."

These helicopters were sold to Iran under terms of a Foreign Military Sales contract negotiated with Bell by the U.S. government, acting as agent for Iran. This included the final unit price under a target/incentive type contract.

The program was a large one to begin with and expanded well beyond what Bell had initially envisioned. The next phases of the program — training, maintenance and support — were to be separately competed. Bell won the first phase which involved training Iranians to operate the helicopters.

At this point, Bell realized that the program was going to need more management than it could give, so Bell Helicopter International was formed. This subsidiary was to provide the training which Bell had contracted, originally, and later took on all of the support functions for the Iranian helicopter program. It became the center of all Bell activities in Iran. BHI was structured as a direct subsidiary of Textron but was assigned to Bell Helicopter for management purposes. The company was headquartered in Bedford, Texas, near the Bell factory, and the chairman was Jim Atkins. He considered the Iranian program to have been more of a challenge to Bell than the Vietnam buildup just a few years earlier. The company met the challenge of the Vietnam buildup with an experienced work force in Fort Worth. The Iranian job had to be done mostly with new hires.

Delk Oden was the first president of BHI. He was a retired Army general. Oden got BHI underway and operating and oversaw the hiring of the first great number of American

workers. Most of these were ex-Army people because the Army was the only place that people with the required talents could be found in the numbers needed. Most were Vietnam veterans, and there were about 400 Vietnamese wives of U.S. expatriates.

In 1975, Robert Williams, another retired Army general, became president of BHI and headed the company for most of its existence.

BHI found out that it was difficult to hire people to go to Iran, and there tended to be a lot of risk in selecting employees. Expatriate Americans employed by BHI in Iran posed special problems. The Iranian government considered that BHI was responsible for every employee and every dependent 24 hours a day." Some of them were pretty hard characters and tended to get into trouble," Robert Williams recalled.

But because they were hired under terms of U.S. Foreign Military Sale contract, the U.S. government ruled that they were covered by the Defense Base Act, which laid down strict rules on how their employer must treat them. These rules were administered by the U.S. Labor Dept. and there was no appeal from their decision. The U.S. rules agreed with the Iranian concept that workers were on duty every hour of the day and that BHI was responsible for all their actions.

The U.S. regulations required that each worker receive a base pay with cost-of-living, housing and travel home allowances. Disability settlements were increased by the inclusion of the cost-of-living allowances to the base pay. A worker adjudged totally disabled got 75% of his base pay for life plus cost-of-living adjustments annually. His wife would receive 50% of his base pay for life.

BHI initially was committed to training 2,500 Iranian pilots and 5,000 mechanics, later increased to 4,500 pilots and 6,000 mechanics. In order to get the equipment needed to Iran, Flying Tigers cargo airline was asked to move 50 transport aircraft loads from Fort Worth to Teheran. Later, an additional 17 planeloads were shipped.

The decision to located the Bell facility in Isfahan was made in late 1973 or early 1974,and BHI designed the flight academy which Iran was to build there. When it was finished, it was found that the Iranians had equipped it with such amenities as marble floors.

Since Atkins was the first Bell official who had come to Iran to negotiate for the contract, Iranian officials seemed to believe that before they made any decision, they must consult with him. "And whatever decision they made today, after talking it over with me, might be changed completely tomorrow," Atkins recalled.

"Eventually, BHI had 5,000 employees and another 8,000 dependents in Iran, and it became a question as to where we could house all of them," he said. Iran volunteered to build a village near Isfahan to house many of the expatriate American workers.

BHI also requested schools for dependent children, and the Iranians offered any one of five new schools, which had just been built and not yet opened near Isfahan. Upon inspection, however, an architect working for BHI found cracks in the walls of all five and feared they would not be safe in case one of the frequent earthquakes in the area proved sufficiently severe.

BHI rejected the schools on safety considerations and within a few days all five schools had been bulldozed. Bell officials never found out what happened to the contractor who originally built the schools. A completely new school was then built in Isfahan for the American children, close to both the expatriate village and the Iranian training academy.

"We used English as the working language in Iran," Williams said. "Originally, we set up a four-week course to bring the students up to the level where we felt they could learn. But we found that many of the students had little English when they came to us, so we expanded the English training to one-year and two-year courses. Based on this, it took us

Bell Helicopter Textron manufacturing complex in Fort Worth has grown markedly during the 43 years of its existence. The original factory is almost lost amid the buildings in the upper left. Old two-lane highway has been widened to five lanes.

This model AH-1J+ built for the Imperial Iranian air force was one of those actually delivered.

about five years to train a pilot.

"The mechanic candidates usually had no English knowledge when they arrived and, worse, they had no experience with machines," Williams added. "Iranian mechanic students usually did not have any experience with automobiles, and the helicopters we had to train them to maintain had no similarity to a camel."

It was quickly learned that instructors must be trained to use consistent terms and not make any deviations at all from the approved vocabulary. Few of the students could, at the beginning, read technical manuals.

The pilots were to be trained to U.S. Army standards and, after some criticism of the level of proficiency they achieved, several U.S. Army check pilots were brought over to conduct check rides with Iranian student pilots. They reported that while the Iranians might not meet the written standards precisely, they had mastered the mechanics of flying a helicopter better than the average U.S. Army trainee pilot. The greatest problem Iranian pilots had was learning to cope with emergencies. They tended to learn by rote and were not able to handle emergency situations unless they had been previously taught to cope with that specific problem.

Eventually, BHI was under contract to train all of Iran's army aviation establishment from scratch, based on a projected size of 1,000 rotary-wing aircraft. Management instructors were selected from the Bell Helicopter management team for limited tours and many instructors were retired U.S. Army officers.

Bell Operations Co. was formed in 1976 to take responsibility for building the helicopter production facility in Iran. The Iranians wanted a factory on the scale of the existing Bell factory in Fort Worth. BOC expected to provide technical assistance to Iran to build transport helicopters there. A twin-engine version of the Model 214 was to have been the first program there.

By the time this complex was nearing completion, the Iranian revolution was imminent and some contracts for interior fixtures and tooling had to be canceled. The air-conditioning for the plant arrived during the revolution and no one would accept it, so it was dumped overboard.

As late as November, 1978, however, the Shah reviewed progress on the entire program with Jim Atkins in Teheran and made no reference to the growing situation in the country. A few blocks from the palace, Atkins's car was stopped by rioting students from Teheran University, demonstrating against the Shah.

"We tried to keep the program going, but Iran had our vouchers for a lot of money and had not paid them. We maintained the program for a while, but eventually had to cancel it. The basic accord we had reached with the Iranian government when we started went overboard," Atkins said.

The Shah was still in power when Atkins pulled the plug on the Iranian program, but it was clear he would not stay there long. The Shah eventually left in 1979.

"In the fall of 1978, I became very worried about our exposure in Iran and stopped all hiring there," Atkins recounted. "In October, I instructed Bob Williams to evacuate the women and children. Most didn't want to leave, but we insisted. They were used to living in an expatriate environment and were getting big pay. The U.S. ambassador even wanted us to bring in more people, but we declined."

Bob Williams remembered other problems of evacuating dependents. "We couldn't pull out too rapidly because it was feared that might have an adverse political impact in Iran.

Bell was big and visible and we were afraid the U.S. government would be upset, also."

Finally, Jim Atkins bit the bullet and canceled the entire program. He called the Textron corporate headquarters first to see if they knew of any reason he should not.

"They told me, 'Jim, it's your call.' It was a hard, hard decision to cancel that program," Atkins said. Many dependents were already out by the time the Shah left the country. Bell had requested that Pan American Airways fly aircraft in with volunteer crews to get as many people as possible out. Still, there were about 2,000 Bell employees in Iran when the Shah left.

Bell moved everyone to the Hilton Hotel in Teheran — leaving behind clothes, household effects and much else at their homes. The revolutionary mobs shot the hotel up, with many Bell people lying on the floor to escape the rain of bullets. Many were Vietnam War veterans who had experienced similar situations during the war and took control of the situation.

Finally, a Bell representative got a message to the Ayatollah Khomeni that the Bell workers had been in Iran under a contract signed by the old government and requesting an escort to the airport so they could leave the country. Surprisingly, Khomeni agreed to provide the needed transport and also allowed more Pan Am aircraft to land to take out the remaining employees — all but one.

One Bell employee — Chet McKeen — remained behind for several days and was at the Hilton when it was taken over by the Iranian mobs. He was not harmed and left the country several days later.

Iran was an "absolute dream program" in the opinion of L. M (Jack) Horner, who later succeeded Atkins as president of Bell. It also was a source of research and development dollars which otherwise could not have been obtained.

Reminiscences: Jim Atkins, former president of Bell Helicopter.

Just after our demonstration team had completed a tour of Iran in 1972, they received a call that the Shah would be arriving at the Teheran airport in a few minutes to inspect the prototype 214ST and AH-1J+ we had been flying there for a month. There was little time to prepare before the Shah arrived accompanied by a dozen or so gold-braided admirals and generals.

The Bell people showed him all the features of the two helicopters, and then he said he wanted to get checked out in both. He was a helicopter pilot, so Elton Smith took him up in each helicopter for a short time and he flew both machines.

When he landed back at Teheran airport, he came over to all the admirals and generals accompanying him and told them all to get on board the 214ST because he was going to take them for a' flight. They all got on board, although some looked nervous, and the Shah took off and flew to a nearby football field, where he landed. Then he brought them back. A Bell pilot accompanied him, but the Shah did all the flying.

Two days later, with only a few minutes warning, I was called to the palace to meet the Shah, and he asked if Bell would train his pilots and mechanics if he ordered any helicopters. I said we would. Then the Shah turned to his defense minister and said, "I want 500 helicopters." And the deal was done.

James Atkins was chief cost accountant at Bell Aircraft in Buffalo when he was asked to come to Fort Worth temporarily to help train people at the Texas Div., which was just starting to make helicopters. He remained more than 30 years, rising to president of the company. Atkins and his wife, Helen, reside in Fort Worth.

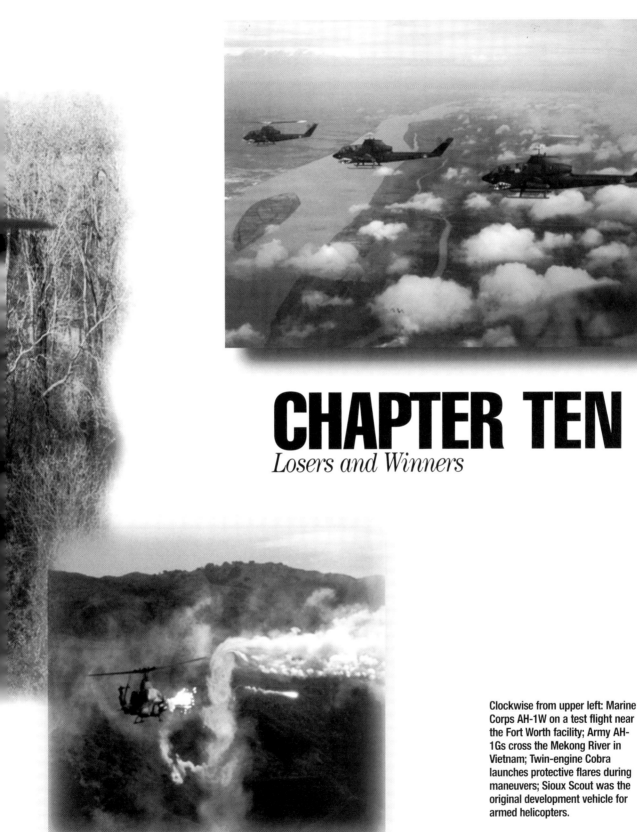

CHAPTER TEN
Losers and Winners

Clockwise from upper left: Marine Corps AH-1W on a test flight near the Fort Worth facility; Army AH-1Gs cross the Mekong River in Vietnam; Twin-engine Cobra launches protective flares during maneuvers; Sioux Scout was the original development vehicle for armed helicopters.

There are old sayings about winning and losing. You can't win them all, is one. For every winner, there's got to be a loser, is another. And, of course, winning isn't everything.

But the history of Bell Helicopter seems to indicate that these sayings are about as valid as the old saw, If God had wanted us to fly . . . .

In the competitive world of helicopters, winning is, most certainly, everything. Coming in second doesn't put bread on the table.

Furthermore, in Bell's case, it would be more appropriate to say that for every loser, there's a winner. In the helicopter industry, losing a playoff game doesn't necessarily mean that you are out of the Super Bowl.

And as to the notion that you can't win them all — you can. And Bell very nearly has.

A few examples will illustrate this point. Back in 1960, the Army called for proposals for a new light observation and liaison helicopter and the service said it planned to buy at least 3,600 of the winning design. The industry agreed that the company which landed this plum would dominate the light helicopter field for decades. Bell lost.

A couple of years later, in 1962, just as the U.S. was beginning to edge into the Vietnam War, the Army began to look for a helicopter designed for the sole purpose of fighting; sort of a fighter plane on rotors. The Army called it the Advanced Aerial Fire Support System (AAFSS). The helicopter industry called it a great challenge, and the general consensus was that the company that won the competition would be sitting in the driver's seat for years to come. Bell lost.

So how did this company, which lost two of the biggest military helicopter competitions of the past 35 years, wind up building thousands of civil and military light helicopters — models which are still in production today. And how was it that the same com-

Marines also evaluated the Bell OH-4, which was Bell's original entrant in the Army's Light Observation Helicopter competition.

Bell's secret 1962 mock-up of an advanced helicopter gunship, the D-255 Iroquois Warrior, excited the Army and led to the development of the Cobra.

pany built thousands of dedicated helicopter combat gunships and is building them still.

It's an interesting story.

In 1960, having replaced its Bell Model 47/H-13 medevac helicopters with the UH-1, the U.S. Army asked for proposals for a new helicopter to replace the Bell H-13 and other light helicopters in its inventory as scout/liaison aircraft. It was called the Light Observation Helicopter (LOH) program.

Bell responded with a proposal called Design D-250, which the Army labeled the OH-4. It was powered by the Allison T63 turboshaft engine and five prototypes were built for testing. The machine proved to be heavy and did not meet the performance level which had been expected of it. It was eliminated from consideration by the Army, which eventually selected the Hughes design, the OH-6.

When the competition was announced, the Army said that it planned to acquire 3,600 helicopters of the winning design over a 10-year period. Before the winner was selected in 1965, however, the nation became embroiled in the Vietnam conflict and all previous forecasts of helicopter requirements were tossed to the winds.

Apparently, one of the major advantages of the OH-6 was its low unit cost, which has been estimated at about $18,000 per helicopter, in 1965 dollars. Many in the industry believe the original price was set artificially low to give the OH-6 a decisive advantage. Within two years, however, the OH-6's unit price had nearly doubled, and the Army's budget was being severely strained. As the demands of the Vietnam buildup increased, the Army decided to reopen the LOH competition and see if it could not acquire a capable helicopter at a more affordable price.

Here, however, the old problem of interservice agreements surfaced. In order to hold costs down, ostensibly, the Army had been directed to agree to the Air Force or the Navy directing the research and development phase

Model 206s are operated in Chile by navy, army and air force. These are naval helicopters.

of new aircraft acquisitions by the Army. The Army feared this meant that they would not get what they wanted, either because the research and development engineering costs would force the unit price up, or because the other service would try to engineer into the new helicopter capabilities the Army did not want.

The Army looked for and found a way out.

Immediately after the OH-4 was eliminated, Bell began work on a civil version of that helicopter, based on a market study which indicated that the company could sell about 500 units over a five year period. The final result was the Model 206 JetRanger, which was certificated by the FAA in October, 1966. Commercial deliveries began in January, 1967. The Model 206 is noteworthy because it was the first Bell helicopter to enter production which replaced the rotor stabilizing bar, developed on the Model 30, with a stability augmentation system. Other than this change, the rotor system was the same as offered on the unsuccessful OH-4.

"When the Army began looking at the possibility of getting a new observation helicopter, it discovered a statement in the agreement with the other services which allowed it to buy a civil helicopter on an off-the-shelf basis, if it could show that the helicopter could meet the Army's requirements," Perry Craddock, who retired from the Army and came to work in Bell's government sales department, recalled.

This would remove the need for the Air Force or Navy to be involved in the selection of the new LOH version and would further reduce costs by allowing an existing airframe to be used, thereby eliminating most of the costs of developing a new helicopter.

Furthermore, the Army planned to get a multi-year contract with fixed prices for the new helicopter to prevent another case of rapid price escalation. The Army's request for proposals for the second LOH design specified that the airframe and engine combination must be certificated by the FAA and must be in commercial production.

"Hughes had won the first competition, but Bell won the second," Craddock said.

One problem that surfaced was the fact that the FAA would not give civil certification to an armed helicopter. This meant the Army had to write its own armament specifications. But the certification on the airframe was acceptable.

Bell was announced as the winner of the competition in early 1968 with the Model 206A, which was designated the OH-58A by the Army. Bell received a multi-year contract for 2,200 OH-58As. Due to the heavy demand for the UH-1 series helicopters at the time, Bell signed a five-year contract with Beech Aircraft to provide airframes and other assemblies for the OH-58 to Bell. This work later was progressively transferred to Bell's new Canadian facility, along with production of the civil JetRanger version.

Prototype Cobra had retractable landing skids, later removed for "simplicity" and replaced with fixed skids.

The Army later had nearly 500 of the OH-58As upgraded to the improved OH-58C version, which had a more powerful version of the Allison T63 engine and improved infrared suppression capability.

The U.S. Navy also purchased nearly 200 TH-57s as trainers for its helicopter pilots. About 35 other nations have ordered military versions of the Model 206A and it has been built in Australia and Italy as well as in Canada and U.S.

The Army continued development of helicopter technology through the Army

Marine Corps AH-1J, above, passes over Lake Arlington during a test flight. Below, an Army AH-1S flies over suburbs of Fort Worth.

Helicopter Improvement Program (AHIP), which had as its goal the development of an interim helicopter to perform scouting and combat missions until a new-technology helicopter could be developed.

Bell proposed the Model 406, which was a much improved OH-58C, equipped with a four-bladed rotor, a more powerful version of the T63 engine, and a mast-mounted sight. The sight, which was developed and produced by the team of Northrop and McDonnell Douglas, permits an armed version of the Model 406 to carry and launch a number of guided weapons such as the Hellfire anti-tank missile. The new helicopter was designated the OH-58D Kiowa by the Army when it announced the selection of the type in 1981.

In addition to air-to-surface weapons, the OH-58D also can carry and launch the Stinger missile in an air-to-air role, which gives the helicopter a limited self-defense capability against attacking aircraft.

Initial plans called for about 600 OH-58Ds to be built. Some of the armed version of the OH-58D, called the Kiowa Warrior, were modified to have the capability of carrying troops on the outside of the fuselage.

The OH-58Ds were first deployed to Europe and, later, to the Persian Gulf. There, based on vessels sailing in the Gulf, they proved highly successful in halting attacks by high-speed

Iranian gunboats on shipping, particularly oil tankers, transiting the area. This success prompted the Army to modify more than 200 of the OH-58Ds to the armed Kiowa Warrior configuration.

The helicopter served in the Gulf War in 1991 and was highly successful as a reconnaissance and target-designator aircraft.

Today, both the civil and military versions of the Model 206 still are in production, with thousands already in service.

Not bad for a program Bell lost.

Having the ability to find and designate targets is one thing. Having the ability to destroy them with a helicopter is a far different thing.

In Vietnam, the Army began arming UH-1 Hueys to permit them to escort transport helicopters to combat zones where they might be attacked. At first, jury-rigged guns were fitted experimentally in the field and later, some Hueys were retrofitted at Army facilities as gunships.

The first helicopters used for the armed escort role were the early Huey A and B models. These helicopters did the job in the early days of their operations, but soon the increasing weight of the armament they were called on to carry and the hot, humid climate showed they were not the best escorts that could be had.

Thoughts both in the Army and at Bell turned to the concept of a helicopter designed as a gunship and dedicated to that mission alone. Bell mocked up a gunship design which it showed to the Army in June, 1962. A few months later, the Howze Board, an Army study group, recommended that the Army form Air Cavalry Combat Brigades and develop armed helicopters to equip them. It took the Army nearly two years to act on this recommendation.

Bell's 1962 mockup was based on the concept that a helicopter designed specifically as an attack aircraft should have great firepower and high maneuverability. It then could take over the escort role and let the Hueys concentrate on their primary medevac and troop transport missions.

The mockup that Bell created was of a helicopter based on the UH-1C power train and rotor system, but with a slim fuselage equipped to carry a variety of weapons.

Actually, the concept at Bell of a dedicated, high-speed helicopter gunship pre-dated the Vietnamese conflict. As early as 1958, studies had been made and small models built of a helicopter which mated the Huey engine, drive

train and rotor systems with a new, slim fuselage with internally mounted weapons. Designated Design D-245, it had swept stub wings and a gun in the fuselage nose firing forward. But it was never built as a full-scale mockup or helicopter.

The design which was secretly mocked up full-scale and shown to the Army was known as the Design D-255 and unofficially called the Iroquois Warrior. The D-255 retained the engine and drive/rotor system from the UH-1C and, like the proposed D-245, it had a slim fuselage with a two-man crew — pilot and gunner — seated in tandem.

When the Army did call for designs for a high-speed, heavily armed helicopter in its 1964 Advanced Aerial Fire Support System (AAFSS) competition, Bell responded with a modified version of the D-255, the D-262. A twin-engine version, called the D-280, also was studied. The D-262 was not selected in the AAFSS competition, a decision which Bell regretted at the time, but eventually hailed. The AAFSS designs, including the winning Lockheed entry, eventually proved to be complex, costly and difficult to develop. Before the helicopter completed development, the Army's experience in Vietnam taught it that a very high speed capability was not a primary requirement, and the service eventually canceled the entire program in the early 1970s.

However, even before the AAFSS, it was evident that the Army needed a gunship which could effectively protect the Hueys in Vietnam as well as fly strike missions. Somebody — there is a difference of opinion just who — conceived the idea of a small, lightweight, high-speed helicopter with good maneuverability and enough firepower to allow it to demonstrate what a real helicopter gunship could do in meeting the anticipated need.

Joe Mashman recalled that a small group — himself, Hans Weichsel, Bob Duppstadt, Phil Norwine, Cliff Kalista and possibly one or two others — got together one day and roughed out a design based on using the Model 47J's engine, power transmission and rotor systems. A two-seat cockpit was penciled in with the pilot sitting behind and slightly above the gunner in a tandem arrangement. Stub wings were mounted on either side of the rotor mast to provide extra lift and possibly additional fuel or weapons.

The forward part of the fuselage was slimmer than that of the Model 47J to reduce drag and provide better vision for both the pilot and gunner. The gunner, who controlled the weapons with an overhead sight, had limited authority side-arm controls for use in an emergency. The Model 201 or Sioux Scout, as it was named, was armed with two .30-cal. machine guns located in a swiveling turret mounted under the fuselage, directly beneath the gunner's seat.

The Sioux Scout was, when it made its initial flight on June 27, 1963, the first dedicated gunship in the non-Communist world to actually get off the ground. Bell test pilot Al Averill was the pilot on that first flight.

With a demonstrator gunship flying, Bell sent its chief salesman-pilot, Joe Mashman, and sales engineer Phil Norwine, out to fly the Sioux Scout at Army bases across the country. The goal was to show what such a gunship could do and to let senior Army officers have a chance to experience this capability. Mechanic Jim Tripp followed the demonstration team in

Gunships that never reached production are the Model 309 KingCobra, top, and the Model 409 YAH-63 prototype, center.

OH-58s stream down the production line at the Globe plant in 1969 or 1970.

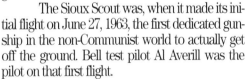

The OH-58/Model 206 found many missions. An OH-58A in Army artic colors hovers, above, while a Navy TH-57A trainer, a version of the Model 206A, is shown below.

a station wagon with the necessary support equipment.

Among the senior Army officers who flew the Sioux Scout while it was on tour were Maj. Gen. Harry Kennard, then commander of the 11th Air Assault Div. and Brig. Gen. Phil Seneff, who later would be chief of Army Aviation. Seneff took the Sioux Scout to a firing range near Ft. Bragg, N.C., and conducted some live firing tests there. Gen. Kennard had reason to remember his flight. It was on Nov. 22, 1963. When he landed, he was informed that President Kennedy had been assassinated.

"After he got back," Phil Norwine recalled, "Seneff asked me 'When are you going to do this with a Huey airframe?' I told him, 'We're thinking about it.' Altogether, we flew some 750 hr. of demonstration flights for

the Army on this tour." A few years later, Gen. Seneff flew the first actual combat mission in a Huey Cobra in Vietnam.

After the tour, Sioux Scout was handed over to the Army for further evaluation and Bell

officials began to again ponder the problem of developing and selling an advanced gunship.

The AAFSS program was still being proclaimed as the answer to the Army's needs at this time, but fairly early on several people began to doubt that it would do what it was expected to do. Among these was Charlie Seibel from the old Gardenville team, who felt that the Army would shortly have to opt for a "quick-and-dirty" method of getting a gunship until the AAFSS program could produce. Seibel, however, was at this time on the Model 206 JetRanger project, so others at first carried the gunship program forward.

By late 1964, proponents of the interim gunship idea — engineers were calling it the Army Scout at this time — felt they had enough data to convince the Bell management that it would pay to go ahead with development of such a helicopter, even though the Army had no stated need for it.

"Hans Weichsel pushed the idea of the Army Scout and provided much of the impetus that got it approved," Cliff Kalista recalled.

Some in the Bell management were reluctant to invest much money in a helicopter for which the Army said it had no need and which might prove extremely costly before it was completed.

"In late 1964," Phil Norwine said, "a group of us briefed Ed Ducayet and other members of the Bell management on the proposed armed helicopter, which we based then on the engine, transmission and rotor system of the Huey C."

First deliveries of the Huey C had been made only the previous September. It had the new Model 540 rotor system, which gave promise of greatly reduced vibration and provided for elimination of speed restrictions imposed on earlier versions of the Huey.

"We told them that if the Army Scout proved successful, we possibly should consider canceling the Huey C for anyone other than the U.S. Army," Norwine recalled. "We figured we stood to lose about 500 export orders for the UH-1C, but we believed we would sell at least 1,000 armed helicopters." Others figured that armed helicopter sales might even reach 1,500.

There were others in the upper echelons of the company who felt there were better uses for $1 million than gambling that the Army might soon want a helicopter gunship. Projects such as the Model 208 twin-engined Huey looked a lot more promising than an unwanted gunship.

Management approval called for the prototype to be completed in not more than six months and to cost not more than $1 million. Final approval took several months and work did not start until April, 1965, which meant that the prototype should be ready to fly in September.

A "green room," as it came to be known, was walled off from the rest of the factory to keep the project secret even from most Bell employees, and all the work on the mockup and later the prototype was done there.

Charlie Seibel, who had first voiced the possibility that the Army would need an interim gunship quickly, was pulled off the JetRanger program and assigned to head the Army Scout effort, as it was thought that he would be able to meet the time and cost constraints, if anyone could.

"How good was Charlie Seibel?" Kalista asked. "Let me put it this way. He was the only man out of uniform I ever met who could call Wright Field collect."

Seibel's job on the new helicopter was not an enviable one. There were many unknowns and some features of the new helicopter had to be devised simply by doing what the development team thought would be needed.

"We thought the cockpit ought to be able to handle a 95th percentile pilot and still not exceed the 36-in. width limit we had set," Kalista said. "Since I met the 95th percentile in terms of height and weight, they made me a model and built the mockup cockpit out of wooden strips around me with a helmet on my head."

One of the unusual design decisions made was to give the prototype gunship retractable skids, unlike any previous Bell design. "The retractable landing gear was one of the keys to the sale of the Huey Cobra. It was put on originally to give the ship sex appeal," Kalista said. "The Army brass liked

to see the helicopter suck it up."

When the landing gear was retracted, it tended to give the Huey Cobra an appearance of attaining a greater speed than it could actually reach. But there were also drawbacks. The retractable landing gear was complex, heavy and expensive, compared with the standard fixed skids. From a practical point of view, it appeared the retractable skids were a waste. But Bell had other ideas for it.

Another problem which had to be faced was the fact that there was no request for proposals for anything like the Huey Cobra. No one had ever considered such a craft and the Army officially was wedded to the AAFSS program. Someone in Bell — both Hans Weichsel and Perry Craddock have been credited by others — came up with the idea of simply putting in an Engineering Change Proposal for the UH-1. ECPs were as common as nails. Every time a screw was changed in one of the designs, an ECP had to be generated. The logic was that the Huey Cobra had the same dynamics as the UH-1. All that was really changed was a slight streamlining of the fuselage and some modified weaponry. And under the rules then governing military aircraft modifications, there was no limit to the extent of changes which could be proposed in any ECP.

This relieved the Cobra from having to go through many tests and qualifications and, even more important, blocked the Air Force or the Navy from having a say about how it was developed.

The new gunship was not originally named the Cobra. It first was designated the HeliCobra. The Cobra part came from one of Bell Aircraft's successful fighter aircraft, the P-

U.S. Army's 1st Cavalry Division introduced the OH-58A to combat in vietnam, with a door gunner for added protection.

Bell 222 patch celebrates the first American-built light twin helicopter.

Dubai (United Arab Emirates) air force operates this Agusta-built AB 206.

Model 206 was used by the Army as a development vehicle in the New Technology Helicopter (NTH) program.

39 Airacobra of World War 2 fame. The Heli-part was to show it was a helicopter, which was pretty obvious to anyone who saw it. But the name Huey had become well-known for the transport helicopter from which the gunship was derived. So Cobra it became.

Even then, the Cobra name came close to being rejected. Someone had suggested that Bell copyright the name Huey and use it as one of the company trade marks. Since the name had to be used on a product to be copyrighted, the suggestion was made to replace the name Bell on one of the two rudder pedals with Huey, so that instead of reading Bell - Bell it would read Bell - Huey.

But the idea was dropped after the Army said it wouldn't be able to formally approve the name Cobra if the Huey portion

were copyrighted.

The Cobra project was kept strictly secret, even from the Army, during the early part of its development, in order to gain and keep a lead over potential competitors. When the program was about half complete, the decision was made to inform a select senior Army officer of what was being done. The lone officer selected was Gen. Phil Seneff, who had earlier flown the Sioux Scout and had asked then about the possibility of using the Huey as the basis of an armed helicopter.

"Gen. Seneff was very futuristic," Kalista said. "He had battled the Army Transportation Corps over the use of the Huey and was known to be in favor of a gunship sooner, rather than later." Other officers, including Gen. Kennard, were not in favor of an interim gunship. They wanted the UH-1D

now and would wait on the AAFSS program to provide the Army with an armed escort helicopter.

The Cobra team chose an unusual method of letting Gen. Seneff know what was going on.

"Harvey Gaylord was then in Washington as president of Bell Aerospace and he was a close friend of Gen. Seneff," Kalista related. "We had a few copies — maybe as few as half-a-dozen — of a very expensive brochure on the Cobra concept printed. Then Mr. Gaylord invited Gen. Seneff to dinner at his house one Sunday night and showed him the brochure.

"Gen. Seneff was ecstatic when he saw the Cobra brochure and asked Mr. Gaylord if Bell had any plans to proceed," Kalista said. "Mr. Gaylord then said very quietly, 'We're building the prototype right now.'"

The next day, Hans Weichsel and Kalista were at the Pentagon to brief Gen. Seneff, who had agreed to keep the secret of the development until Bell was ready to announce it.

"He saw photos and charts and graphs and within a few days, he went to Fort Worth to see the prototype development," Kalista recalled.

The major question that confronted both Seneff and Bell was how to get funding to complete development and begin production. Luck played a role in achieving this.

Kaman, in 1963, had been seeking orders for a high-speed version of the H-2 helicopter, which originally had been developed for the Navy. That service had told the company they probably would not buy any more H-2s for the foreseeable future. Development of the H-2 reached the point where the helicopter demonstrated a top speed of about 150 kt. and Kaman engineers thought they could push it to 200 kt. or more. This was enough to worry Bell that it might be selected to replace the UH-1B, which was then the gunship used in Vietnam.

This knowledge originally helped get the Cobra development program approved. Now it would help get the Cobra funded.

In August, 1965, the Army announced that it was seeking an interim helicopter gunship pending the outcome of the AAFSS program. Bell immediately proposed the Cobra. Before the month was out, an Army team had been briefed on the program.

Charlie Seibel guided his development team to an on-time finish and only slightly broke the budget line. Official figures show the Cobra development costs at just $40 thousand over the

million dollar limit. However, some team members recall that before development was complete, the total investment was about $1.25 million. The prototype Cobra was rolled out on September 2, 1965, and made its first flight on September 7.

"By the middle of the month it was routinely exceeding 150 kt.," Norwine said. Top speed achieved during the first month was more than 160 kt.

Still, there was concern among senior Army officers about the effect the Cobra might have on the development of the AAFSS helicopter. Army Chief of Staff Gen. H. K. Johnson was at best lukewarm to the further development of the Cobra and others were opposed for various reasons. One of these was Gen. Delk Oden, who a decade later was president of Bell Helicopter International.

"Some of us got Gen. Oden aside when he visited Fort Worth one time and told him that we could have the Cobra in Vietnam within a year and that while it might not be any better than a Huey B or C, it would look better and would help raise morale," Perry Craddock said. "We also told him it would provide a new lease on life for Army Aviation." Soon after, Gen. Oden persuaded Gen. Johnson to come see the Cobra. He rode in it and was a supporter of it from then on.

There also was a problem with the Army-Air Force roles and missions agreement. The Air Force had the mission of close support, but didn't have anything that could escort helicopter troop transports and provide the kind of support the infantrymen in Vietnam needed.

"Gen. Seneff really put his career on the line here and finally persuaded senior Army commanders that the Cobra was needed," Norwine said.

With the knowledge of the Cobra development and the H-2 effort, the Army decided to hold a technical competition for the interim armed helicopter. Bell, with the Cobra; Kaman, with the high-speed H-2, and Sikorsky, with an armed version of the H-3, were selected as finalists.

"By this time the Army wanted the Cobra and the competition was a bit loaded in Bell's favor," Phil Norwine recalled. "We developed a flight demonstration to prove the value of the tandem seating arrangement which was pretty radical at that time. Joe Mashman and I called it the 'teardrop turn.' Joe would come in at about 30 ft. off the deck, overfly the target, pull up sharply, get his guns on the target and do a two-and-a-half G turn holding the guns on the target with the turret swiveled about 90 deg. The maneuver became the criteria for the evaluations at the competition."

The competition proved to the Army that no other helicopter could fill the requirements. But in the heat of Vietnam, nothing was allowed to enter production without an OK from the commanders in the Vietnam combat zone.

So the prototype Cobra was sent to Vietnam in a transport aircraft to show its wares to the 1st Cavalry Div. there.

"I talked to Maj. Gen. Jack Tolson, who commanded the division, about the Cobra and what it could do and I came to believe that if the 1st Cav bought the Cobra concept, it's in," Cliff Kalista remarked. After inspecting the machine, Tolson said he didn't like the Lycoming T53-L-11, but would accept the -13 version. Production versions of the Cobra did have the -13 version of the T53.

"Tolson was reluctant, but he eventually bought the concept," Kalista said.

Once the Army had accepted the Cobra, only two more obstacles had to be overcome — the Defense Dept. and the Congress.

The OH-58D Advanced Scout, a development of the Model 206L, carries a mast-mounted sight and uses a four-bladed rotor. The armed version, the Kiowa Warrior, carries a variety of weapons.

Shoulder patches from the Army, Navy and Marines all celebrate the use of the Cobra.

Three Spanish Navy AH-1Gs fly in formation. For a time, they were based onboard a Spanish aircraft carrier.

Army AH-1S Cobra, equipped with TOW missel launch tubes, is pictured on a test flight near the Bell factory in Fort Worth.

Marine Corps AH-1T+ SuperCobra prototype, painted with Cobra insignia on side, was powered by two General Electric T700 engines.

Taiwanese AH-1T carries TOW missile tubes on a test flight near the Fort Worth factory.

The Army and Bell took their case to the Pentagon with a request for funding and got turned down. Robert S. McNamara, then Defense Secretary under President Johnson, did not see any benefit to having another armed helicopter when armed Hueys already were in operation in Vietnam.

"We decided to write a reclama to McNamara's decision, pointing out the great savings because the Cobra was so much more effective as a gunship than the Huey. "We stressed that the Cobra would improve mission effectiveness because it could bring greater firepower to the battlefield for the same amount of money," Kalista recounted. "Members of his staff accepted the idea and helped sell McNamara on the concept."

When the Army took its case for production money to a Congressional committee, Bell's foresight in putting retractable skids on the prototype paid off. When committee members balked at the cost of the new helicopters — two Cobras would cost about the same as three UH-1Bs — it was suggested that the cost could be reduced by taking some of the "frills" off of the machine. The frill first mentioned was the retractable skid. The cost of this skid was considerably greater than the old standard Huey fixed skid and when the Army and Bell agreed it could go without seriously detracting from the Cobras' performance, opposition to the funding melted away.

"We got a development contract in April, 1966, and a production contract a week or so later and we had that helicopter in action in Vietnam in 15 months," Phil Norwine said. "Between April of 1966 and August of 1967, we completed development, testing, qualification and manufactured and delivered the first Cobras to the Army in time for them to train pilots and get the helicopters into action in August, 1967."

When the U.S. Army put the Cobra into combat in Vietnam, it validated the concept of

the tandem cockpit design, which today is standard on virtually all helicopter gunships. It also opened the floodgates to literally hundreds of orders for the Cobra.

The initial version ordered by the Army was designated the AH-1G. It has been followed by the AH-1E, F, P, Q, R and S versions. The Navy and Marines ordered the twin-engined AH-1J, AH-1T and AH-1T+, which was later redesignated the AH-1W. The AH-1W — the Super Cobra or Whiskey Cobra — still is in production and an advanced version, the AH-1W-4BR, is being developed with the four-bladed Model 680 advanced rotor system.

In addition to Vietnam, the Cobra has seen combat in a number of small conflicts and in the 1991 Desert Storm operation, where both AH-1S Cobras of the U.S. Army and AH-1W Cobras operated by the Marines ran up impressive records.

Not all of the Cobra versions or derivatives were successful. Bell worked to develop the Model 309 KingCobra, a larger and more powerful version, but it never was ordered into production. On the whole, however, the concept has been validated many times over. Versions of the Cobra are in service with the military forces of at least 10 other nations and is being evaluated by several other countries, including some NATO members.

And there was the Model 409/AH-63, a new design which Bell entered in the Army's Advanced Attack Helicopter competition. Test Pilot Gene Colvin swears the helicopter tried to kill him at least three times. Cliff Kalista recalls a "wild ride" with Colvin in the AH-63, which ended with the helicopter making an emergency landing in Mansfield, Texas, some miles from the Bell test site.

Needless to say, the Model 409 didn't win the competition. But the loss didn't noticeably slow the Cobra program. The winner of the AAH competition is nearing the end of its production life, while the Cobra continues on.

Phil Norwine summarized the Cobra program best: "We sometimes wondered when we were struggling to develop the helicopter, if we would ever see a profit from the Cobra, but now that we've delivered more than 2,000 units, I guess you could say it was a good gamble."

Reminiscences: Charlie Seibel, engineer and designer

I think I was the first — certainly one of the first — college aeronautical engineering students to specialize in helicopters. I was an undergraduate at Cal Tech in the early 1940s and I had heard of the Sikorsky VS-300, which was just starting its flight test work then. It was the only helicopter I knew of. I was then writing my thesis on helicopter control systems.

All four years I studied at Cal Tech, I worked in the Cal Tech wind tunnel, which, during the early days of World War 2, was kept running 24 hr. a day. Because I worked there, I got to meet many of the nation's top aeronautical engineers when they would come in to work on various projects.

In January, 1943, I heard of this fellow with a broken arm who was visiting the wind tunnel. It turned out to be Bob Stanley, who had been injured in a recent accident with the Bell Model 30. One thing led to another, and pretty soon I accepted a job with Bell to work on their helicopter program after I graduated. During spring break that year, I flew from Los Angeles to Buffalo on a DC-3 just to spend a week seeing what the program was like. In June, after I finished school, I shared a ride across the country to Buffalo to go to work.

One of my first jobs after I got to Gardenville was model testing. I would take Art Young's small models and measure their performance. Later, when the Model 30 was first flying, it developed a severe two-per-rev vibration problem. The vibration was so severe that Floyd Carlson, who was our only test pilot, wouldn't try to fly any faster when he got to 30 mph.

Art, who had researched previous helicopter work and who had a fabulous memory, recalled two research papers. One had been written in Britain and the other was published by NACA. Using them, we calculated when the greatest rotor vibration should occur and it was at 30 mph. forward speed. Bart Kelley studied the resonant conditions of the rotor and came up with the idea of stiffening the blade near the hub. Floyd Carlson then designed the famous Swedish Yoke and the vibration stopped. Floyd, incidentally, taught himself to fly, and I later figured that he had more than 100 hr. of piloting time before he ever saw a helicopter fly from the ground.

As a result of these vibration problems and the resulting tests, I wrote my first NACA technical paper, which outlined the work we had done.

Charles Seibel left Bell in 1948 to establish his own company. He later returned until his retirement. Mr. Seibel died in 1994, shortly after being interviewed for this book.

Clockwise from upper left: Model 230 in Petroleum Helicopter Inc. markings near Fort Worth; A militarized Model 230 with nose radar in Slobbovian naval markings; AH-1J Cobra with TOW launchers in Imperial Iranian Air Force markings, about 1977; Model 47H in pre-Castro Cuban civil markings.

CHAPTER ELEVEN

The Way It Was; The Way It's Going To Be

Back in 1960, when Textron bought Bell Helicopter and other defense-oriented divisions of the old Bell Aircraft Corp., a major financial publication ran an article commenting on what a terrible mistake Textron had made, investing in a company and an industry which had a future so cloudy and insecure. And Bell grew from a company with annual sales of $51 million then to one with sales of $1.400 billion now.

In 1963, when Bell lost the Army's Advanced Aerial Fire Support System (AAFSS) competition, and later, the Advanced Armed Helicopter competition, industry speculation was that the company's future was limited and that a merger was the likely fate of Bell. And while the AAFSS program was subsequently canceled, Bell built thousands of Huey Cobras in the following years and is still building them.

In 1965, when Bell lost the Army's Light Observation Helicopter (LOH) competition, many foresaw a bleak future for a company which had previously dominated the light util-

Model 412 in Canadian military markings is shown in flight. Improvements include a four-bladed rotor and Pratt & Whitney PT6 Twin Pac powerplant.

ity helicopter market. And Bell has to date sold more than 9,000 military and civil versions of its basic LOH design and continues to build hundreds each year.

In 1972, when Bell was eliminated from the Army's Utility Tactical Transport Aircraft System (UTTAS) competition, there were those who predicted the company would be shut out of future civil markets for medium-lift helicopters. Bell, they prophesied, would not have the advanced technology in its helicopters to compete with the builders of the new generation of rotary-wing aircraft which would flow from the UTTAS design. And Bell followed with the development of the 214 series of helicopters which have to date sold 500+ units. There are still no civil versions of the winning UTTAS design.

"With the exception of the XH-40 program [later redesignated the HU-1 Huey], almost all of Bell's most successful major programs have come from a defeat," Phil Norwine, vice president and sales engineer during the development of the Cobra, noted. "Even with the Huey, we put a lot of effort into the C model and lost. But we came back with the D model which has been very successful."

This capacity to rebound from defeat, to continue even after severe setbacks, and to see and capitalize on opportunities which competitors did not, has been the most notable facet of Bell's often turbulent, occasionally surprising and always forceful history.

This characteristic goes all the way back to the very earliest days of the helicopter program, when the decision was made to abandon the Model 30 in favor of the Model 42. The Model 42 was unsuccessful, but the Model 30, which was continued for a time on an almost surreptitious basis, evolved into the Model 47, which sustained the company through its first decade and continued in production for more than 25 years.

In the early years, when there was no civil market, Bell led the way in creating one, by showing what the helicopter could do that nothing else could. And it was a leader in developing the basis for a military need for helicopters, including such widely varying roles as medical evacuation, troop transport and armed combat helicopters.

Bell's history of determination to beat the odds and success in doing so is easy to recall. What is much more difficult to relate is the human side of this history. The people who built Bell and those who sustain it today exhibit a wide range of char-

acteristics. They have been ingenious, intelligent, devoted, unwilling to admit defeat, determined, forceful, and at times, even belligerent or maniacal.

They have found pathways to their goals through lollipops and insects, through rain and heat and cold, with ingenuity and stubbornness and an amazing ability to succeed where others failed. Whatever it took, they found it and gave it.

Whatever they did, they considered themselves part of a family, the Bell Family.

The future at times may look just as bleak and unpromising as it did in 1946, when Bell certificated the first civil helicopter and delivered its first H-13 to the Army for evaluation. There are still predictions of doom, gloom and catastrophe.

And Bell still faces the future with intelligence, initiative and confidence — mostly because of the people who today are still doing what their predecessors did in the past half-century.

"Bell has the potential to have a greater future than it has a past," Webb Joiner, current president of the company, predicted. "Bell today is well positioned for the future if we really build on what's been given to us. Matter of fact, when you look at the [helicopter] industry, I think Bell is probably the one company which really has a foundation on which to build. And it is a foundation that was laid by all the people who have made up the Bell family.

"They were extroverts and rather flamboyant at times," Joiner said. "But we've always been blessed with an innovative management which has never let Bell be limited by what they had in hand. They were always willing to go out and find a way to get what they needed."

Now, he noted, the helicopter business has changed and matured.

"It is basically a mature business," Joiner said. "As a result, I think

the opportunity to look into the future and see where you ought to be going with products and who the customers should be and what the size of the market will be is much better today than it was 30 years ago.

"As a result, I think that having a good, sound business is a big part of what is going to make a helicopter company successful in the future, as opposed to the entrepreneurs who originally built the industry," Joiner added. "Now, that does not replace the imagination and the creativity and the vision to see where the industry can go and what the product to match that vision will be. I think another thing has changed from the early days. That entrepreneurial spirit that existed carried over to every employee. They all felt a part of things;

Model 206L LongRangers are outfitted for delivery at the Bell Factory in Mirabel, Quebec.

Model 47G flies near the Fort Worth factory in Cuban military markings in the early 1950s.

as we said during Vietnam, 'I'm on the Huey team.' Everybody felt a part of that. Today, I think it becomes much more important that that relationship and communication within the company has to be much better than it was in the early days. I think there has to be much

future — the Bell Family.

"We can never take our eyes off the future and have a vision of where we want to go, but by the same token I don't think we can ever forget where we've been and how we got to where we are today," Joiner

The first Model 214A transport helicopter delivered to Iran is shown during test flight near Fort W.orth

more of an openness and inclusion of everyone in the process [of operating the business]. This openness existed before because of the spirit — the industry was just so tiny and so new that people were drawn in because they wanted to be part of it."

As industries get older, there tends to be great divisions between parts of the companies, Joiner said. "It becomes a we and they situation within the company. I think that's been one of the secrets of Bell Helicopter — that there really has been a Bell Family. And that's going to be the secret of our success in the

said. "That winning spirit really is the thing that sets an individual, a team, a company up to succeed in the future."

Another factor which will contribute to future success is the fact that Bell understands that it has to be the leader in every market in which it competes, Joiner believes. These are the U.S. government market, the U.S. civil market and the international market.

"We have to have the number one position in order to have the resources to keep improving the product line. You have

to continually improve your product line so that you can offer a broad range to the customers. And if you aren't really the dominant player in the market, the resources just won't be available to do it," Joiner emphasized.

The overall military market will over the next few years experience some further cutback, Joiner predicted, but he believes the aerospace industry is getting close to the bottom of the present decline.

"But as far as Bell Helicopter is concerned, I think that over the next five to 10 years, we will actually grow in that market," Joiner added. "And one of the big reasons is tilt-rotor technology. I think we'll still have a growing sales base in helicopters, but the tilt-rotor will expand the size of our market even more."

Over the past 10 to 15 years the international market has become a "very competitive market," Joiner said. "And it will continue to be. There are a lot of manufacturers in the world and there are a lot of people who build good helicopters. And there is a small market, so the competition is tough."

The U.S. domestic market is itself crowded with competing helicopter manufacturers, which is going to force some changes on the helicopter industry, Joiner said.

"It seems obvious to me that in the next few years one of two things has to happen — either a consolidation or some folks are going to have to go out of business, or become subcontractors," Joiner stated. "We've got four manufacturers in the market place today and there is just no way to have enough market to support four manufacturers. The competition is going to get more difficult and the sales are going to get smaller."

Composites and systems integration development are likely to be the technologies which drive the helicopter industry in the next 20 years, Joiner predicted. Similarly, the tilt-rotor will require a 20-year period before it is fully developed and is fully meeting the needs of the market, he said.

"And these technologies are not only going to have to make better performing helicopters, but also more cost-efficient aircraft. I think we as an industry have to get our arms around continuously growing costs. In a business like ours, you'll find that people are either not doing what they want to do, or going out and finding another way to do it," Joiner stated. "One of our operators used to frequently get calls to carry newlyweds off to their honeymoon. It was part of the ceremony and a lot of fun, but he doesn't get these calls any more. When they find out what he has to charge, the couple will decide to get a big limousine. It won't be quite as much fun, but they can afford to do it. On a larger scale, that's what is going to happen to the whole industry if we let costs drive us.

"Bell can never be comfortable with where we are."

Model 214ST prototype in Iranian colors during flight test program at Bell's Arlington, Texas facility. Vertical fins on horizontal tail were eventually discarded in light of improved directional stability offered by larger vertical tail.

Like It Is: Naomi Caruthers, supervisor of telecommunications and administrative services.

Naomi Caruthers resides in Fort Worth and has not made any plans yet for retirement.

I got up before it was light and drove off with my headlights on because I didn't want to be late for work on my first day. It was June 15, 1951, and I had just graduated from high school in Paradise, Texas. Bell had moved to the old Globe plant in January, and things were just starting to pick up there when I was hired. By the time I got to the plant in Saginaw, it was daylight and I forgot to switch my headlights off.

The first thing that happened was they took me for a ride in a Model 47. It had no doors on it and only a little belt to hold me in. I was scared, but I also enjoyed it. I was hired to run the telex machine. I had never seen a telex machine, but they said they would teach me. Bill Gunderson was the plant manager and Rufus Ivey, his assistant, was the one who hired me.

Another 'employee' also went to work for the first time that day. It was a dog we named Lady Bell, and she just took up residence in the guard house. The guards fed her and she accompanied them on their rounds. She was still there when I left.

After I finished work that first day, I tried to start my car and, of course, the battery was dead because the lights had been on all day. I was too shy to ask anyone for help, so I just sat there until somebody came over and asked me if everything was alright.

At first, our offices were in an area that ran right down the middle of the Globe plant, which we called the Tin Barn. The assembly lines were on either side of our offices. Later, we moved over to what was called the Army Building. It was so cold in the winter that I typed with my gloves on and in the summer there was no air conditioning.

When the new plant opened here at Hurst, they asked me to come over and open the communications department. I really intended to go back to Globe, but it was so much nicer here that I decided to stay.

Things grew rapidly and, at one time, I had 18 girls working for me on the telephone switchboard and telex machines. Our Direct Inward Dialing system has reduced that number quite a bit, but we still use the telex.

Like It Is: M. L. (Put) Putnam, lead production worker

A friend of mine and I were driving down [Texas] Highway 114 and we saw this big sign that said "Help Wanted at Bell Helicopter." We talked about it, but we had already been interviewed at another aircraft manufacturer in the area, so I went to work there.

I got laid off in the middle of 1962, and decided to try working for myself as a carpenter for a while. In about three months, a friend called me, and said I ought to get a job at Bell. I was a little bit skeptical, because I had just been laid off, but he said that he thought Bell had enough work to see me through the winter. That was 32 years ago and I'm still here.

I started out doing subassembly work, and later moved over for a time to the Model 205 when it was just entering production. I worked in a number of different departments, and am now in final assembly, supervising about eight men. They all know their jobs pretty well, so I have time to get my paperwork all done. Everyone is used to his job, and it's not bad at all.

The program I remember best is the Model 214ST. I was on it from the first day it came into production, and I was still on it the day the last one rolled out the factory door. I later worked on the Model 206 and the Model 209, with a lot of time spent on the Model 206. I got a ride in one of those helicopters once, but I turned down a chance to ride in a Model 209 because I just wasn't sure about that big machine. I wish now I had flown in it.

I worked at Hurst when we had five production lines and three shifts during Vietnam and every 2 hr. 45 min. we would roll another helicopter out the door. We had 12,000 workers or so then.

Even with that many people, Bell has been just like a big family. I can say that because the other company where I worked didn't have that feeling. It's been a very good company to work for.

Like it is: Pete Hardy, security guard

I've been a security guard at Bell for 29 years, and I would guess that I know about 70% of all the employees here — by face if not by name. I know where most of them work and what they do, too. In fact, I've recognized Bell employees in places as far away as Hawaii and Colorado. They always ask me what I'm doing there.

A lot of the security job nowadays is public relations. We operate all the lobbies and have to get visitors signed in and make sure they get where they are supposed to go. We also check employees in each day and clear contractors and delivery people in and out. We handle all emergency calls and that can be nearly anything. Just this week a person at the Bell plant had a heart attack and we were responsible for getting the ambulance in to him and making sure he got proper treatment.

Bell's like a city within itself. We have physical problems, people lost, even a little crime once in a while. A man got over the fence one day and lit some paper in the cockpit of a Cobra parked on the ramp. We got the fire out before it did any damage and we got the man, too. Another time, a mentally deranged former soldier got in and went to the military liaison office, pointed his finger at the officer there and said 'Bang — I could have got you.' We got him out and on the way to help.

My work takes me to all of the Bell plants in the area, so I have the opportunity to see and meet many of the workers that people working in just one plant don't have. It seems to me like we're a working family in which pride in our accomplishments flows through each level. I think there's a pretty close relationship between all the workers and between the work force and the management.

One thing I'll always remember is locking the gate at the old Globe plant. I was the last Bell employee out when we shut it down. That plant was where Bell first started when they came to Texas, and an awful lot of us have fond memories of the place.

Bell Helicopter Family Tree

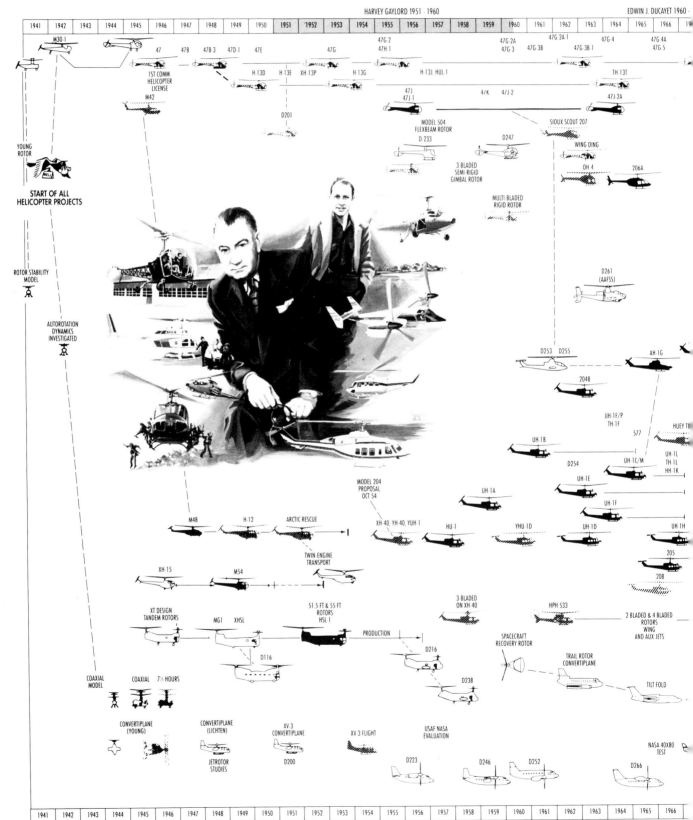

JAMES F. ATKINS 1972 - 1983

LEONARD M. HORNER 1983 - 1991

WEBB F. JOINER 1991 - PRESENT

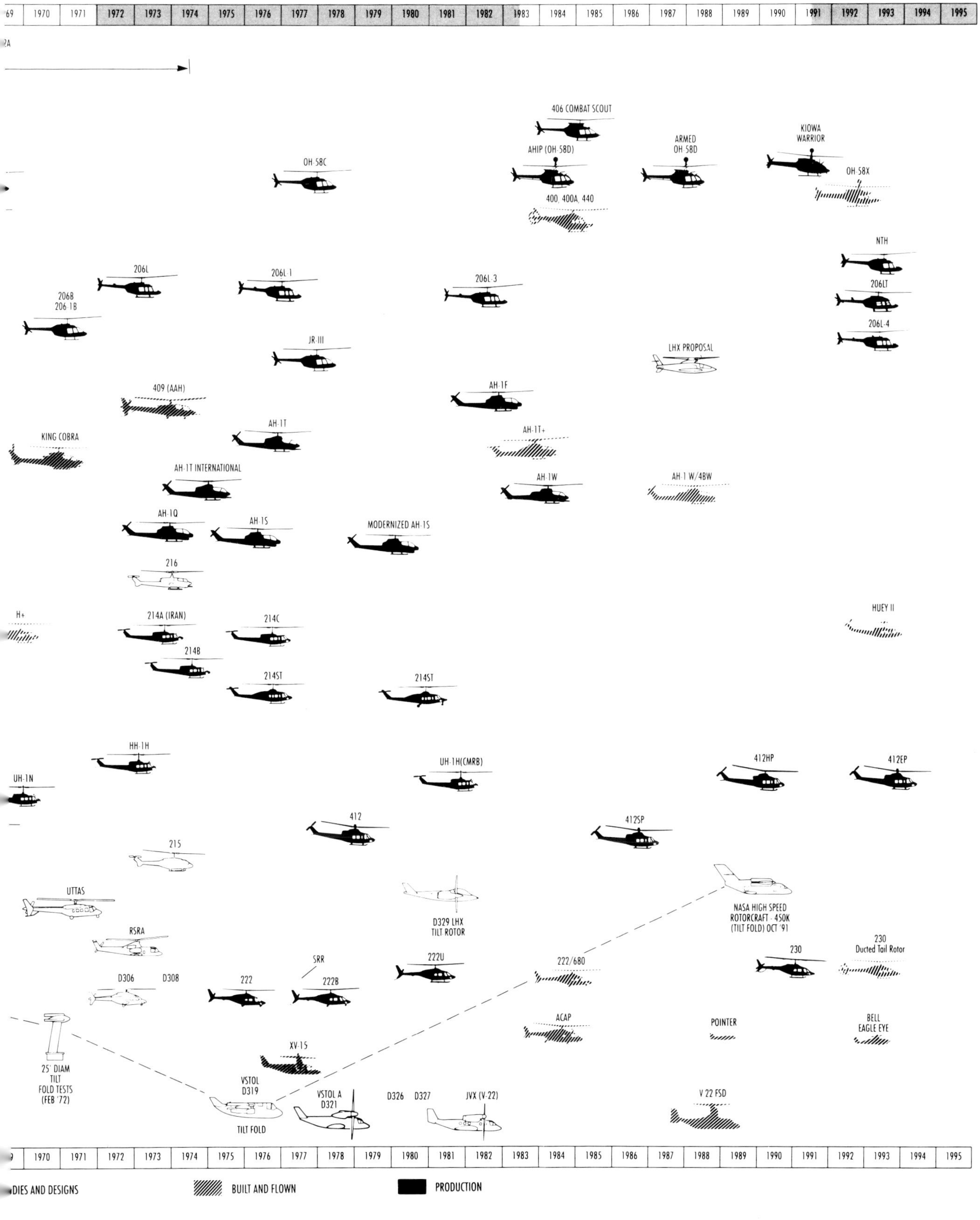

| 69 | 1970 | 1971 | 1972 | 1973 | 1974 | 1975 | 1976 | 1977 | 1978 | 1979 | 1980 | 1981 | 1982 | 1983 | 1984 | 1985 | 1986 | 1987 | 1988 | 1989 | 1990 | 1991 | 1992 | 1993 | 1994 | 1995 |

406 COMBAT SCOUT

AHIP (OH-58D)

ARMED
OH-58D

KIOWA
WARRIOR

OH-58C

OH-58X

400, 400A, 440

NTH

206L

206L-1

206L-3

206LT

206B
206-1B

206L-4

JR-III

LHX PROPOSAL

409 (AAH)

AH-1F

AH-1T

KING COBRA

AH-1T+

AH-1T INTERNATIONAL

AH-1W

AH-1W/4BW

AH-1Q

AH-1S

MODERNIZED AH-1S

216

HUEY II

H+

214A (IRAN)

214C

214B

214ST

214ST

HH-1H

UH-1H(CMRB)

412HP

412EP

UH-1N

412

412SP

215

UTTAS

NASA HIGH SPEED
ROTORCRAFT - 450K
(TILT FOLD) OCT '91

D329 LHX
TILT ROTOR

RSRA

230
Ducted Tail Rotor

SRR

222U

222/680

D306   D308

222

222B

ACAP

POINTER

BELL
EAGLE EYE

XV-15

25' DIAM
TILT
FOLD TESTS
(FEB '72)

VSTOL
D319

VSTOL A
D321

D326   D327

JVX (V-22)

V 22 FSD

TILT FOLD

| 1970 | 1971 | 1972 | 1973 | 1974 | 1975 | 1976 | 1977 | 1978 | 1979 | 1980 | 1981 | 1982 | 1983 | 1984 | 1985 | 1986 | 1987 | 1988 | 1989 | 1990 | 1991 | 1992 | 1993 | 1994 | 1995 |

DIES AND DESIGNS   BUILT AND FLOWN   PRODUCTION

Bells that never were...

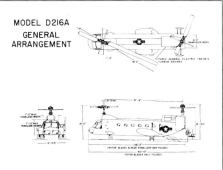

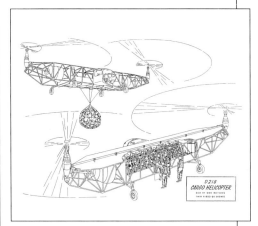

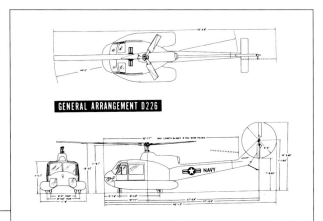

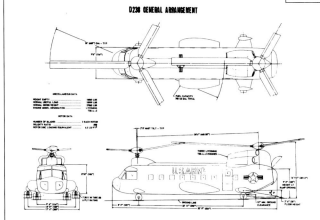

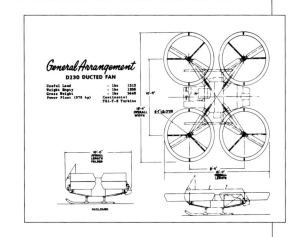

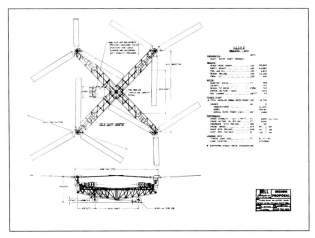

Bell's nuclear-powered helicopter project of the 1950's.

Army H-13H, military version of the Model 47G-2, entered service with the military in 1956. Here one hovers in front of others ready for delivery.

Predecessor of a large family, the fourth (of five) OH-4A protypes hovers at the Bell factory in Fort Worth. The unsuccessful candidate for the Army's light observation helicopter was the basis for the Model 206 and 406 designs.

Recently restored all-weather instrument trainer version of the classic HTL-7 (later designated TH-13N) is now civil registered N5710 and owned by a private-sector operator.

The old and the new pose together. The 36th Bell Model 47B constructed, registered N116B, is parked in front of one of only two XV-15 tilt-rotor test aircraft built. N116B is the second oldest Model 47 known to exist.

The XV-3 tilt-rotor, modified after its accident, flies fully converted to airplane mode. Two-bladed rotors replaced the original three-bladed design.

A brightly painted early production version of the Model 47G sits on the ramp at Fort Worth. The helicopter was the first designed after the move from Buffalo.

Presidential helicopter, one of two UH-13J-1s acquired by the U.S. Air Force for use by President Eisenhower, is run up on the ramp at the Fort Worth factory prior to delivery.

The XV-3, first of Bell's tilt-rotor designs, is res-died for testing in the 40 x 80 ft. wind tunnel at NASA's Ames Research Center about 1963.

Bell Design D-292 was tested as part of the Army's Advanced Composite Airframe Program in 1985. Three aircraft were built, but only this one ever flew.

UH-1B gunship lifts off the launch pad in Vietnam, early in the war there. On the ground are both additional gunships and unarmed troop-carring "slicks."

The XV-15 tilt-rotor development aircraft flies over the Potomac River with its rotors in a near-vertical position.

Navy TH-57A SeaRanger trainer, a version of the Model 206, was delivered to fleet training facilities beginning in 1968.

Model 205/UH-1Ds for the Venezuelan Air Force. These aircraft have been used for a variety of VIP transport, air/sea rescue, and counter-insurgency missions.

Armed Model 412 demonstrator is equipped with a nose-mounted gun pod and associated fire control system.

Ron Bower set a new round-the-world helicopter speed record of 24 days, 4 hours, and 36 minutes in this JetRanger during mid-1994.

Another operator of the AH-1W Whiskey Cobra is the Turkish army, which received five of the helicopters in 1990.

Marine Corps Ah-1W is the ultimate development of the AH-1 HueyCobra now in service. A version with a four-bladed rotor is envisioned.

Marine Corps AH-1T
Cobra was developed
using components origi-
nally devised for heli-
copters sold to Iran.

An AH-1F Cobra for
Pakistan Army Aviation is
test flown by Ned Gilliand
before delivery from the
Fort Worth factory about
1984.

Three Jordanian AH-1F
Cobras, of a total of 24
delivered, fly in formation
near Fort Worth before
delivery, about 1983.

Demonstrator OH-58D Kiowa Warrior, was all black except for Indian head on the fuselage and an identification racing stripe on the tail boom.

Model 407, Bell's latest, a four-bladed version, introduced in early 1995.

A Model 230 demonstrator, an improved version of the Model 222, flies past the World Trade Centers on lower Manhatten Island in New York.

BELL HELICOPTER HIGHLIGHTS

YEAR 1935
July 10   Lawrence D. Bell founds Bell Aircraft Corporation with 56 employees.

YEAR 1941
November 1   Development work begun by Bell on first helicopter.

YEAR 1942
May 1   Building in Gardenville, New York, near Buffalo, leased for Bell helicopter project.

YEAR 1943
July 29   First formal flight of Bell helicopter, at Gardenville, New York.

YEAR 1944
May 10   Aviation history is made when Bell helicopter is flown inside 65th Regiment Armory, Buffalo, New York; first U.S. indoor flight.

YEAR 1945
January 5   Bell helicopter flies doctor to injured pilot, who had bailed out of an airplane and became snowbound in a western New York farmhouse.

YEAR 1946
March 8   Bell Model 47B granted world's first commercial helicopter license.
May 8   Bell receives Helicopter Type Certificate No. 1, first to be granted by Civil Aeronautics Administration.
December 31   First production line Bell helicopter delivered to U.S. Army.

YEAR 1947
January 6   First two YH-13A helicopters built for Army Air Force leave plant in C-82 for Alaska.
April 11   Delivery of 13 helicopters for Army Air Force and Navy represents largest single delivery of rotary wing aircraft to date.

YEAR 1948
February 1   Floyd Carlson rescues, by Bell helicopter, three fishermen marooned on Lake Erie ice.
September 27   Air Force announces two-place liaison XH-15 helicopter is being built by Bell.

YEAR 1949
March 18   Bell Helicopter sets altitude record of 18,550 feet.
March 28   Bell Helicopter sets speed record of 133.9 miles per hour.
April 1   Bell announces Model 47D-1 utility helicopter, capable of carrying three passengers or 500-pound payload.
May 13   Bell Aircraft Supply Corporation formed to fly helicopter oil surveys in South and Southwest and to service helicopter operations on the West Coast.

YEAR 1950
September 21   Bell 47-D becomes first helicopter to fly over the Alps.
October 21   Bell Model 48 announced.
November 10   Eight H-13D helicopters, first of new Army order, sent to Korea.

YEAR 1951
January 30   55-acre site at Hurst selected for Bell Aircraft Corporation's helicopter division.
February 12   Navy's Bell XHSL-1 announced.
February 15   Globe Plant north of Fort Worth occupied and extensive Texas hiring started.
May 21   Ground-breaking for Hurst plant.
December 3   Personnel begin occupying Hurst plant.

YEAR 1952
September 17   Bell Pilot Elton J. Smith set world's record for helicopter distance flight in straight line without payload. Smith flew a Bell 47D-1 non-stop from Hurst, Texas, to Buffalo, New York, a total of 1,217.137 miles.

YEAR 1953
March 3   HSL's first flight.
April 10   1,000th model roles off assembly line.
July 1   First Army order (21 ships) for H-13H.

YEAR 1954
January 26   First delivery to Navy of HSL-1.
April 5   Last B-36 pod delivered to Convair.
June 17   HSL-1 completes 1,465-mile flight from Fort Worth to Patuxent River, Md.
October 20   First flight of XH-13F turbine helicopter.

YEAR 1955
February 10   XV-3 convertiplane rollout.
February 23   Bell wins industry competition for Army's first production line turbine-powered utility helicopter (Bell 204/Army UH-1 Model), first all-Texas designed and developed model.
August 11   First flight of XV-3 convertiplane.
August 12   First order of 10 ships for Navy HUL-1 helicopters.

YEAR 1956

September 3   Army pilots at National Air Show, Oklahoma City, set unofficial record for helicopte endurance flight by keeping H-13H aloft for 57 hours, 50 minutes.
September 4   Pilot Joe Mashman and Service Rep. Joe Beebe leave Hurst in 47J on 83-day introductory tour of the new model through Central and South America.
October 20   Lawrence D. Bell dies.

YEAR 1957
January 1   Bell Helicopter Corporation founded as wholly-owned subsidiary of Bell Aircraft Corporation.
January 18   Navy announced order for HTL-7 helicopters.
March 29   Two H-13J helicopters delivered to Air Force for presidential use.
July 12   President Eisenhower rides in H-13J from White House lawn to command post as part of civil defense exercise.

December 1   12,000th Model 47 rolls off assembly line, with Lyndon B. Johnson witnessing the ceremony.

YEAR 1958
September 5   Brazilian president receives one of four 47J Rangers bought by that country.
December 18   XV-3 makes aviation history with first 100 percent conversion of tilt prop-rotor aircraft.

YEAR 1959
March 13   Bell receives order for Army HU-1A helicopters.
April 17   XV-3 convertiplane becomes first VTOL craft to shift gears in flight.
July 10   Bell announces Navy contract for turbine-powered HUL-1M.

YEAR 1960
April 27   First flight of HU-1B system.
May 26   Ten HU-1A Army medical evacuation helicopters air lifted to Chile for Operation Amigo relief mission.
July 2   Textron Inc. of Providence, R.I., purchases defense activities of Bell Aircraft Corp. and sets up Bell Aerospace Corp. as wholly-owned subsidiary with three operating divisions: Bell Helicopter Co., Bell Aerosystems Co., and Hydraulic Research and Manufacturing Co.
July 19-26   Army pilots fly HU-1 to seven world helicopter records.

YEAR 1961
January 10   Initial flight of Navy's HUL-1M, first aircraft to be powered by 250 shp, T-63 turbine engine.
January 31   Al Averill, flying 47J-2, sets world helicopter record in Class E-1.c for 100-kilometer speed in closed circuit. His speed 107.081 mph, breaking Russian-held mark.
January 31   Lou Hartwig, flying 47J-2, sets world helicopter record in Class E-1.b for 100-kilometer speed in closed circuit. His speed was 104.613, breaking Czechoslovakian-held mark.
February 2   Lou Hartwig, flying 47G, sets three class E-1.b world records on one flight. One is non-stop distance in closed circuit, 631.436 miles. Second is 500-kilometer speed in closed circuit, 73.985 mph. Third is 1,000-kilometer speed in closed circuit, 73.351 mph. All three marks are first records to be set in these categories and weight classes.
February 8   Al Averill, flying 47G, sets world helicopter record in Class E-1.b for non-stop distance in straight line without payload, 731.22 miles. New record for this category.
February 8   Dr. Dora Dougherty, flying Bell 47G, sets feminine world helicopter record for altitude with-out payload, 19,385 feet. Old record held by Russians.
February 10   Dr. Dora Dougherty, flying Bell 47G-3, sets feminine world helicopter record for non-stop distance in straight line without payload, 405.83 miles. Old record held by Russians.
April 17   Bell receives $4,000,000 order for eight Model 204B/HU-1B helicopters for Royal Australian Air Force.
April 19   Bell announces whole new range of high-altitude capabilities for helicopter operations opened by new turbo-supercharged 47G-3B in Pikes Peak test.
April 27   Vice President Lyndon B. Johnson and West German Chancellor Konrad Adenauer arrive at Austin, Texas in HU-1A.
May 19   Bell OH-4 announced as one of three LOH design winners
June 9   HTL-6 sets unofficial world record for helicopter flight endurance of 72 hours and two minutes at Navy's Ellyson Field, Pensacola, Fla.
November 13   Bell receives $6,000,000 contract for procurement of five HO-4 light observation helicopter prototypes.
December 8   Bell announces receipt of $70,000,000 worth of new government business, including HO-4, RAAF contracts and follow-on production of HU-1B and HU-1D Army helicopters.

YEAR 1962
January 20   Mitsui & Co., Ltd. licensed to manufacture Bell commercial model 204 in Japan.
March 3   Bell's UH-1E wins competition for production contract for U.S. Marine Corps' ASH (Assault Support Helicopter).
April 13   U.S. Army's Capt. Boyce B. Buckner sets world record in Bell YHU-ID by climbing to 6,000 meters (19,686 ft.) in five minutes 51 seconds.
April 14   U.S. Army's Lt. Col. Leland Wilhelm sets world record in Bell YHU-1D by climbing to 3,000 meters (9,843 ft.) in two minutes 17 seconds.
April 20   U.S. Army's Capt. W. F. Gurley sets world class record in Bell YHU-1D by flying 1,000 kilometers in closed circuit at average speed of 134.9 miles per hour.
May 2   Bell President E. J. Ducayet elected president of American Helicopter Society.

YEAR 1963
January 7   Harvey Gaylord, president of Bell Aerospace Corporation, is elected executive vice president of Textron Inc.
February   Bell UH-1B carries 32 flood refugees and crew of four in one flight in Morocco.
March   High-performance UH-IB flies more than 170 miles per hour.
April 15   FAA certificates Bell Model 204B
May 31   U.S. Army accepts first Bell UH-1D.
June 7   Bell wins competition to build UH-IF for the U.S. Air Force.
October 29   Bell plant cognizance changes from U.S. Navy to U.S. Army; noted in elaborate ceremonies at Hurst plant. In same program, $108,320,407 contract for UH-1B and UH-1D ships announced by Congressman Jim Wright.

YEAR 1964
January 6   Bell receives $7,662,257 production contract from U.S. Marines for UH-11E helicopters.
February 15   New Engineering and Research facility occupied at plant.
February 20   Bell delivers 850th UH-1; first flight of UH-1F series; and first delivery of UH-1E made to operational Marine unit.
March 20   British Army orders 150 47G-3B-I helicopters.
May 25   YUH-1B flies 222 mph in unofficial new world record.
June 18 $5,762,850 contract for 103 47G-3B-I's modified to trainer configuration fo Army.
September 24   First operational UH-1F delivered to Air Force.
November 6   Ten world flight records set by UH-1D.
December 7   Four bladed rigid rotor flown in high speed flight.
December 17   Eleven more world records claimed by UH-1D making total of 21 for the Iroquois model and a total of 27 records held by Bell helicopters.
December 24   Bell receives $98,517,345 contract for 720 UH-1B's and UH-1D's.

YEAR 1965

January 5 — 204B sling lifts and assembles the first oil well cementing unit built for helicopter transport for remote drilling operations. (Halliburton Company, Duncan, Oklahoma.)

January 27 — First delivery of U.S. Army's Instrument Trainer, TH-13T.

March 2 — Bell wins industry-wide competition to produce turbine-powered UH-1Es for U.S Marine Corps.

March 2 — Production record believed to be unprecedented in aerospace industry with 100 consecutive months of on-schedule deliveries to U.S government

March 19 — New V/STOL design -- Trailing Rotor Machine.

April 5 — West German Parliamentary Committee in Bonn approves selection of UH-1D with order of 406 helicopters costing approximately $125 million.

April 29 — Development and first flight of helicopter with Twin-Turbine power plant (UH-1D).

July 14 — Bell receives additional U.S. Army order for 720 helicopters (225 UH-1Bs and 465 UH-1Ds). Bell also received a 720-ship order for UH-1 models in December 1964, the largest number of UH-1 models ever purchased in a single order. This follow-up procurement is approximately $100 million.

September 20 — Bell announces development of Cobra, a modified version of UH-1B. It features streamlined fuselage configuration for maximum speed, armament payload and crew effectiveness.

October 12 — Bell unveils new 5 place high-speed JetRanger for addition to its 1966 commercial line. It will fly at speeds in excess of 140 mph and will carry a 1500-pound useful load.

October 25 — Cobra records sustained level flight cruise speed of 200 mph. Official world speed for its weight class is 180.1 miles per hour.

November 17 — A $297,000 contract for preliminary design study for new research VTOL (vertical take off and landing) rotary-wing composite aircraft awarded to Bell.

YEAR 1966

January 10 — Roll-out of JetRanger, new 5-place utility ship, at Fort Worth facility. Ship immediately enters flight test program.

April 13 — U.S. Army awards Bell production order for 110 Cobras.

May 20 — A three-bladed spacecraft recovery rotor system that could allow astronauts to safely land their capsules at low speeds is successfully tested.

June 28 — Bell receives largest contract in its history and the largest ever awarded by U.S. Army Aviation Material Command, totalling $249,457,443 for 2,115 UH-1 Iroquois helicopters.

August 25 — Halvorson-Lent's Transcanyon Pipeline Project nears completion at Grand Canyon. It is one of the greatest construction challenges in history, using exclusively helicopters to lay water pipe in floor of canyon.

September 1 — U.S. Army awards Bell $44,377,858 letter contract for 708 UH-1D helicopters.

September 21 — A unique radar antenna built into the blade of a helicopter is successfully tested.

October 17 — Delivery of three UH-1D helicopters completes order for 11 ships constituting New Zealand's first armed forces rotary-wing fleet.

November 30 — Army continues helicopter buildup by placing $21,795,000 order for 210 more Cobras.

YEAR 1967

January 13 — First two deliveries of production 206A JetRangers made at HAA convention to Hollymatic Corp. of Park Forest, Ill., and to National Helicopter Service & Engineering Co. of Van Nuys, Calif.

February 15 — Dominion Helicopters Ltd. and Pegasus Airlifts, Canadian operators, establish joint air taxi service using four JetRangers and four 47J-2s at the Canadian International Exposition of 1967 (Expo '67).

March 10 — The Brazilian Air Force purchases its first UH-1Ds acquiring 6 aircraft to supplement 47G and 47J fleet.

March 14 — First export delivery of production model 206A made to Helicopter Sales (Aust) Pty. Ltd., Bell dealer in Australia.

March 14 — Los Angeles County Fire Department becomes first municipality to purchase 204B.

March 16 — Army officially accepts AH-1G name of "Cobra."

June 15 — First delivery of a production AH-1G is made to Army.

June 22 — Army contract is awarded for 141 TH-13T instrument trainers.

August 1 — German Army accepts first UH-1D assembled in Germany under coproduction contract between Bell and Dornier, GmbH for 380 helicopters.

August 14 — The UH-ID is selected as the first helicopter to be used in the all-around ground support operations of the Canadian Forces (Army, Navy, Air Force.) Ten aircraft are ordered.

October 4 — Bell announces a new 15-place commercial model, the 205A, to be available in 1968. It is the largest model ever manufactured by Bell.

October 7 — Army announces it has deployed the Cobra in Vietnam. First combat kill is credited to Maj. Gen. George P. Seneff, commander of First Aviation Brigade, who destroyed a sampan with four Viet Cong aboard.

YEAR 1968

January 31 — U.S. Navy selects JetRanger as its light turbine trainer, orders 40 for delivery by end of 1968.

February 8 — Bell announces it will open Overhaul & Modification Center at Amarillo, Texas, in buildings being phased out by U.S. Air Force. William Humphrey named general manager of facility, which will repair and refurbish battle-damaged Army helicopters.

March 6 — Brazilian Air Force orders seven JetRangers and six more UH-1Ds to update and expand its helicopter forces.

March 8 — JetRanger named winner of the U.S. Army's re-opened light observation helicopter (LOH) competition. Bell awarded $123,000,000 contract for 2,200 aircraft, with deliveries scheduled between 1969 and 1972.

April 24 — Canadian Government approves development of a twinengine UH-1 powered by United Aircraft of Canada Pratt & Whitney PT6T-3 turbine. The contract is expected to lead to Canada's equipping its armed forces with the new aircraft.

May 14 — Bell delivers its 10,000th helicopter, a JetRanger, to Petroleum Helicopters, Inc., world's largest operator.

May 16 — Navy picks Huey as its advanced rotary-wing trainer, orders 45 TH-ILs, plus eight UH-1L utility aircraft.

May 29 — U.S. Marines order 49 Cobras, becoming second branch of armed forces to buy high-speed gunship.

August 5 — Army awards Bell contract for 900 UH-1Hs, second largest order ever received for Hueys.

September 17 — New York City Police Department, pioneer in use of helicopters by law enforcement agencies, marks 20th anniversary of purchase of first Bell. NYCPD has all-Bell fleet.

October 8 — Bell announces that its Model 212, nation's first twin-engine, medium-size commercial helicopter, will be ready for delivery early in 1970.

December 11 — Atlantic Aviation Corporation, headquartered at Wilmington, Del., named to the first Bell Helicopter dealership in U.S., serving the populous eastern seaboard area.

YEAR 1969

April 15 — Bell compound research helicopter attains speed of 316 mph in level flight-- an unofficial record which still stands today.

April 17 — U. S. Air Force awards Bell contract to define design characteristics of folding proprotor aircraft.

May 1 — Bell announces that its Twin Two-Twelve flight testing is well underway. Certification expected in 1970 to touch off full-scale production.

May 23 — U. S. Army accepts first OH-58A light observation helicopter from Bell. Aircraft is designated as Kiowa.

August 19 — Republic of China and Bell Helicopter sign license agreement for co-production of Model 205 helicopter.

August 28 — Navy and Marines join Air Force in ordering the new twin-engine Huey helicopter, designated UH-IN. Order for 62 includes 40 Navy, 22 for Marines. Air Force previously had ordered 79.

September 19 — Canadian government orders 50 twin-engine Bell helicopters, designated CUH-IN, for its armed forces.

October 10 — U.S. Marines' AH-IJ SeaCobra, a twin-engine version of the Cobra, unveiled by Bell before a gathering of armed forces representatives. Marines have ordered 49.

November 3 — U.S. Navy accepts first UH-1L utility helicopter from Bell for deployment to Pacific Fleet.

December 8 — Army announces first deployment of OH-58A Kiowa helicopter to battle units in Vietnam has taken place.

YEAR 1970

January 30 — U.S. Army awards contract for 170 additional Cobras with $5 million initial funding.

March 20 — Army orders 289 UH-1Hs with $20 million initial funding.

April 30 — Canadian Government selects OH-58A as LOH for Canadian Forces, orders 74.

July 24 — Bell opens factory-operated sales and service center in Van Nuys, California.

September 30 — PHI reaches millionth flight hour.

October 2 — Air Force formally accepts first UH-IN Twin Huey at Eglin AFB.

October 30 — Bell's 212 Twin gets FAA type certificate.

November 24 — Bell acquires its Australian dealership and will operate it as separate corporation.

December 22 — First 212 Twin logbook is presented to Mack Trucks Inc., during delivery ceremony.

YEAR 1971

January 8 — U.S. Army contracts for 300 UH-1H helicopters, funded at $37.5 million.

February 24 — Bell Helicopter and Government of Australia announce co-production program for 191military and civil helicopters during next eight years.

April 15 — U.S. Marine Corps takes delivery on first UH-1N Twin Huey of quantity order.

April 22 — Bell JetRanger-II receives FAA Type Certification. Powered by Allison C-20 engine.

April 30 — Canadian Armed Forces accepts first of 50 twin-engine Bell CUH-IN helicopters.

May 21 — Fort Worth mayor proclaims Bell Week in honor of Bell's 20th year in Texas.

May 25 — First production model of Bell's JetRanger-II delivered to Okanagon Helicopters Ltd. of Canada.

July 1 — Bell 212-Twin receives FAA Category A Certification.

September 23 — 1963 experimental Sioux Scout helicopter presented to U.S. Army Aviation Museum.

September 23 — KingCobra premieres for U.S. Military. KingCobra's role: performing anti-armor missions in adverse weather, terrain and threat environments.

December 13 — E. J. Ducayet named chairman and James F. Atkins elevated to president of Bell.

December 16 — First of 74 COH-58A light observation helicopters delivered to Canadian Armed Forces.

YEAR 1972

January — Prototype #2 KingCobra enters total systems integration phase of its development program.

February — Commercial and International Marketing break all-time records with firm orders for 105 helicopters valued at $23,000,000 during month.

March 6 — Bell receives $24,732,793 contract for U.S.Army as prime systems integrator of the Improved Cobra Armament Program (ICAP). Contract called for the integration of TOW system into eight Bell/Army AH-1G Huey Cobras.

April 24 — U.S. Army Mobility R & D Lab, Ft. Eustis, awards Bell $600,000 contract for investigation of new flexbeam (rigid) rotor system.

May 19 — Bell Chairman E. J. Ducayet receives the Alexander Klemin award from the American Helicopter Society for "notable achievement in the advancement of rotary wing aeronautics".

July 28 — Bell and Agusta (Costruzioni Aeronautiche Giovanni Agusta) mark 20 years of manufacturing under licensing agreements.

August 2 — Twenty-four UH-1Hs added to co-production contract between Bell and Republic of China.

August 21 — U.S. Air Force takes delivery of first two of 30 Bell HH-1H local base rescue helicopters.

October 24 — Bell selected winner of 1972 James S. Cogswell award for outstanding security performance on classified defense contracts.

November 11 — First Cobra (N209J prototype) is donated to George S. Patton Museum at Fort Knox during dedication of museum.

November 16 — Petroleum Helicopters Inc. orders 33 new Bell helicopters valued at $5 million--largest single commercial order in history.

November 30 — Bell announces breakthrough in elimination of helicopter vibration by suspending fuselage from "nodalized" beam.

December 6 — Four Bell UH-1's assigned to launch site recovery force team during last prgrammed Apollo lunar mission--the first night launch from Kennedy Space Center.

December 22 — Congressman Wright announces sale of 287 new Bell 214A's and 202 Model AH-1J's to Iran through the U.S. Government. Total value of purchase exceeds $500 million.

YEAR 1973

January 12 U.S. Army orders 74 additional Bell OH-58A helicopters. Contract valued at $6.5 million.

February Bell Helicopter International Inc. formed as separate division of Textron to conduct business in Iran. Maj. Gen. Delk M. Oden, U.S. Army, ret., named president.

February 28 U.S. Marines order 20 additional AH-1J SeaCobras. Contract valued at $5 million.

March 15 U.S. Army orders 180 UH-1H helicopters. Contract set at $27.4 million.

March 20 U.S. Army orders 16 additional UH-1H helicopters under March 15 option. Contract valued at $2.6M.

March 1,000th JetRanger delivered.

April 2 U.S. Navy orders 24 additional UH-1N helicopters. Nine-and-one-half million dollar contract.

April 13 Bell awarded NASA/U.S. Army contract to build and test two tilt-rotor research aircraft. Estimated cost of the four-year program to be $28 million.

April 18 Bell announces $6 million capital investment program. Includes $1.7 million for test and evaluation lab.

May Bell President James F. Atkins named president of American Helicopter Society. Jan Dress, Bell chief of flight technology, awarded AHS' Grover Bell Award for developing nodalized support system.

June 22 U.S. Army awards Bell $44.7 million contract to initiate development of Advanced Attack Helicopter system. Total development funds could reach $120 million. Three-year program to design and fabricate two flying prototypes and one ground test vehicle. Army will select production contractor for estimated $500 million run in three to five years.

June All-time, single month record of 70 commercial deliveries established during June.

September Development of new Model seven-place, light-turbine 206L Long Ranger announced. Initial deliveries targeted for 1975.

YEAR 1974

January 17 Construction of a $2 million Paint Facility is approved for Bell's Hurst Plant.

January 31 Bell receives a $59.2 million U.S. Army contract to modify 101 of the Army's existing AH-1G Huey Cobras into AH-IQ TOW/Cobras.

February 14 Bell dedicates new $1.7 million Engineering Test and Evaluation Center.

March 1 A Bell Helicopter Supply Center is established at Schiphol East Airport, Amsterdam, The Netherlands.

March 22 ranian Model 214A makes initial flight.

April 19 Bell Model 222--the first U.S. built commercial light twin helicopter, receives a total development go-ahead.

April 23 A ceremony at the Hurst Plant commemorates the delivery of the 20,000th Bell helicopter.

April 30 Bell's integrated YAH-63 Advanced Attack Helicopter mockup is unveiled for inspection by the U.S. Army at the Fort Worth facility.

June 20 The first AH-1J Sea Cobra arrives in Iran.

September Bell's new 214B "Big Lifter" makes its performance debut symposium for U.S. and Canadian representatives from logging, electrical utility & petroleum industries.

September 11 Bell's new model 206L LongRanger makes its initial flight.

October 1 U.S. Army awards Bell modifications to two existing contracts, calling for 54 additional UH-1H utility helicopters. Value of the awards is nearly $12 million.

December 16 An additional 189 Bell Cobra helicopters will be modified to AH-1Q TOW/Cobra configuration for the U.S. Army under a $54 million contract.

December 20 Bell announces the establishment of a Marketing Services & Supply Center in Ottawa.

YEAR 1975

January 31 Bell's YAH-63 Advanced Attack Helicopter Ground Test Vehicle is rolled out at a brief ceremony at the Fort Worth facility.

February 8 Plans for a 200,000 square foot addition to the company's transmission and gear facility (Plant 5) in Grand Prairie are announced.

April 29 An Iranian Model 214A helicopter sets five world records in altitude and time-to-climb categories.

June 10 Delivery of the first of 290 production Model AH-1Q TOW/Cobra helicopters is made to the U.S. Army at Bell.

June Development of Bell's Model 222, the first U.S. built light twin turbine commercial helicopter, moves from design phase to manufacturing of prototypes.

September 22 Bell's Model 206L LongRanger, the new seven-place light-turbine helicopter, receives FAA certification.

October 1 Bell's YAH-63 Advanced Attack Helicopter prototype makes its first flight.

October 8 A major technical breakthrough is achieved by Bell when the main transmission of a Model 214A helicopter runs for one and a half hours without oil.

October Bell's first XV-15 tilt-rotor research aircraft goes into final assembly.

October 29 Bell and Collins Radio Group announce the development of an IFR system for the JetRanger and the LongRanger.

November 21 The Government of Iran names Bell as its partner in a joint venture that will be organized to establish a modern helicopter industry in Iran. The program includes co-production of 400 Model 214 transport aircraft.

December 18 The U.S. Army awards Bell a $37 million production contract for 44 units of the AH-1S, an improved version of the AH-1G Cobra.

YEAR 1976

January Bell Operations Corporation is formed to carry out Bell's long term co-production and joint venture agreement with the Government of Iran.

January Company adopts new name, Bell Helicopter Textron.

January 27 Bell's new Model 214B BigLifter receives FAA certification.

May 21 Ceremonies at the main plant mark the company's 25th Anniversary in Texas.

June The AH-1T, an improved version of the U.S. Marines AH-IJ SeaCobra, makes its initial flight.

June Delivery of the first of 198 AH-IS, modifications of existing Army aircraft, is made to the U.S. Army at Bell's Amarillo facility.

July The 2,000th Fort Worth-built JetRanger is delivered to McDonald's Corporation.

August 13 Bell's 222, America's first light twin turbine commercial helicopter, makes its initial flight.

October The U.S. Army awards Bell a production contract for 22 additional units of the AH-1S, an advanced version of the Cobra, increasing the total on order to 66.

October 22 First NASA/Army tilt-rotor XV-15 is rolled out at the Arlington Flight Research Center.

October 27 Dedication ceremonies of Bell's Machining Center are held at Grand Prairie.

November 11 Bell is awarded a contract for 82 additional AH-1S improved Cobra helicopters.

December 17 The first of 38 Model 214C advanced utility helicopters.

December 31 90 commercial helicopters delivered during December sets one-month delivery record.

YEAR 1977

February 6 Bell's Model 222, America's first commercial mid-size turbine helicopter, makes its initial public flight at the Helicopter Association of America's annual meeting.

February Bell announces the development of a JetRanger-III, a more powerful version of the world's most popular helicopter.

March 16 The U.S. Army formally accepts the initial production model of the AH-1S, its most modern anti-armor helicopter.

May 3 Bell's XV-15 tilt-rotor research aircraft makes its first hover flight at the company's Arlington Flight Research Center.

July JetRanger-III began deliveries to customers all over the world.

July 28 U.S. Marines order 22 additional twin-engine AH-1T improved SeaCobras.

August Petroleum Helicopters, Inc., records 1,100,000 flight hours on its Bell Model 47's--a mark unequalled in commercial rotary wing operation.

September Bell announces the development of the 214ST, a 19-place twin-engine, stretched version of the Model 214 utility helicopter.

September 27 Plans for production of a new model, the LongRanger-II, are announced at the annual National Business Aircraft Association convention.

October 15. U.S. Marines formally accept the first production model of Bell's AH-IT twin-engine armed helicopter.

December 21 U.S. Army exercises option to purchase 83 additional units of Bell's AH-1S improved Cobras.

YEAR 1978

January 19 Construction begins on the two-story, 135,000 square foot Bell Technical Center at the Main (Hurst) Plant.

January 30 A single pilot IFR system designed for the new seven-place LongRanger-II is announced. The system was developed by Bell and Collins Avionics.

March 23 Bell's XV-15 tilt-rotor research Aircraft No. 1 is shipped to NASA-Ames Research Center, Moffet Field, California for extensive wind tunnel tests.

April 10 U.S. Marines order additional AH-1T improved SeaCobra helicopters.

May 19 Bell's LongRanger-II receives FAA type certification. First customer deliveries take place in June.

July 24 FAA certifies the first American-made fiberglass helicopter main rotor blade. The all- composite blade was developed by Bell for the Model 214 helicopter.

August Bell's XV-15 Aircraft No. 2 commences ground run tests at the company's Arlington Flight Research Center.

September President James F. Atkins announces development of the Model 412, an advanced technology four-bladed variant of the 15-place, twin turbine Bell 212.

November 1 The U.S. Army orders 66 more production units of the AH-1S Cobra.

November 27 Bell selects FlightSafety International to provide crew training for operators of the new Model 222 mid-size, twin-turbine helicopter. In 1979, FlightSafety will build a 13,000 square foot learning center adjacent to Bell's Training & Delivery Center in Fort Worth.

December 20 The LongRanger-II receives FAA certification for single pilot IFR.

YEAR 1979

February 20 Bell receives order for eight of its commercial Model 212s from the People's Republic of China. The sale is the first by a U. S. helicopter manufacturer to the PRC.

April The first Model 214B helicopter equipped with fiberglass main rotor blades is delivered to Paramount Helicopters Inc., Bend, Oregon.

April 23 XV-15 Aircraft No. 2 tilt rotor research aircraft makes first flight in the helicopter mode.

July 21 Bell's 19-place Model 214ST Super Transport makes initial flight.

July 24 The first in-flight conversion from helicopter to airplane mode is made by the XV-15 tilt rotor research aircraft (Aircraft No. 2).

August 3 Model 412 makes first flight. It's destined to become Bell's first four-bladed production helicopter.

August 16 Bell's Model 222, in pre-production configuration, receives FAA type certification.

November Construction begins on a 270,000 square foot $10 million manufacturing building at Bell's main Hurst complex.

November 14-16 During Bell sponsored program called ImaginEighties, orders are received for more than 200 commercial aircraft valued at $200 million. Included are $150 million in customer commitments for the 214ST.

December 20 Production Model 222 receives FAA approval for Visual Flight Rules Operation.

December 21 Bell closes year with record setting delivery of 585 commercial helicopters to domestic and foreign customers.

YEAR 1980

February 1 First production Model 222 is delivered to Petroleum Helicopters. Schiavone Construction, New Jersey, receives first 222 in executive configuration.

February 7 L. Knight & Co. Ltd., a Canadian manufacturing firm, is the first customer to take delivery of a JetRanger-III equipped with the new Collins VFR flight control system.

February 10 Ron Erhart and Dorman Cannon, XV-15 project pilots, receive the Fredrick L. Feinberg Award from the American Helicopter Society. The honor is presented for the most outstanding piloting achievement during the preceding year.

May 15 Bell's Model 222 twin-turbine helicopter receives FAA approval for single-pilot IFR operation.

June 17 The XV-15 tilt rotor research aircraft exceeds an unofficial world's speed record for rotorcraft by achieving a true airspeed of 301 knots (346 mph) The flight was made at the company's Flight Research Center in Arlington, Texas.

August 6 Bell awards contracts to FlightSafety International to provide crew training for operators of the new Model 412 and 214ST SuperTransport helicopters.

August 13 Bell completes contractor portion of XV-15 flight tests. Aircraft No. 2 is shipped to NASA's Dryden Research Center for additional envelope expansion and proof concept flight tests.

September 8 A seven-place LongRanger-II helicopter completes a 5,100 mile flight from Dallas, Texas to Bern, Switzerland. The historic flight by German pilots Karl

Wagner and Warner Roschlau, is believed to be the first trans-Atlantic crossing by a light helicopter.

October — Bell announces development of the TexasRanger, a multi-mission 206L, capable of rapid in-the-field conversion to anti-tank configuration.

October 1 — XV-15 Project Pilots Ronald Erhart and Dorman Cannon are named test pilots of the year by the Society of Experimental Test Pilots.

December 31 — Bell delivers record 783 commercial helicopters in 1980, a 30 per cent increase over the previous year.

YEAR 1981

January 18 — Delivery of the 25,000th Bell helicopter--a Model 222 is made to Omniflight Helicopters.

January 18 — ERA Helicopters accepts the first Model 412 at the Helicopter Association International convention.

February 23 — Bell forms a new Customer Support and Service Division.

March 31 — Bell is selected as a contractor for the U.S. Army's Advanced Composite Airframe Program (ACAP).

April 10 — The first AH-1S Modernized Cobra/TOW helicopter produced for the Army National Guard is delivered.

May 20 — Bell is named a co-recipient of the American Helicopter Society Grover P. Bell Award for outstanding tilt-rotor technology in developing the XV-15.

June 4 — The XV-15 makes its first international flight demonstrations at the Paris Air Show.

August 20 — Bell pilots John Williams and Morton Meng flying a LongRanger-II, help the U.S. win the World Helicopter Championship in Poland.

September 18 — Bell receives a contract for $56 million to convert 70 Model AH-1G's to AH-1S Modernized Cobras.

September 21 — U.S. Army names Bell winner of its Army Helicopter Improvement Program (AHIP) competition.

September 28 — Maj. Gen. Story Stevens becomes the first non-test pilot to fly the XV-15. Stevens is Commanding General of the U.S. Army Aviation Research & Development Command.

October 27 — XV-15 completes its longest cross-country flight (1,600 miles) from NASA's Ames Research Center, Moffett Field, California to the Arlington Municipal Airport.

October 30 — Sen. Barry Goldwater, R-Ariz. pilots the XV-15 at Bell's Flight Research Center in Arlington.

December — The first Model 412 delivered to the Middle East is accepted by the State of Bahrain's Public Security Flying Wing.

December — Secretary of Defense Weinberger's office announces decision to develop a multi-service aircraft. The following year, a Joint Services Operartional Requirement (JSOR) identified ten service-specific missions for the proposed joint services aircraft. Working in tandem with the JSOR study, a joint services technical evaluation group studies VTOL alternatives and determines that tiltrotor develompent offers the best military and technical choice for a self-deployable aircraft that could fulfill missions for every branch of the armed forces. This finding leads to the establishment of the joint services tiltrotor, of JVX program. The JVX program marks the first time that an aircraft has been assigned a multi-mission role to serve all four services.

YEAR 1982

January 4 — Bell is awarded a $35 million contract by the Department of the Navy for 55 Model TH-57 Advanced Instrument Trainers.

February 14 — Bell President James F. Atkins announces 1982 availability of the Model 222B, an improved version of the series.

February 19 — The Model 214ST SuperTransport receives FAA Type Certification for VFR and IFR operations.

May 28 — Bell and Mitsui & Co. sign a contract to co-produce AH-1S Modernized Cobras for the Ground Self Defense Forces of the Japanese Defense Agency.

June 7 — Bell and Boeing Vertol Co., announce teaming agreement to participate in the Joint Services Vertical Lift Aircraft Program (JVX) competition.

July 29 — The improved 222B becomes the first transport category helicopter to be certified by FAA for single pilot IFR without stability augmentation.

August — Australian pilot Dick Smith departs from Bell on Aug. 5 in a JetRanger-III, the first leg of an attempt to make the first helicopter solo flight around the world. On Aug. 19 he lands in U.K. to mark the world's first solo helicopter crossing of the Atlantic.

August 5 — The XV-15 Tilt Rotor Research Aircraft successfully completes three days of seaboard trials on the U.S.S. Tripoli, assault carrier. Earlier, it had undergone Special Electronics Mission Aircraft (SEMA) evaluation at Fort Huachuca, AZ.

September 24 — Bell receives $113 million contracts for helicopter sales to Jordan, Pakistan and Turkey.

September 30 — Ross Perot Jr. and Jay Coburn become the first pilots to make an around-the-world helicopter flight. The pair departed from Dallas in a LongRanger-II, dubbed the "Spirit of Texas" on September 1.

October — The Army exercises option for Bell to manufacture and test three composite airframes in the second phase of its Advanced Composite Airframe Program (ACAP). Contract value is $21 million.

November — The Nurtanio Indonesian Aircraft Industry and sign a license agreement to co-produce at least 100 Model 412 helicopters.

November 16 — U.S. Navy accepts first Model TH-57 Advanced Instrument Trainer during formal ceremonies at Bell.

YEAR 1983

February — Development of the Model 400 TwinRanger is announced at HAI's annual meeting (Feb.13-16).

March — Flight testing begins in a modified LongRanger to evaluate Model 406 dynamics that will be used in the aircraft that Bell will manufacture for the U.S. Army's Helicopter mprovement Program (AHIP). The components are also being developed for the new Model 400 Twin-Ranger.

April — The Naval Air Systems Command awards a contract to Bell and Boeing Vertol Company for the preliminary design phase of the Joint Services Advanced Vertical Lift Aircraft (JVX) Program.

May — The 222UT receives FAA Type Certification and is approved for single-pilot IFR operation without additional stabilization.

May 21 — Harvey Gaylord, Bell Helicopter's first president, dies after a lengthy illness.

July 20 — Textron Inc. appoints James F. Atkins as BHT chairman. Leonard M. (Jack) Horner succeeds Atkins as president of Bell Helicopter Textron.

July 22 — Australian adventurer Dick Smith becomes the first pilot to complete a solo flight around-theworld by helicopter. When his JetRanger-II touched down here at Bell, he had flown 35,258 miles.

October 7 — The Canadian Federal Government selects Bell to establish a helicopter industry in Canada. First production aircraft of a new helicopter family will be the Model 400 TwinRanger.

October — An AHIP prototype makes its first contractual flight and completes initial tests with a full-up Mast Mounted Sight (MMS).

October 26 — Bell Helicopter Asia (Pte.) Ltd. is established, with headquarters in Singapore, to coordinate Southeast Asian operations.

November 16 — The AH-IT+ SuperCobra makes its first flight at Bell's Flight Research Center in Arlington.

December — Jim P. Schwalbe is named president of Bell's new division of Textron Canada Ltd.

YEAR 1984

January — A definitive contract is executed between Bell Canada and the Government of Canada toestablish a helicopter industry in Canada.

February — William A. Anders is named executive vice-president-Aerospace at Textron Inc.

March — Bell receives a $58.5 million contract for long lead items and related ground support equipment for 16 aircraft in the Army Helicopter Improvement Program (AHIP).

April 9 — Floyd W. Carlson, Bell Helicopter pioneer whose aviation career spanned more than 40 years, dies after a lengthy illness.

May 3 — Bell receives initial funding for 22 U.S. Marine AH-1T-- SuperCobras. Total amount of the contract is $105 million.

May 21 — Development of the Model 406 Combat Scout, a new four-bladed light combat helicopter with a quick change weapons system, is announced.

June — The Naval Air Systems Command awards the Bell-Boeing team a $23.4 million contract addition for the second stage of the JVX program's preliminary design effort.

July 4 — A prototype model 400 successfully completes the Canadian Government's flight requirements.

July 7 — The first of five OH-58D (AHIP) advanced scout helicopters is delivered to the U.S. Army.

August — Increases of 300 lbs. in gross weight and 50 shp in takeoff horsepower increase the capabilities of the Model 412.

September — Bell signs a Memorandum of Understanding with Dornier GmbH of Germany to explore several joint advanced technology projects, including improvement proposals on UH-I helicopters.

October 5 — The XV-15 tilt rotor aircraft completes a four-week, 3,500 mile demonstration and evaluation tour of the Eastern United States.

November — Paul Powers, director of Safety and Certification, is recipient of the Aviation Week and Space Technology Flight Safety Service Award for 1984.

November — Donald L. Bloom, senior experimental test pilot, receives the Iven C. Kincheloe award as "Test Pilot of the Year" from the Society of Experimental Test Pilots.

YEAR 1985

January — The OH-58D, being developed for the U.S. Army Helicopter Improvement Program (AHIP) exceeds or meets all performance and specification requirements during the development tests.

January — Bell introduces the Model 412SP (Special Performance) helicopter, an improved version of the four-bladed 412, at the HAI Convention in New Orleans.

February — A research aircraft (a four-bladed Bell Cobra) performs a series of tactical maneuvers without hand control manipulation by the pilot. The tests are applicable to the Army's Advanced Technology Integration (ARTI) program.

April — Bell receives $49.1 million in additional funding for 22 Model AH-1T+ (redesignated AH-IW) SuperCobras.

June — Dornier GmbH and Bell announce plans to develop an advanced rotor, a higher thrust version of the Model 680 bearingless rotor.

June — The Government of Brazil orders 16 JetRanger-III aircraft to upgrade navy pilot training.

June — JVX is now known as the V-22 program. Bell/Boeing begins full-scale development without contract and with its own funds.

July — The People's Republic of China orders six JetRangers-IIIs for pilot training by the Civil Aviation Administration of China.

August 30 — The Model D292, being developed for the Army's Advanced Composite Airframe Program (ACAP) by Bell, makes its initial hover flight.

September — The Department of the Navy orders 36 additional Bell Model TH-57B primary trainers. This will raise the Navy's T-57 inventory to 140.

October — Bell receives a definitized contract in the amount of $223 million for additional production and support of the Army Helicopter Improvement Program (AHIP).

November — The Honduras Air Force orders five Model 412SP helicopters with an option to acquire five additional aircraft.

YEAR 1986

January — The Republic of Honduras orders five additional 412SP helicopters. An initial order was received in 1985 for five aircraft.

March 25 — The U.S. Army Aviation Center, Fort Rucker, Ala., takes delivery of the first production OH-58D Advanced Scout.

March 27 — The Marines take delivery of the first production AH-1W SuperCobra during ceremonies here.

April 9 — Bell and McDonnell Douglas Helicopter Co. annouce an agreement in principle to form a team to develop the U.S. Army's LHX (Light Helicopter Experimental) aircraft.

May 2 — Bell-Boeing V-22 tilt rotor team wins a $1.714 billion fixed-price incentive award from the Navy for a seven-year, full-scale development program.

June — Bell introduces armed version of the Model 412SP helicopter.

June — Plans are announced for an 80,000-square-foot expansion to the Flight Research Center for ground and air testing of the V-22 Osprey.

June — New V-22 contract is awarded by NAVAIR following a year of program reassessment and negotiations. Six prototype aircraft are to be built under the full-scale development contract.

July — A new agreement is signed with the government of Canada to restructure its aircraft production plans at Bell's Mirabel, Quebec plant. Plans call for assembly of the JetRanger and LongRanger.

July — Bell, Samsung Industries Co. Ltd. and the newly founded Korea Bell Helicopter Co. in Seoul announce a memorandum of understanding to coproduce helicopters in the Republic of Korea.

September Bell completes transfer of JetRanger production line to the Canadian facility.
October Company receives contract awards from the U.S Army in the amount of $89.2 million for spare parts to support the Model UH-1, AH-1 and OH-58.
December 18 Bell Helicopter Canada makes the first delivery of a JetRanger-III assembled at the Mirabel facility. Accepting the aircraft is Turbo West of Broomfield, Colo.
December 18 The Department of Defense approves the full-scale development program for the V-22 Osprey.

YEAR 1987
February Bell, Sperry Commercial Flight Systems and Helidyne Systems announce the formation of a team to design and certify a Search and Rescue package for the Model 214ST.
April 1 The first wing structure is completed on the V-22 Osprey. The structure will be used on the ground test article.
April 3 The Norwegian Air force accepts its first Model 412SP. The program calls for 18 aircraft to be co-assembled by Helikopter Services in Norway.
April A second-generation 680 rotor, being flight tested on a Model 222, meets or exceeds design goals set by the LHX team of Bell and McDonnell Douglas Helicopter Company.
April 29 Bell and Boeing announce development of the world's first tilt-rotor unmanned air vehicle (UAV), known as the Pointer.
June Workers begin loading components into assembly fixture for construction on the wing for the V-22 Osprey that will make the first flight in 1988.
June 11 Twelve OH-58Ds were loaded aboard a giant Air Force C-5A at Bell's Amarillo facility. The shipment represented the first delivery of Advanced Scouts to units in U.S. Army Europe.
July 17 Quick action by two UH-IH Hueys operated by the 50th Medical Company (Air Ambulance Unit) at Fort Sam Houston, Texas, saves 33 lives during the Guadalupe River Flood.
August 27 A full scale ACAP airframe crash test demonstrates that the all-composite airframe is capable of meeting stringent military crash survivability requirements.
August 30 Washington, D.C. area and Chicago that shows the feasibility of using tilt rotor applications in civil aviation.
September E.H. Industries of Canada is selected as the winner of a competition to replace the Navy's older CH-124 Sea King with the new EH101 helicopter. BHT Canada will responsible for the assembly and flight testing of the aircraft.
December Bell Helicopter Services, a subsidiary of Textron Inc., purchases the holdings of Inchcape Aviation Corp., to assume total ownership of Bell Helicopter Asia (Pte) Ltd.

YEAR 1988
January 21 Boeing V-22 fuselage for Aircraft No. 1 arrives at Bell's Flight Research Center to be mated with Bell's first flyable wing.
January The Bell Boeing Pointer, the world's first tiltrotor unmanned vehicle (UAV) completes drive system tests at the Fort Worth facility.
February Commercial production of the JetRanger reaches 4,000 mark.
March Bell reveals that eleven armed OH-58Ds were modified to light attack helicopters in response to a request by the U. S. Army.
April 26 The 100th OH-58D (AHIP) produced by Bell is delivered to the U. S. Army at the company's facility in Amarillo, Texas.
May 23 The Bell Boeing V-22 Osprey is unveiled at rollout ceremonies at the Flight Research Center.
August Bell receives a $146 million contract in funding for 30 Model AH-1IW SuperCobras for the U. S. Marines.
August Company is awarded a $22 million contract covering long lead time items for 15 Model 406CS (Combat Scout) for Saudi Arabia.
August 15 Initial ground run tests are completed on V-22 aircraft number 1.
September 1 Bell delivers 100th helicopter built in Canadian facility during ceremonies at the Mirabel, Quebec plant.
October 27 First powered operation of the Bell Boeing V-22 Ground Test Article equipped with proprotors begins.
November 21 The Bell Boeing Pointer makes its first flight at Bell's Globe Plant in Saginaw, Texas.
December 28 The V-22 enters critical ground tests in preparation for the first flight.

YEAR 1989
January 24 Bell flies its Model 680 all composite, fourbladed bearingless rotor system for the first time on an AH-1W SuperCobra.
February The 1988 Army Aviation Material Readiness Award is presented to Bell for efforts by employees to arm the OH-58D for operations in the Persian Gulf.
March 19 The Bell-Boeing V-22 Osprey makes its first flight in the helicopter mode at the Flight Research Center.
April 21 Defense Secretary Dick Cheney submits FY 1990 defense budget that includes termination of the V-22.
May Bell and McDonnell Douglas begin a series of national tours of Army installations to demonstrate LHX (Light Helicopter Experimental SuperTeam technology).
June During the Paris Air Show, customers place orders for 24 aircraft, including 19 LongRanger-IIIs and four JetRanger-IIIs.
August 10 The second V-22 Osprey makes its first successful flight in the helicopter mode.
August Air Logistics Inc., one of the largest charter operators in the world, orders 3 LongRangers and a Model 412SP for offshore support in the Gulf of Mexico.
August The U.S. Marine Corp's AH-1W SuperCobra fleet of 46 helicopters reaches 25,000 flight hours. The first aircraft was delivered in March 1986.
September Using OH-58Cs, the U.S. Army Precision Helicopter Team wins the World Helicopter Championship in Chantilly, France.
September 14 The V-22 Osprey achieves its most significant milestone--accomplishing full conversion from helicopter mode to airplane while in flight.
October Bell announces development of the Model 230, an updated version of the popular Model 222.
October The V-22 flies at a speed of 250 knots equivalent airspeed.
Oct/Dec Success of V-22 flight tests leads Congress to approve $255 million in R&D funding for the program.
November 30 The U.S. Defense Investigation Services names Bell as a recipient of the 1989 Cogswell Award for Security excellence.
December 21 A third Osprey makes its successful flight at the Boeing Flight Test Center in the Wilmington Delaware Municipal Airport.

YEAR 1990
January James F. Hardymon appointed as Textron's president and chief operating officer as well as elected a director of the company.
February 2 Colonel Hommod Al-Reshoodi, commander of Saudi Arabian Land Forces Army Aviation visited Bell Helicopter Textron's Flight Research Center in Arlington, Texas for the first official flight of the 406 Combat Scout.
February Bell Canada delivers 250th aircraft, a model 206B-III Jet Ranger, purchased by Chevron USA Inc.
March 15 Model XV-15 sets five (5) world altitude records during engineering performance flight tests conducted at the Flight Research Center.
April 25 The XV-15 tiltrotor demostrator performs at the East front of the Capitol Building.
May 9 Fourth Osprey takes its maiden flight from Bell Helicopter Textron's Flight Research Facility.
August 21 Bell breaks ground for multi-million dollar expansion product which will add 3200 sq. feet to the Aviation and Simulation Center.
September 5 Announcement made at the Farnborough Air Show that the intermediate twin-engine Model 230 will be built at the company's commercial helicopter facility near Montreal, Quebec, Canada.
October V-22 aircraft No. 1 flew for the 100th time, the first V-22 to do so.
Oct/Dec Congress adds $611 million in V-22 funding to FY 1991 DoD budget. Aircraft #1 makes its 100th flight during October. Two V-22 aircraft undergo successful shipboard compatibility tests in December.
November 6 Osprey given both research and development and long-lead procurement funds in the House and Senate Conference authorization bills. President Bush signed on November 6.
December First fully integrated OH-58D Armed Kiowa Warrior prototype made its first flight at Bell's Flight Test Research Center in Arlington, Tx. This OH-58D contains a highly sophisticated integrated computerized armament system.
December 12 Two V-22's, designated as aircraft No.'s 3 and 4 successfully complete initial ship-board capability tests aboard the USS Wasp (LHD-1).

YEAR 1991
January V-22 Osprey Completes Phase One Shipboard Compatibility Trials; New OH- 58D First Flight Test.
February Direct Deposit Introduced To BHTI Employees Bell Helicopters Support Desert Storm.
February Sling load evaluations began testing the V-22's sling load capability. Tests began using a 2,000 pound metal weight using the aft hook located on the V-22's underside. Both aft and fore hooks were used in the successful demonstration.
March Bell Announces Ma jor Helicopter Sale; TiltRotor Team Honored by Aviation Week.
April 1 Tiltrotor Team wins Collier Trophy; NASA/FAA study on civil tiltrotor results released; Bell team called to support Desert Storm.
April 15 Program completed on Model 406 Combat Scout.
April V-22 program selected to receive the Collier Trophy "for the greatest achievement in aeronautics or astronautics in America...the value of which has been thoroughly demonstrated by actual use during the proceeding year.
May 1 Bell gets high marks for support of Small Business. New transmission work started at Plant 5.
May 15 Pilots fly in safer skies due to new radar system Bell Employees' Humanity Fund Board facing tough challenges.
June 1 U. S. Park Police takes delivery of Bell Model 412; V-22 Osprey activity gaining momentum.
June 15 Reorganization of senior management announced; Collier trophy awarded to Bell Boeing Team; Strategic Direction for the '90s: Cycle Time Reduction - the key to our future.
July 1 Textron names Webb F. Joiner Bell president; Tiltrotor Team Signed Contract; The Grover E. Bell Award recognizes the 4BW engineering team effort for rotor dynamics.
July 15 Research and Engineering restructures personnel; New VP named for Washington office; Governor supports the tiltrotor.
August 1 Bell products praised for Desert Storm performance; Bell announces New Commercial Marketing Chief.
August 15 New co-production contract signed; Air Force Squadron marks 150,100 safe flight hours.
September 1 100th AH-IW SuperCobra Delivered; Bell Model 230 makes first flight.
September 15 Bell submits bid on unmanned tiltrotor program; PHI honored for flight hour feat; Helicopter safety in South America.
October 1 Osprey Flies...Again! Bell Helicopter Canada unveils Model 230; Employees witness Soviet coup attempt.
October 15 Procedure changes made to support FOD prevention; Humanity Fund approaches goal.
November 1 Osprey #1 Returns Home; New appointments made within Bell; The Birth of An Industry, The 50th Anniversary of the Bell Helicopter; Serving the Pacific Rim with Bell Helicopter Asia
November 15 House science group visits Osprey; Textron earnings up, dividend declared.
November Congress approves $790 million in Navy R&D funding to fund full-scale development of the V-22. $15 million also included in DoD budget of Air Force SOF variant.
December 1 Arthur Young visits Bell! New Textron board member elected.
December 15 Bell-Boeing and FAA working on civil certification of tiltrotor aircraft.

YEAR 1992
February 23 V-22 No. 4 began extreme climate testing phase of the full-scale development program. The Osprey's four-month trial subjected the aircraft to extremes of both heat and cold as well as humidity, dust, snow and intense sunlight.
March Transport Canada Aviation and the FAA issue simultaneous certification for the Bell 230.
April 7 The Canadian Ministry of National Defence announces the purchase of 100 Bell 412 medium twin helicopters for its Utility Tactical Transport Helicopter program to replace its existing mixed fleet of aircraft.
April 9 Bell unveils its advanced technology OH-58D Kiowa Warrior Technology

Demonstrator at the annual meeting of the Army Aviation Association of America at Atlanta.

May 6 — At a press conference in London, Bell and the British firm GEC-Marconi announce a teaming agreement to offer a modified AH-1W called "Venom" for the British Army's future attack helicopter requirement.

May 8 — Former Bell President Edwin J. "Duke" Ducayet dies.

May 21 — Bell delivers the first of 36 AH-1W SuperCobra attack helicopters destined for the U.S. Marine Corps Reserve.

June 3 — General Accounting Office releases reports finding that DoD action on V-22 constitutes an illegal impoundment and ordering that DoD obligate FY 1992 funds by August 4, 1992, or face possible court action.

June 4 — U.S. Army conducts a ceremony at Fort Rucker to honor Bell UH-1H Iroquois (serial #62-02109) achieving 20,000 flight hours. The aircraft was built in 1962 and was flown in Vietnam for five years before it became a training helicopter at the Army's Aviation School.

June 24 — Bell delivers a 206L-3 LongRanger to the Moscow Police.

July 2 — Secretary Cheney sends letter to Congress outlining new V-22 proposal. DoD would use most of the $1.5 billion ($790 million in FY 1992 funding, plus $755 million expected to be approved by Congress in FY 1993) in V-22 development funding to complete current phases of program. Some money would be used to study technology of possible new helicopter alternative for USMC medium lift mission.

July 20 — Osprey #4 crashes during landing approach to Quantico Marine Base, killing all seven on board. Flights of remaining three V-22 aircraft suspended pending investigation.

August 5 — In hearing devoted solely to issue of V-22 development, acting Navy Secretary Sean O'Keefe testifies before members of House Armed Services and Defense Appropriations panels. O'Keefe reiterates Cheney statements that DoD lawyers had found that V-22 funds could be legally obligated in a way that complied with law as written by Congress. Members express doubts that DoD ever intended to comply with intent of Congress on V-22 and question if DoD plans to ease Marine Corps medium lift requirements to make it possible for helicopter alternative to compete with the V-22. O'Keefe says Cheney compromise offers way to proceed with tiltrotor development and avoid court battle over whether DoD had made and illegal impoundment. He also says that DoD wants to build V-22, but wants to give contractors chance to develop lower-cost tiltrotor variant that can fulfill lessened USMC medium lift requirements only. O'Keefe announces that two RFPs will be issued -- one to Bell Boeing for lower-cost tiltrotor variant and one for concept studies of helicopter alternatives.

August 26 — Bell unveils the Huey II demonstrator aircraft to 60 representatives from 60 nations around the world that operate the UH-1H. The Huey II is a major upgrade program for the UH-1 H, which enables the legendary Huey to operate well into the next century with greater performance than currently found on the aircraft.

September — Preliminary report on Navy investigation of V-22 crash indicates that a chain of events caused the drive train to fail, a correctable mechanical problem. The investigators found no basic flaws in tiltrotor design or concept .

September — Bell Boeing team completes response to Navy RFP, meeting requirement for lower-cost tiltrotor variant.

October 22 — As a result of major efforts by its supporters, the V-22 Osprey program comes to a successful conclusion for the year with the announcement by NAVAIR of a new Engineering and Manufacturing Development letter contract awarded to the Bell Boeing team. The letter contract provides initial funding of $550 million on a contract that will total more than $2 billion. The contract is publicly confirmed by Vice President Dan Quayle during a visit to the Boeing Helicopters plant near Philadelphia on Friday, October 23. Under terms of the contract, Bell Boeing will build four "production representative" V-22 aircraft designed to meet the new requirements of the Marine Corps' medium lift replacement (MLR) aircraft. Two existing V-22s built during the first phase of the development program will also be modified for an early evaluation phase. The contract calls for eventual full qualification of the V-22 aircraft. This latest development effort is scheduled to conclude in 1998 with the completion of operational evaluation. The six aircraft built or modified under the contract will undergo flight testing primarily at the Navy Air Warfare Center at Patuxent River Naval Air Station in Maryland. Requirements changes made by the Navy allow the Bell Boeing team to develop plans for a V-22 derivative that weighs less, and costs less, than the current Osprey. The Navy lowered the desired cruising speed from 245 knots to 180 knots and eliminated the need for a maximum unrefueled flight range of 2,100 nautical miles. Working to the new specification, Bell Boeing engineers plan to reduce the aircraft's weight by about 2,000 pounds and cut its cost by about 12 percent December 4 Bell JetRanger N206BH, owned by Edwards & Associates of Bristol, TN achieves 30,000 flight hours.

December 9 — Bell is one of 75 Texas companies to pledge to voluntarily reduce waste by 50% by 2000.

YEAR 1993

January — Bell begins deliveries of the newest version of the LongRanger, called the Bell 206L-4. The helicopter has an uprated transmission improving lift capability by 500 pounds.

February 25 — At a press conference at Heli-Expo '93, Miami Beach, Bell President Webb Joiner launches the Bell 430 as the first new product to come from the company's Product Plan 2000.

February 27 — Carl L. Harris, Bell's Director of Public Affairs and Advertising receives the coveted Communicator of the Year Award from the Helicopter Association International during ceremonies conducted at Miami Beach.

March 30 — U.S. Army awards Bell an $85 million contract to build 102 TH-67 Creek new training helicopters. The TH-67 is a modified Bell 206B-3.

March 28 — President Clinton includes funds for the V-22 in his first defense budget submittal. The proposed budget calls for an additional $77 million for V-22 R&D. This amount is added to nearly $1.4 billion in FY 1992 and 1993 funds that Congress had previously provided for the program but were unspent by the previous administration.

April 15 — Bell Boeing submits a proposal to definitize the EMD statement of work and cost. The proposal is for a cost plus fixed fee contract to modify two full-scale development aircraft, and to design, build and test four new "production representative" aircraft with producibility improvements and cost reductions incorporated. These aircraft will feature weight reduction of 2,200 pounds relative to the FSD aircraft and will incorporate all safety enhancements learned from the Aircraft #4 crash investigation.

June 4 — PHI of Louisiana takes delivery of the first new Bell 230 helicopter to be used for the petroleum industry.

June 17 — U.S. Army qualifies first female attack helicopter pilot in a Bell AH-1F.

June 17 — Aircraft #3 resumes flight testing after the aircraft is modified to incorporate safety enhancements. Aircraft will explore the flight envelope and provide pilot familiarization. Aircraft #2 is scheduled to return to flight status in1993.

September — All V-22 flight testing is consolidated at the Naval Air Warfare Center, Patuxent River Naval Air Station, MD.

August — Bell and IBM Federal Systems Company announce a teaming agreement to pursue the U.S. Marine Corps AH-1W SuperCobra Integrated Weapons System program .

October 5 — U.S. Marine Corps Commandant General Carl Mundy praised Bell employees for the quality of their work during a visit to Bell Plant 6.

October 15 — Bell delivers the first TH-67 Creek to the U.S Army Aviation Warfighting Center, Fort Rucker, Alabama.

October — Bell begins flight testing a ducted tail rotor on a modified 222.

November 19 — Bell receives FAA certification of a twin-engine version of the 206L-4, to be called the 206LT TwinRanger.

December 5 — Bell opens first phase of the Hall of Heritage.

December 17 — V-22 emergency cabin egress demonstrations were completed. The demonstrations proved that combat troops ladened with equipment can successfully egress from the V-22 within one minute of the initiation of and emergency.

YEAR 1994

January 17 — The Dallas Convention Center formally opened its new "vertiport" to business. Located in the Dallas business district and built to withstand tiltrotor operations, it includes the largest elevated, urban heliport/vertiport in the United States. The facility will also accommodate the city's light rail system, taxis, buses and private autos.

January 31 — V-22/KC-135 wake evaluations completed demonstrating that the V-22 can fly safely behind the Air Force tanker. These evaluations were necessary so later icing tests behind the aircraft could be conducted at Patuxent River Naval Air Station, MD.

February 23 — The U.S. Army exercises its option to purchase an additional 35 TH-67 Creek training helicopters at a cost of $28 million

April 6 — Bell Helicopter named Texas Business of the Year by the Texas Association of business.

April 12 — Bell and Boeing executives testified before a congressional subcommittee that the V-22 Osprey must be produced if a successful civilian tiltrotor is to be developed and encouraged the government to establish a partnership with industry to focus on developing tiltrotor technology.

April 15 — V-22 icing tests conducted for more than three weeks at Duluth, MN completed. Osprey #2 made a series of ice-related flights including four behind a U.S. Army CH-47 Helicopter Icing Spray System helicopter for more than eight flight hours.

April 21 — First flight of Model 407.

May 5 — Bell delivers 1,000 aircraft manufactured at Mirabel plant, a 206LT TwinRanger for Niagara Helicopters.

May 13 — Two V-22s paid a first-time visit to a Marine Corps Capabilities Exercise staged at Camp Lejeune, NC, landing zone. CAPEX is designed to provide important visitors a cross-section of Second Expeditionary Force (II MEF) capabilities. Four European nation marine commandants witnessed the V-22 demonstration.

May 15 — Bell delivers 15 Armed OH-58D Kiowa Warriors to the Mississippi Army National Guard, the first reserve forces unit to receive the aircraft.

May 20 — The Congressionally-mandated Civil Tiltrotor Advisory Committee met for the first time to determine how civil tiltrotor technology will benefit the nation and to explore the economic viability of incorporating civil tiltrotors into an updated national transportation system.

June 15 — Bell delivers the first AH-1W SuperCobra equipped with a Night Targeting System to the U.S. Marine Corps.

June 21 — Bell Boeing V-22s accumulate 900th flight hour in combined full-scale development and engineering and manufacturing development testing. The milestone was achieved during a flight conducted at Patuxent River NAS, MD.

June 28 — Texan Ron Bower departs Bell plant in a 206B-3 JetRanger on a solo flight around the world.

July 7 — V-22 program completes initial operational flight testing by military air crews. Called OTIIA, this primary flight assessment was completed in 21 flying days accumulating 14.8 flight hours on V-22 #2.

July 22 — Ron Bower returns to Bell plant after setting a new record for an around the world helicopter flight of 24 days, 4 hours, 36 minutes.

July 30 — V-22 high altitude testing began in the mountains of Virginia.

August 14 — Joe Mashman, legendary retired Bell test pilot died. Helicopter Association International names a new helicopter safety award in his memory.

August 29 — Deputy Secretary of Defense John Deutch visited Bell Helicopter to study the merits of the V-22 at the invitation of Texas Governor Ann Richards. He said he was impressed with the technology, but the issue was affordability.

October 14 — Bell delivers first of 100 modified 412 helicopters to Canadian Minister of National Defence, the Honorable David Collenette for Canada's Utility Tactical Transport Helicopter program. The helicopter is designated CH-146 Griffon.

October 25 — First flight of the Bell 430. Based on the 230 design, the 430 has an 18-inch cabin stretch and is equipped with Bell's 680 type rotor system.

December 20 — Bell Boeing and NAVAIR completed the final executive session for the V-22 program's Critical Design Review, ratifying the final configuration for the production representative V-22 and "freezing" the aircraft design.

YEAR 1995

January 29 — Bell President Webb Joiner announces the development of two new commercial helicopters, the Bell 407 and a twin engine variant, the Bell 407T. Based in part on the 206 LongRanger, the 407 has a wider fuselage and the combat tested four-blade flight dynamics of the OH-58D Kiowa Warrior.

BELL HELICOPTER AND BELL HELICOPTER TEXTRON PRODUCTION, CO-PRODUCTION, AND MODIFICATION PROGRAMS 1946 THROUGH 1994

Total Helicopters Manufactured From 1946 Through 1991

Bell Helicopter Textron

Commercial Helicopters	10,217
Military Helicopters	17,479
Commercial and Military Total	**27,696**

Co-Production

Commercial Helicopters	3,803
Military Helicopters	668
Commercial and Military Co-Production Total	**4,471**

Total

Commercial Helicopters	14,020
Military Helicopters	18,147
Commercial and Military Helicopters Total	**32,167**

Buffalo, New York

Commercial Helicopters	202
Military Helicopters	205
Buffalo, New York Total	**407**

Fort Worth, Texas

Commercial Helicopters	9,374
Military Helicopters	17,274
Commerical and Military Total	**26,648**

Mirabel, Quebec, Canada

Commercial Helicopters	641

Total

Commercial Helicopters	10,217
Military Helicopters Total	17,479

Total	**27,696**

Military Helicopters Manufactured at Fort Worth, Texas From 1951 Through 1991

Model	Quantity
HTL-4	25
HTL-5	39
HTL-6	48
HTL-7	18
HUL	23
HUL-1G	2
H-13D	32
H-13E	490
XH-13F	1
H-13G	264
H-13H	466
H-13J	2
H-13K	2
UH-13R	2
OH-13S	396
TH-13T	415
XHSL-1	3
HSL-1	50
XV-3	2
XH-40	3
YH-40	6
HU-1	9
HU-1A	173
HU-1B	1,010
UH-1B (RAAF)	24
UH-1B (RAN)	8
UH-1C	749
UH-1E	209
TH-1F	27
UH-1F	119
YHU-1D	7
UH-1D	1,741
UH-1D (w/L-13 engine)	820
UH-1D (FRG)	10
UH-1H (w/L-11 engine)	172
UH-1H	4,824
UH-1H (AF)	25
UH-1H (Turkey)	25
UH-1H (GRC)	1
UH-1N	288
CUH-1N (Canada)	50
VH-1N	6
HH-1H	30
HH-1K	27
TH-1L	45
UH-1L	8
OH-4A	8
TH-57A	173
OH-58A	2,202
COH-58A (Canada)	74
OH-58B	50
AH-1G	1,119
AH-1G (Spain)	8
AH-1J	67
AH-1J (Iran)	140
AH-1J TOW (Iran)	62
AH-1J (Korea)	8
AH-1S	354
AH-1S (Israel)	37
AH-1S (Jordan)	24
AH-1S (Korea)	74
AH-1S (Pakistan)	20
AH-1T	57
AH-1W	78
ACAP	1
XV-15	2
YAH-63	3
V-22	6
406CS	15
Total Military	**17,276**

Commercial Helicopters Manufactured From 1946 Through 1991

Model	Quantity
47 (Buffalo)	195
47 (Ft. Worth)	2,400
Model 47 Total	**2,595**
204B	6
205	29
205A	39
205A-1	270
205A-1A	20
Model 205 Total	**358**
206A	685
206B (Ft. Worth)	3,137
206B (Australia)	15
206B (Canada)	238
Model 206A/B Total	**4,075**
206L	170
206L-1	637
206L-3 (Ft. Worth)	207
206L-3 (Canada)	314
Model 206L Total	**1,328**
400	5
400 Total	**5**
212 (Ft. Worth)	751
212 (IAF)	62
212 (Canada)	50
212 Total	**863**
412 (Ft. Worth)	187
412 (Canada)	39
412 Total	**226**
222	8
222B	26
222UT	71
222 Total	**186**
214A	296
214B	70
214C	39
214ST	100
214 Total	**505**
Total Commercial	**10,210**

Commercial Helicopters Manufactured At Mirabel, Quebec, Canada From 1986 Through 1991

Model	Quantity
206B	238
206L	314
212	50
412	39
Total Commercial	**641**

Commercial Helicopters Manufactured At Fort Worth, Texas From 1951 Through 1990

Model	Quantity
47D-1	90
47E	1
47G	208
47G-2	334
47G-2A	51
47G-2A-1	25
47G-3	38
47G-3B	80
47G-3B-1	337
47G-3B-2	158
47G-3B-2A	40
47G-4	86
47G-4A	269
47G-5	226
47G-5A	110
47H	33
47J	135
47J-2	104
47J-2A	75
204B	69
205	29
205A	39
205A-1	270
205A-1A	20
206A	685
206B	3,137
206B-1 (Australia)	15
206L	170
206L-1	637
206L-3	207
212	751
212 (IAF)	62
214A	296
214B	70
214C	39
214ST	100
222	89
222B	26
222UT	71
400	5
412	187
Total Commercial	**9,374**

Total Helicopters Manufactured At Buffalo, New York From 1946 Through 1951

Commercial

Model	Quantity
30	3
42	3
47	11
47B	43
47B-2	1
47B-3	33
47D	67
47D-1	40
49	1
Commercial Total	**202**

Military

Model	Quantity
XH-12	11
XR-12	2
YH-13	18
XH-15	3
HTL-1	10
HTL-2	12
HTL-3	9
HTL-4	21
H-13B	65
H-13D	54
Military Total	**205**

Co-Production Programs From 1954 Through 1990

Commercial Helicopters

Country	Partner	Model	Years	Quantity
Australia	CAC	206B-1	1971-77	56
England	Westland	47	1965-69	237
Indonesia	IPTN	412	1988-	16 (as of 1991)
Italy	Agusta	47	1954-79	762
Italy	Agusta	204/205	1962-85	780
Italy	Agusta	206B	1966	904 (as of 1991)
Italy	Agusta	212	1972-	293
Italy	Agusta	412	1982-	84
Japan	Kawasaki	47	1954-76	423
Japan	Fuji	204/205	1961-	238
Norway	Helikopter Service	412	1987-	15
Argentina	?	?	?	?

Co-Production Commercial Total	**3,803**

Military Helicopters

Country	Partner	Model	Years	Quantity
Japan	Fuji	AH-1S	1984-	47
Taiwan	AIDC	UH-1H	1970-76	118
Turkey	TLFC	UH-1H	1984-87	45
W. Germany	Dornier	UH-1D	1965-70	458

Co-Production Military Total	**4,471**

Modification Programs Through 1991

Model	Quantity
AH-1G/S	487
AH-1T/W	31
OH-58D (AHIP)	226
Modifications Total	**744**

INDEX

220